The Complete Idiot's Reference Card

To help you start and use Microsoft Works for Windows 95 as fast as possible, here are all the main component toolbars, button-by-button:

The Word Processing Toolbar

Drop-down list of fonts

Drop-down list of font sizes

Task Launcher, for running two or more documents at once

Saves the open document

Prints the open document

Print Preview: on-screen look at how your document will print

Cuts selected item and stores it in the Windows Clipboard

Copies selected item and stores it in the Windows Clipboard

Pastes the contents of the Clipboard at your insertion point

Bold; toggles on and off

Italic; toggles on and off

Underline; toggles on and off

Left aligns text on page

Center aligns text on page

Right aligns text on page

The Communications Toolbar

Communication settings: modem, properties, location

Terminal settings: emulation, font, and font size

Phone settings: dial, redial, or answer calls

Transfer settings: protocol, directory for received files

Standard modem setting: 8 data bits, no parity, 1 stop bit

Alternative settings; rarely used

Easy Connect, for dialing up another computer

Dial/Hangup: does what it says

Pauses the online proceedings

Capture Text; saves text sent from a bulletin board

Send Text; saves you time online

Send Binary File (uploading)

Receive Binary file (downloading)

tear here

QUe®

The Spreadsheet Toolbars

 AutoSum automatically totals a row or column of figures

 Currency formats your figures as money

 Easy Calc creates formulas to do more complex math

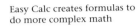 New Chart opens Works' charting tools

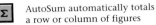 Cancel deletes the contents of a selected cell

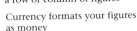 Enter works just like the Enter key

 Get Help when you need it

The Database Toolbar

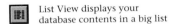 List View displays your database contents in a big list

 Form Design View lets you format records

 Insert Record lets you do just that

 Form View displays your database one record at a time

 Report View lets you summarize your data

Filters lets you filter out unwanted records

The Works Keyboard Shortcuts

Keyboard shortcuts give you an easy way to perform common Works functions without having to click a button or select from a menu.

All Modules

New File	Ctrl+N
Open File	Ctrl+O
Save File	Ctrl+S
Print File	Ctrl+P
Undo last	Ctrl+Z
Clear	Del
Cut	Ctrl+X
Copy	Ctrl+C
Paste	Ctrl+V
Select All	Ctrl+A
Find	Ctrl+F
Replace	Ctrl+H
Go To	Ctrl+G
Page Break	Ctrl+Enter
Spelling	F7

Word Processor

Thesaurus	Shift+F7

Spreadsheet

Fill Right	Ctrl+R
Fill Down	Ctrl+D

Database

Cut Record	Ctrl+Shift+X
Copy Record	Ctrl+Shift+C
Paste Record	Ctrl+V
List View	Shift+F9
Form View	F9
Form Design View	Ctrl+F9

Communications

Copy Text	Ctrl+C

The
COMPLETE
IDIOT'S
GUIDE TO
Microsoft Works
for Windows 95

by John Pivovarnick

A Division of Macmillan Computer Publishing
201 W.103rd Street, Indianapolis, IN 46290

International Standard Book Number: 0-7897-0451-X

Library of Congress Catalog Card Number: 95-71451

98 97 96 95   8 7 6 5 4 3 2 1

Interpretation of the printing code: the rightmost double-digit number is the year of the book's first printing; the rightmost single-digit number is the number of the book's printing. For example, a printing code of 95-1 shows that this copy of the book was printed during the first printing of the book in 1995.

Publisher
Roland Elgey

Vice-President and Publisher
Marie Butler-Knight

Publishing Manager
Barry Pruett

Director of Editorial Services
Elizabeth Keaffaber

Managing Editor
Michael Cunningham

Development Editor
Faithe Wempen

Senior Editor
Michelle Shaw

Copy Editor
San Dee Phillips

Designer
Kim Scott

Cover Designer
Dan Armstrong

Technical Specialist
Cari Skaggs

Cartoonist
Judd Winick

Indexer
Kathy Venable

Production Team
*Steve Adams, Angela D. Bannan, Maxine Dillingham,
Chad Dressler, Damon Jordan, Bobbi Satterfield, Michael Thomas*

*Special thanks to C. Herbert Feltner for ensuring the technical
accuracy of this book.*

Contents at a Glance

Introduction   xx
This is a fine "how do you do" that explains what this book will do
for you, and how to use it.

Part 1: The Basics   1

1 The Top 10 Things You Need to Know   3
The absolute bare minimum of information you need to get started.

2 Getting to Know Windows 95   9
A quick overview of Windows 95, what it is, what it does, and how to find
more tips and tricks on using it.

3 Works Gives You "The Works"   25
A general look around Works, focusing on each of the component applications
(like the word processor and database).

4 Starting from Scratch with Works   31
Step-by-step instructions for installing Works on your PC, with helpful tips
and illustrations.

5 The BIG Concepts   45
Simple explanations for some important ideas, like: what "integra-
tion" is; what Wizards are; plus a look at Works' menus and
toolbar.

6 Works: Beyond the Basics (Sounds Like A Movie of the Week)   59
Takes the big concepts from Chapter 5 and gives you intimate
details about them—from entering information to printing it out.

Part 2: Works' Word Processor—Getting Your Word's Worth   73

7 Processing, Not Typing   75
Explains what typing habits (if you have any) you should break
while learning Works.

8 Editorial Skills   83
All the tools at your disposal for creating perfectly polished prose.

9 Fun With Paragraphs   97
Everything you could possibly want to do with (or to) the
paragraphs you create.

10 Format This!   113
Funky and fun font and formatting fanaticism, for friends and
foes alike.

11 Getting Fancy-Schmancy: Works as a Page Layout Tool   127
Turning Works into a high-powered page-layout program to
create flyers, news-letters, and other interesting creations.

Part 3: Spreadsheets: Dollars and Sense   **143**

12 Spreadsheets Explained   145
Why spreadsheets and bed sheets are two different things.
(Because spreadsheets are easier to fold, and do better with math.)

13 Spreadsheets 101   153
Info on spreadsheets that will save you time and effort (and keep
you from making the same goofy mistakes everybody makes—
even me).

14 Secret Formula Secrets   161
How to make sense out of SUMS and such, and how to get Works
to figure them out for you.

15 Editing: The Art of Fiddling With Spreadsheets   171
Editorial skills spreadsheet style: tinkering with rows, columns,
and formulas to save time and energy.

16 Lovely to Look At: Spreadsheet Beautification   181
How to get beautiful spreadsheets, painlessly.

17 What Chart Is This, I Think I Know...   195
Turning your spreadsheet information into a meaningful chart.

Part 4: Your Basic Database   **213**

18 Database, First Base   215
What a database is and does, and some of the terms and tools
you'll be using.

19 Getting to Second Base: Entering Data and Printing   225
Entering information, then moving it around and printing it out.

20 Prettying Up a Database   237
Using fonts, labels, and other pretty options to make your data
beautiful and practical (not to mention readable).

21 Reports: Data, Reporting for Duty   253
Turning your data into a report that can be shared with your
friends and neighbors (or not).

Part 5: Works Working Together   **269**

22 Picture Perfect: Art Accessories   271
Using Draw, and Works' other artistic options, to accessorize all
of your documents.

23 Spreading Information Around   283
Sharing your Works files (and parts of files) with other applica-
tions you own, or friends and co-workers—and vice versa.

24 Grow Your Own Junk Mail: Form Letters   295
How to take names and addresses from a database and get Works to automatically drop them into letters.

25 Address Book Details   313
How to use (and abuse) Works Address Book Wizard so you can keep tabs on everybody you know.

26 Communications Basics   323
Using Works, your computer, modem, and telephone line to communicate with this big, wide, wonderful world we live in.

27 Communication Skills: The Next Generation   329
A rogues' gallery of documents created with Works that you can recreate yourself—quickly and easily.

28 Works' Customizing Options   347
Make Works behave and look the way you want it to.

Speak Like a Geek: The Complete Archive   357
A major concatenation of all the geeky buzzwords used and defined throughout the rest of the book.

Index   367

Contents

Part 1: The Basics   1

1 The Top 10 Things You Need to Know   3

1. Works Is a Complete Package 3
2. You Have to Install It Before You Can Use It 4
3. Starting Works Is Simple 4
4. TaskWizards Give You a Head Start.............................. 5
5. ...But It's Easy to Create Documents
   of Your Own, Too 5
6. Save Early, Save Often 6
7. Editing Is Easy! 6
8. You Can Dress Up Your Documents with ClipArt or
   WordArt 7
9. Printing Is a Pleasure.. 7
10. Help Is All Around 7

2 Getting to Know Windows 95   9

What Is Windows 95? 9
Launching Windows 95 10
Icons Everywhere 11
    On Your Marks! Get Set! Start Button! 13
Let Your Mouse Do It 14
    The Drag 14
    The Click 14
      The Drag and the Drop 14
    The Double-Click 15
    Other Assorted Mouse Activities 15
Anatomy of a Windows Window 16
Menus Out the Wazoo 19
    File Me! 19
    Edit Me! 20
    View Me! 21
    Help Me! 22
    For the Forgetful Like... What Was I Saying? 23
Closing Windows 23
The Least You Need to Know 24

3 Works Gives You "The Works" 25

A Typical Works Workday 25
Write Up a Storm 26
Crunch Those Numbers 27
Data for Days 28
Pretty As a Picture 29
Other Goodies 29
The Least You Need to Know 30

4 Starting from Scratch with Works 31

Let's Start at the Very Beginning 32
  It's a Setup! 32
  Direct Me To Your Directory 34
  Works? Or Works Lite? 35
  Taking the Shortcut and Shuffling Floppies 36
  Done! 37
Launching Works 37
Taking the Nickel Tour 39
Help Yourself to Help 41
  A Helpful Window 41
  A Helpful Menu 42
  First Time Help 43
  Instant Help Is Gonna Get You 44
The Least You Need to Know 44

5 The BIG Concepts 45

Start Your Engines! 46
Integration Means Easy Pickin's 46
Integrate the World 47
We're Off to See the Wizards 48
Save Me! 52
Creating a New Document 55
The Works Menus and Toolbar 56
  The Works Menus 56
  The Toolbar 57
The Least You Need to Know 58

6 Works: Beyond the Basics (Sounds Like A Movie of the Week...) 59

Open Up. It's the Law! 60
   Using the Task Launcher 60
   Using the Open Command 61
Opening More Than One File 62
   Use the Window Menu 62
   Which Window Is Which? 63
   Managing Windows: A Minimalist Approach 63
   Playing with Windows 64
Entering Text 64
Overstrike Mode 65
The Unkindest Cut of All: Editing 66
   Inserting New Text 66
   Selecting Text 66
   Deleting Text 67
   Replacing Text 68
Save Me II 68
Prettying Up 69
   Changing Fonts 69
   Size Matters 69
Save Me III 70
A Peek Before Printing 70
About Printing 71
I Quit! 71
The Least You Need to Know 72

Part 2: Works' Word Processor— Getting Your Word's Worth 73

7 Processing, Not Typing 75

Typos Begone! 76
Editing Without Retyping 76
Typing Habits You Should Break
(And Why You Should Break Them) 77
   Don't Double Space at the End of Each Sentence 77
   Don't Indent Five Spaces at the Start of Paragraphs! 78
   Lay Off the Enter Key, Why Don'tcha? 79
Some Typing Habits You Should Keep 80

Some Typing Habits I've Never Been Able to Break 80
The Least You Need to Know 81

8 Editorial Skills   83

The Selection Process: A Quick Brush-Up 83
More Things to Do with Selected Text 84
   Cut! 84
Copy, Anyone? 85
   Paste Me! Paste Me! 85
   Paste Special 85
   Select It All, Then Clear It All 86
Drag-and-Drop Editing: An Easier Way to
  Move Your Words Around 87
Lost And Find 87
Please Replace Me, Let Me Go… 88
Check Yourself 90
   Checking Your Spelling 90
   Editing Your Custom Dictionary 92
   Other Spelling Options 93
I Need A Synonym for Cinnamon 93
When in Doubt, Save As 94
The Least You Need to Know 96

9 Fun with Paragraphs   97

Marginalia 98
   Setting Your Margins 99
   Changing Paragraph Margins 100
Spacing Out 101
   Setting the Spacing for a Whole Document 103
   To Change Spacing for a Paragraph or Two 104
In-nie And Out-ie Indents 104
Madonna: Justify My Paragraph 106
Love and Bullets 107
The Tab Stops Here 108
   Setting Tabs 109
   The Lazy Way to Set Tabs 110
   Moving Tabs 111
A Sneaky Editing Trick 111
The Least You Need to Know 111

10 Format This!   113

"What Formatting Means to Me" 113
Take It Easy with Easy Formats 114
   Using an Easy Format 114
   Changing an Easy Format 116
   Creating New Easy Formats 117
Confessions of a Font Addict 118
Font Varieties 118
   Fonts for Text 118
   I Shot the Serif—Headlines and Signs 119
   It's a Novelty 119
   Edith, You Dingbat 119
Trying Fonts on for Size 120
Headings, Subheadings, and Captions 121
   Head This Way 121
   Under Your Head 121
   Caption 122
Headers, Footers, and Footnotes 122
   Getting a Header 123
   My Left Footer 123
   Footnote Notes 124
Some Formatting Rules of Thumb 124
Breaking Pages and Other Niceties 125
   The Broken Page 125
   Other Special Goodies 126
The Least You Need to Know 126

11 Getting Fancy-Shmancy: Works as a Page Layout Tool 127

Need It in a Hurry? Use a Wizard! 127
What's Your Page Orientation? 128
Margins Revisited 129
Doric or Ironic Columns 130
   Staying Within the Lines 131
Borders and Color Draw Attention 132
   Putting a Border Around Text 133
   110 Boxes in the Shade 134
   Slap a Border on a Whole Page 135
   Add a Spot of Color 136
Add Some Art 137
   Insert a Clip 137

Resizing a Clip 138
Wrapping Text Around a Clip 140
Add a Chart or Table 140
A Gussying Up Review 141
Layout Tips and Tricks 141
The Least You Need to Know 142

Part 3: Spreadsheets: Dollars and Sense   143

12 Spreadsheets Explained   145

Some Special Spreadsheet Info 146
Spreadsheet Tools 147
The Toolbar 147
The Formula Bar 148
Sister Margo's Mystic Math Symbols 149
You Can Pick a Cell, And You Can Pick a Row... 150
You Can Use TaskWizards to Create
a New Spreadsheet 151
Before You Start a New Spreadsheet 151
After You Start a New Spreadsheet 152
The Least You Need to Know 152

13 Spreadsheets 101   153

Have a Plan 154
Start a New Spreadsheet 155
Stick a Label on It 156
Entering Information: Some Nitty-Gritty Details 157
Enter Those Receipts! 158
Nice and Easy 158
A Little Complicated: Multiple Categories
on the Same Receipt 159
Carry on Entering Data 160
Coming Attractions 160
The Least You Need to Know 160

14 Secret Formula Secrets   161

Formulas Defined 162
Entering a Formula 162
Prepare for Manual Entry! 163

Using Auto(Sum) Pilot 163
Sneaky, Underhanded Formula Copying 164
Grow Your Own Formulas 165
Any Two Cells Can Play 165
Three or More Can Play 165
Multiple Math 166
Getting Complicated 166
Functions: Predefined Formulas 167
Easy Calc: Uniting Form(ula) and Function 167
Common Calculations 167
Other Functions 169
A Quick Recap, Then Onward 170
The Least You Need To Know 170

15 Editing: The Art of Fiddling With Spreadsheets   171

Back to Editing Basics 172
Ye Olde Delete and Backspace Keys 172
Cutting, Copying, Pasting, & Other
Words That End In -ING 172
When You Do That Undo That You Do So Well......... 173
Inserting Rows and Columns 173
Deleting Rows and Columns 174
Drag-and-Drop a Row or Column 174
Taller Rows and Wider Columns 175
Changing Column Width 176
Changing Row Height 177
The Sneaky Way To Adjust Height And Width 177
Sorting All Sorts of Stuff 178
The Least You Need to Know 180

16 Lovely to Look At: Spreadsheet Beautification   181

Do It Yourself? Or AutoFormat? 182
Just Fonting Around 184
General Spreadsheet Font Tips 184
Formatting, Body and Cell 185
Playing the Numbers 185
Proper Alignment Makes for Easy Reading 187
Borders and Shading Suggestions 189
Special Spreadsheet Printing Concerns 190
Specify a Print Area 191

Landscape or Portrait? 191
But Is It Legal (Sized)? 192
Freeze, Mister! 192
Other Printing Options 192
Printing (Finally!) 193
The Least You Need to Know 194

17 What Chart Is This, I Think I Know... 195

Mommy, Where Do Charts Come From? 196
A Chart Warning 196
Chart Varieties 197
How Charts Work 198
Creating a Chart 199
    Select What You Want Charted 200
    Pick a Chart, Any Chart... 200
    Oh, Those Advanced Options 201
Change That Chart! 203
    Making Changes on the Spreadsheet 204
    Refining the Chart (or Changing It Completely) 204
    What I Did... 206
If You Have an Axis to Grind... 207
    X Marks the Axis 207
    Y Axis Y? 208
    Other Options 210
Chart Tips and Tricks 210
    Pretty but Simple 210
    Stylize Those Indicators! 211
    KISS Me Again 212
Printing a Chart 212
The Least You Need to Know 212

Part 4: Your Basic Database 213

18 Database, First Base 215

Forms and Fields: Database Building Blocks 216
Before You Start 216
Before You Start, Part II 217
Starting a Database 218
Creating a New Database 218

If You're Playing Along with My Sample... 220
When Your Fields Have All Been Entered... 221
The Database Tools 222
    Déjà Vu: The Entry Bar 222
    The Toolbar Tools 222
Save It or Lose It 223
The Least You Need to Know 223

19 Getting to Second Base: Entering Data and Printing   225

Entering Data 225
    Telling Works That You're Entering Text 226
    What About Entering Numbers? 226
    Entering Formulas 227
Editing Data 227
The Four Faces of Your Database 227
    Form View 228
    Form Design View 228
Renaming Fields 229
Resizing Fields and Records 229
    Wider Fields 230
    Taller Records 230
    Two, Two, Two Dialog Boxes in One 231
    The Lazy Eyeball Method 232
Adding and Deleting Fields 232
    Add A Field Here... 232
    Delete This Field 233
Adding and Deleting Whole Records 234
    Add One 234
    Delete One 234
Moving Stuff Around 234
Printing Out a Database 234
    Printing from List View 234
    Printing in Form View 235
    Other Printing Stuff 235
The Least You Need to Know 236

20 Prettying Up a Database   237

Design That Form! 238
Labeling Your Data 240
    Using the Insert Label Command 240

Just Type It—Entering the Label Manually 241
My Label Choices 241
Stylize Your Fonts 241
Font Changing Recap (It Has Been a While) 242
My Font Choices 242
Alignment Options 243
Boxes, Color, and Shading 244
Insert Rectangle 244
Bordering and Shading Labels 246
Adding Some Art 248
The Last (Re)Sort 249
Drumroll, Please! The Finished Product 250
The Least You Need to Know 251

21 Reports: Data, Reporting for Duty   **253**

So, Why Create a Report? 254
Filtering Data 254
Easy Filter 254
Filter Using Formula 257
Using ReportCreator 259
ReportCreator Is… 259
ReportCreator: Title 260
Database Fields Forever 260
Sorting Things Out 262
Grouping Groupies and Groupers 262
Filters Revisited 263
Summarizing Your Summary Options 265
Preview It 266
Modify It 267
The Least You Need to Know 268

Part 5: Works Working Together   **269**

22 Picture Perfect: Art Accessories   **271**

Draw! 272
The Drawing Tools 272
Line And Fill Colors 274
Learn by Playing 275
On the File Menu 275

On the Edit Menu 275
On the Draw Menu 276
Creating a Logo 276
The Logo, and How to Swing It 276
Using That Logo 277
ClipArt Revisited 278
A Word Can Be Worth a Thousand Pictures 279
Starting with WordArt 279
The WordArt Tools 280
The Least You Need to Know 282

23 Spreading Information Around   **283**

Thanks for Sharing: Works 4.0 to Works 4.0 284
Share and Share Alike:
Works 4.0 to Other Applications 284
Opening a Foreign File Format 286
Sharing Within Works 287
Sharing Information with Other Applications
on Your PC 289
The Copy and Paste Special Method 289
Inserting an Object 291
Create New 291
Create from File 291
Working with Objects 293
The Least You Need to Know 294

24 Grow Your Own Junk Mail: Form Letters   **295**

Why Use a Form Letter? 296
Creating a Form Letter: How It Works 296
The Urge to Merge 296
Take a Letter, Maria... 297
Design That Letter 298
Letterhead 299
Address 300
Assemble the Address 301
Greetings! 302
Fresh or Canned Contents? 303
Stylize Your Text 304
Extras! Extras! 305

Check That Checklist! 306
Anatomy of a Form Letter 306
Editing a Form Letter 307
Smooshing the Data into the Letter 308
Do-It-Yourself Form Letters 308
All This, and Mailing Labels, Too 309
The Least You Need to Know 312

25 Address Book Details   313

Start Here… 314
What Flavor Do You Want? 314
Adding Details 315
    Additional Fields 316
    Do Your Own Fields 316
    Reports Will Tell 317
    Are You Sure About That? 317
The Address Book Proper 318
Save It or Lose It 319
Entering Names and Such 319
Customizing the Address Book 319
The Report Report 320
Address Book Suggestions 320
    The Obvious Idea: Birthday/Anniversary Warnings 321
    Phone Lists 321
    Emergency Numbers 322
    Holiday Card Craziness 322
    Year-in-Review Letters 322
The Least You Need to Know 322

26 Communications Basics   323

Before You Get Your Hopes Up… 324
    Stuff You Need 324
    Call Waiting? 324
    Where to Find the Items You Don't Have 325
    Things You Won't Be Able to Do (Sorry) 327
Computer Communications Explained 327
The Least You Need to Know 328

27 Communication Skills: The Next Generation   **329**

  Your First Time Online 329

    Where Are You Calling? 330

    Dialing… 331

  If At First You Don't Succeed… 332

    Number Is Busy or No Answer 333

    Works Can't Find My Modem 334

    I See Garbage Characters on My Screen 334

    Transfer Settings 336

  Save Your Settings 338

  The Communications Toolbar 338

  Sending and Receiving Text 340

    Sending Text 340

    Receiving Text 341

  Sending and Receiving Files 343

    Gimme Files! 343

    It's Better to Send Than to Receive 345

  Be Legal In All Things 345

  The Least You Need to Know 346

28 Works' Customizing Options   **347**

  Customizing the Toolbar 347

    Removing Buttons 348

    Adding a Button 348

    Other Toolbar Options 349

  Options, Options, And More Options 350

    Editing Options 350

    Data Entry 351

    The Default Address Book 352

    Generally Speaking… 353

    A View to a Window 354

    Finally: Proofing Tools 355

    The Least You Need to Know 356

Speak Like a Geek: The Complete Archive   **357**

Index   **367**

What Is This Thing Called "Works"?

In my line of work, I often find myself feeling like *The Great Carnak*—remember him? Johnny Carson's psychic alter ego? Johnny would be behind his desk, wearing that big ol' glittery Pasha hat. He'd hold an envelope up to his forehead and say, "Jessie Helms, The Scarecrow, and Frankenstein's Monster!" Then he'd open the envelope and read the question inside: "Name three 'poster children' for the Better Brains Foundation." Then Ed McMahon would laugh like a goof, whether the joke was funny or not.

In my case, I sit here behind my messy desk and hold floppy disks up to my forehead and try to anticipate all the various things people will want to do with the software they contain. The result may not be as side-splittingly funny as a Carson routine, but I'll give it a shot.

Who This Book Is For

This book will be useful to anyone trying to fake his way through Microsoft Works for Windows 95 without cracking that too-long, too-complete, too-tedious user's manual that seems to be written completely in geek-speak.

Chances are, you got Microsoft Works for Windows 95 bundled with your brand spanking new PC—that's how many folks acquire it—so, in addition to wanting to be productive with Works, you're also in the throes of learning your way around a new computer. There's a recipe for stress if I ever heard one; just add gray hair and mix.

You want to be productive *now,* not after six days (or weeks, or months) of wrestling with your computer. That can be *so* frustrating. This book is here to help speed you through the process.

As I've maintained in all of my *Idiot's Guides*: you are not an idiot. Your computer, or your software, may make you *feel* like one, but you aren't really a bona fide idiot. True idiots are, thankfully, rare and are usually found working as infomercial hosts.

How to Use This Book

This book flows from beginning basics (installing and starting the software) through advanced Works features (such as mail merge). In between, there are sections devoted to each of Works' main components (the word processor, spreadsheet, database, and so on).

If you're starting from scratch, start at the beginning. There's a *Top 10 Things You Need to Know* chapter (Chapter 1, which everyone should read), a chapter on Windows 95 basics (Chapter 2), and chapters that talk about Works in general terms, including installation and major ideas you'll use time after time (Chapters 3, 4, and 5).

If this isn't your first experience with Works (you've used an earlier version), you may want to skim or skip the introductory info and move on to the chapters devoted to the different parts of Works.

You may want to read the whole book, and then keep it handy for easy reference. Or you may not. You may just want to put it near your computer and read the chapter(s) that cover whatever you're trying to do at the moment. I leave that up to you.

Some Convenient Conventions

To make it easier for you to bull your way through all of the information here, there are some easy-to-spot conventions used throughout the book. One is the use of **boldface type** so key information or instructions jump out at you. For example, if I want you to type something, I'll say:

Type **this**.

If I want you to press a key, or a set of keys, on your keyboard, I'll say:

Press **Enter**. Or press **Ctrl+S** (which means press and hold the **Control** key, and while you're holding it down, also press the **S** key—that's a *keyboard shortcut* for the Save command, but don't worry about it now).

If I want you to go through a series of steps, I'll give you a list of things to do, like this:

1. Do **this**.

2. Then do **that**.

3. Finally, do **the other thing**.

When you run into a new term that isn't fully explained in the text, you'll find a box like this one somewhere in the vicinity.

> **Check This Out...**
>
> **A Keyboard Shortcut for Save** A combination of keystrokes (such as Ctrl+S) that you can use instead of a menu item (in this case, selecting **Save** from the **File** menu). Most use the Control or Alt keys on a standard keyboard, plus a letter, number, or function key (such as the F1 key).

These boxes may also contain information you'll need eventually, if not right now. You should at least read the titles of these boxes to make sure they don't answer a question you may have, solve a problem, or contain a warning, before you choose to ignore them. It couldn't hurt.

If I have a bit of technical information to share with you (maybe why, or how, Works does what it does), it will be set off in a box like the following:

Insert Technical Babbling Here

You can read this stuff, or not, at your own discretion. It's in a box so you can easily find it, or ignore it, quickly.

Assumptions

This is a *Complete Idiot's Guide*, after all, so I'll try not to assume anything about your level of expertise with a PC. However, some information will fall outside the scope of this book. Whenever I refer to a skill or a concept you should know that isn't covered here, I will tell you where you can find the information.

For example, you should know how to format a floppy disk. If you don't know how, you can find that information in your Windows 95 manual (in the chapter on the My Computer feature) or from Windows 95's Help menu.

With a Little Help from My Friends

Nobody, but nobody, gets through writing a book without help and support from the people in their lives—like my mother who's afraid to call, in case I'm working; or T Greenfield who *likes* to call in case I'm working too hard.

Thanks to Karen Razler for getting me the movie extra job I mention in Chapter 15; it's a great way to waste Sunday night through Monday morning. I'm *still* yawning.

Many thanks to Carmen Kahn, Eleanor Holdridge, and the cast of the Red Heel Theater's staged reading "Much Ado About Nothing." The reading was another fun distraction to keep me from getting too serious about life in general, and work in particular. Bill's words bring out the best in folks, I think.

Also thanks to the crew of distracting regulars: Jaqueline Yancey for being brave enough to go fishing for the first time in her life; Mark Yannick for the "If it weren't for caffeine, I'd have no personality at all" T-shirt. The sentiment is sadly true.

Copyrights, Trademarks, and Other Legal-Speak

Whenever I write about computers, I always wind up mentioning a lot of products, goods, and services that are somehow owned by somebody else. Microsoft Works and Microsoft Windows, for instance, are both registered trademarks of the jolly folks at Microsoft Corporation.

Wherever I knew that words and names were the property of a corporate entity, I indicated it by using the proper capitalization (IBM, Intel, Apple Computer, or whatever). That spares me, and the typesetters, from remembering how to put all those annoying ™, ©, and ® symbols into the text.

If, by some chance, I've screwed up and missed one or two, the lack of capitalization in no way takes away from their ownership of the mentioned product, goods, or services. Thanks for not litigating.

Don't Forget to Breathe

Even if you have a major "I've got to get this done now or my butt is grass" project waiting in the wings, don't forget to take your time and take a break now and then. If it's possible (sometimes it isn't), I think you'd do better trying to learn Works with no real project in mind (homework that needs to be done, a business report, anything else). Learn by playing, rather than by doing.

If you have an important deadline breathing down your neck, you won't feel free to make mistakes (or learn from them), or wonder "What happens if I do *this*?" So, if you can, work through the book with pretend projects, or nonjob- or nongrade-threatening stuff— why add pressure if you can avoid it?

If you can't avoid it, still take your time. Take breaks. Get an occasional hug if you can, or at least a "Poor baby" from somebody. Let me give you your first: *Poor baby!*

On a Sad Note...

While writing this book, on June 3, 1995, I learned of the death of Dr. J. Presper Eckert. It received little media attention in the Philadelphia area (in spite of Dr. Eckert's status as home-town boy), so I doubt it got any elsewhere in the country.

Dr. Eckert, along with the late Dr. John W. Maunchly, designed and built ENIAC, the world's first electronic digital computer, at the University of Pennsylvania just after World War II. This 30-ton behemoth was the forerunner of the PC that sits on your desk, and on millions of desks around the world.

Considering the impact of their work, I felt his passing should be noted by more than a footnote in some obscure engineering text somewhere.

Part 1
The Basics

If you are dealing with a computer, Windows 95, and/or Microsoft Works for the very first time, Part 1 provides some basic information about Microsoft Windows 95 and Microsoft Works for Windows 95: what they are, what they do, some skills you'll be using on a regular basis, that sort of thing.

So, everybody who's coming along, stay with me now. Emergency exits are located fore and aft of the wings. In the event of a loss of brain pressure, portable televisions will drop from the overhead compartment and cool your brain with reruns of "I Dream of Jeannie" and "The Partridge Family." If you are computing with small children, please make sure that they are firmly stowed beneath the seat in front of you, or in the overhead compartment…or is that luggage? Prepare for take off.

Chapter 1

The Top 10 Things You Need to Know

Even if you don't plan to *ever* read the rest of this book (but please do), there are a handful of things you should know before you plunge into Microsoft Works for Windows 95. Here they are:

1. Works Is a Complete Package

Microsoft Works for Windows 95 is an integrated suite of applications that help you compose letters and more complicated writing (see Part 2); track financial and other numerical data (see Part 3); and organize, search, and create reports from other sorts of data (see Part 4).

Works also includes communication software (see Chapter 26) so a modem-equipped PC can chat with other modem-equipped computers, and you can use Works to tinker with graphic images (that's pictures to you and me—check out Chapter 22).

Works for Windows 95 is actually version 4.0 of Microsoft Works, a venerable software package that has been around almost as long as there have been computers. The reason it's called "Microsoft Works for Windows 95," and not "Microsoft Works 4.0," is because Microsoft designed this new version for you to use with the new version of Windows— Windows 95. Works won't work with earlier versions of Windows. Trust me; I tried—it laughed at me.

For a more detailed overview of Works, take a look at Chapter 3. For a gander at Windows 95, take a peek at Chapter 2.

2. You Have to Install It Before You Can Use It

"Duh!" you say. Hear me out.

You probably know that your Works software must be installed on your computer before you can use it. If your computer came with Works installed, you don't have to worry about it.

If you got ahold of Works on disks or a CD-ROM, you need to install it. Chapter 4 has more detailed instructions, but here's the bare minimum:

1. Insert the first floppy disk (labeled **Setup Disk 1**) in your floppy drive, or the Works CD in your CD-ROM drive.

2. Open the **Start** menu and choose **Run**.

3. In the Run dialog box, type the drive letter for the drive into which you just inserted the disk (or CD), followed by the word **Setup**.

   For a floppy disk, it will probably look like this:

   A:\Setup

   For a CD, it will probably look like this:

   D:\Setup

Follow the directions on-screen, and you'll be home free.

If you're installing from a CD, don't be surprised if Windows asks if you want to install Works shortly after you pop in the disc. Windows 95 has this spooky AutoRun feature that checks CDs for setup routines. It could work for Dionne Warwick and her Psychic Friends.

3. Starting Works Is Simple

To launch Works after you install it, click on the **Start** menu (at the bottom-left corner of your Windows 95 desktop).

Drag your mouse pointer up the menu until it touches the **Programs** menu item. A list of all your installed applications will pop up.

Move your pointer over the list until it touches the entry for **Microsoft Works 4.0** (you'll know you have selected it because the entry will turn white on a blue bar). Another menu will pop up.

Move your pointer over the new menu until it touches the entry for **Microsoft Works 4.0**. Click on it once, and Works will start right up.

You can also use this opportunity to start up the Works tour. Just click on the **Introduction to Microsoft Works 4.0** entry in the Microsoft Works 4.0 pop-up menu.

Launching Works and taking the Works tour, are covered in Chapter 4.

4. TaskWizards Give You a Head Start...

When you first start up Works, you'll see the Works Task Launcher. The Task Launcher gives you access to Works TaskWizards, which are predefined documents that Works will help you customize to your personal needs.

There are TaskWizards for Common Tasks (such as letters, résumés, and newsletters), Correspondence (more letters, fax cover sheets, certificates), Envelopes and Labels (pretty much what you'd expect—envelopes and labels), Business Management (employee profiles, time sheets, business inventories), Names and Addresses (self-explanatory), and Household Management (household inventories, phone lists, and so on).

There are also TaskWizard categories for Students and Teachers, Billing, Employment, and Volunteer/Civic Activities.

With these TaskWizards, you can quickly start producing professional-looking documents. Later, when you feel more comfortable with Works, you'll be ready to create some exciting designs of your own. TaskWizards are covered in Chapter 5, and then in application-specific chapters.

5. ...But It's Easy to Create Documents of Your Own, Too

Even if there are dozens of TaskWizards, there may not be a wizard that meets your unique needs. No problem. To create a completely new, original document, click on the **Works Tools** tab in the Task Launcher (select **File**, **New** to reopen the Task Launcher, if you closed it).

From the Works Tools dialog box, simply click on the button in front of the type of document you want to create (Word Processor, Spreadsheet, Database, or Communications) and Works will present you with a new, blank, unsaved document in the appropriate style. Go to town with it.

You can read about the various modules throughout the book (Word Processing in Part 2, Spreadsheets in Part 3, Database in Part 4, and Communications in Chapter 26). Check the appropriate chapters for more information.

6. Save Early, Save Often

Once you begin a new document (whether from scratch, or with a TaskWizard) you should save it right away, and then save it regularly afterward. That will protect you from losing your work, should anything untoward happen (like a power outage, say, or something like the ever-popular "my three-year-old was at the keyboard when I wasn't looking" trauma).

To save a document, open the **File** menu and choose **Save**.

The first time you save a document, you'll be asked to give it a name. Give it an obvious one, so you'll know what the file is when you see it (call your résumés MYRESUME, perhaps). When you've named it, click the **Save** button, and Works will save a copy of the file on your hard drive.

After that first save, when you select **Save** from the **File** menu (or use the keyboard shortcut **Ctrl+S**), Works will automatically update the saved copy of the file. Windows 95 (and therefore Works for Windows 95) has new, easier rules for naming files—no more trying to come up with a meaningful name in eight characters or less! (So instead of MYRESUME, you can name your résumé "Second draft of resume for dog catcher job." The scoop on saving is in Chapter 5, with little reminders salted throughout the rest of the book.

7. Editing Is Easy!

If you've never used a word processor before, you will be stunned and amazed at how easy it is to edit your work: no more retyping whole pages because of one !#*%! typographical error. (I *hated* it when that used to happen—of course, that was *waaaay* back in the olden days, back before Liquid Paper).

You can check the spelling of a single word, a phrase, a paragraph, or a whole document, just by opening the **Tools** menu and choosing **Spelling**. You can find an entirely new word, just by selecting **Thesaurus** from the **Tools** menu.

Even if you've used word processors before and have used the usual Cut, Copy, and Paste commands in the Edit menu, you'll still be floored by drag-and-drop editing, which lets you select text, and then simply drag it to its new home—elsewhere in the same document, or even to a completely different Works document.

There are chapters on editing for each of the main Works applications. Word processing's editing chapter is Chapter 8; for spreadsheets check out Chapter 15; for databases try Chapter 19.

8. You Can Dress Up Your Documents with ClipArt or WordArt

Page after page after page of words and numbers is not the most exciting way to present information. To keep your readers interested, you can jazz up your documents with ClipArt and WordArt.

ClipArt lets you insert pictures into your document—so you can illustrate the report on your trip to Hawaii with palm trees and beauties in grass skirts.

WordArt lets you turn boring words into works of art, by adding color, shadows, and by bending them into all manner of bizarre shapes.

To begin, select **ClipArt** or **WordArt** from the **Insert** menu. If you want to add a drawing of your own, select **Drawing** from the **Insert** menu, and you'll find tools to help you create your own work of art. (Chapter 22 covers these and other art accessories).

9. Printing Is a Pleasure...

Once you've worked so hard (well, not *that* hard, but hard enough) creating a beautiful document, there's nothing quite as satisfying as printing out a paper copy you can hold in your hot little hands.

Naturally, there are some small picky things you need to do or have before you can print—a printer couldn't hurt, for one. You should also have your document set up to print (using the **Page Setup** command in the **File** menu) on the proper size paper, with appropriate margins. That's all covered in Chapter 6.

Once you take care of those basics, printing from Works is as easy as selecting **File**, **Print** and then waiting for your printer to hand it over.

10. Help Is All Around

(I almost broke into a chorus of the theme from "The Mary Tyler Moore" show. That kind of help, *nobody* needs.)

No matter where you are in Works, or what you're doing, there's help available so you can get the job done. It's as close as Works' Help menu. You can set Works up so that its Help menu is visible all the time. Just select **How to use Help** from the **Help** menu.

When you try to do something new, Works will even offer to give you step-by-step instructions. You can't miss. Read about the details on getting the help you want, when you want it, in Chapter 4.

Chapter 2

Getting to Know Windows 95

In This Chapter

- ➤ Windows is…
- ➤ Getting it started
- ➤ Doing stuff with it
- ➤ Shutting it down

Before you get your hopes up, this is only the most general glance at Windows 95. This tiny little chapter will in no way replace your manual or a good book (such as *The Complete Idiot's Guide to Windows 95*) devoted to the ins and outs of Windows. It's simply meant to give you a few basics, so you can do what you need to with Works and get on with your life.

That said…

What Is Windows 95?

Windows 95 is the newest incarnation of the most popular operating environment for IBM-compatible computers (PCs).

Check This Out...

MS-DOS An acronym for Microsoft Disk Operating System (pronounced "em-ess-doss" to rhyme with "toss"). MS-DOS is the most popular operating system for IBM-compatible computers.

OS Operating System. The basic set of instructions that tell a computer how to deal with software, hardware, and commands. All computers require an operating system. PCs can use MS-DOS or Windows 95, among others.

Your real-life work environment may include a desk, filing cabinet, and telephone. A computer's environment contains similar elements. Instead of a desk, you have a *desktop*, a home base from which you access the rest of the tools available to your computer. It also includes the PC's filing system and software accessories.

Earlier versions of Windows were "shell programs" that acted as an intermediary between users and the dreaded MS-DOS C:\> prompt. Instead of remembering an obscure command to make your PC, say, format a disk, you'd simply select a command from a menu that said (in plain English) **Format a disk**. Windows 95, while retaining the menus and plain English commands, eliminates your dependency on MS-DOS. Windows 95 *is* your computer's operating system.

While Windows 95 replaces MS-DOS as the operating system for your PC, you can still run Windows 95 in MS-DOS mode, to take advantage of the huge number of MS-DOS programs still available from your favorite software vendor. For details, check your Windows 95 manual, or online help available from the Help menu.

Launching Windows 95

This one's a no-brainer. To start Windows 95, turn on your computer. Since Windows 95 replaces MS-DOS as the operating system, it starts up automatically when you start your PC.

And you thought this was going to be difficult.

Techno Talk
blah blah blah blah blah bl b

Restarting in MS-DOS Mode

If you have a non-Windows game or application you want to install or use, you can restart Windows 95 so it runs like MS-DOS. To restart into MS-DOS Mode, open the **Start** menu. Next, **choose Shut Down**. Finally, click **Restart The Computer In MS-DOS Mode**.

Your PC will go through its startup routine, and when it's done, you'll see that old, faithful C:\> prompt. *Yippee*.

Icons Everywhere

The very first time you start up Windows 95, you'll see a special one-time-only welcoming box that will offer you some special information. You may take advantage of it, or not, as you see fit—but it would be a good idea to read through it.

Techno Talk

Gone But Not Forgotten...

If you decide you want to see that special information at a later date, double-click on the **WELCOME** file in your Windows directory (you can use either Windows Explorer or My Computer to do this). The official name is WELCOME.EXE, but you probably won't see the file extension since Windows 95 tends to hide them.

You'll also get a **Tip of the Day** window, with a handy/annoying (I haven't made up my mind which, yet) tip. Once you whack through all that underbrush, you'll see a desktop like the one shown here, dotted with *icons* and with a *taskbar* across the bottom of your screen.

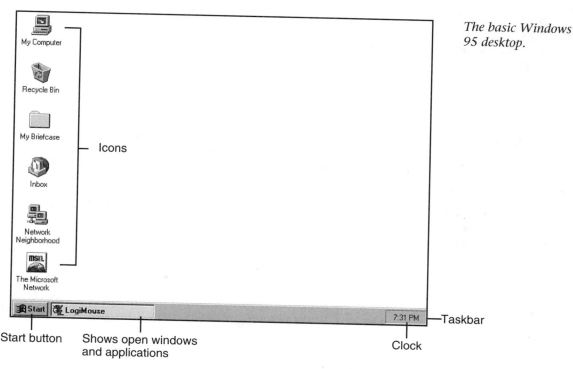

The basic Windows 95 desktop.

My Computer

Recycle Bin

My Briefcase

Inbox — Icons

Network Neighborhood

The Microsoft Network

Start | LogiMouse   7:31 PM —Taskbar

Start button | Shows open windows and applications | Clock

The first thing you'll probably notice is the string of icons running down the left side of the screen. These icons give you quick access to a number of Windows features and functions.

My Computer

Gives you instant access to your floppy drive, hard drive, and (if you have one) CD-ROM or other storage drive. It also gives you a quick way to access your Windows Control Panels and Printer(s).

Recycle Bin

A politically correct "trash can" where deleted files land until you finally confirm that you want to get rid of them. It acts as a safety net and gives you a chance to change your mind.

The Microsoft Network

The Microsoft Network is an optional feature. If it's installed on your system, this icon will launch the software that lets you connect (via a *modem* and telephone line) to Microsoft's online service.

Inbox

Launches the Microsoft Exchange application, useful for sending and receiving information on a network. Most home users won't have/need it, though.

Check This Out...

Icon A graphical representation of a computer command or feature. Usually, you issue a command by double-clicking on an icon with your mouse.

Taskbar The bar that runs across the bottom of the Windows 95 screen. It contains buttons for all of your currently open windows and applications so you can easily switch between them. To go to an item in the taskbar, just click on it.

Modem A device that allows computers to communicate with each other over standard telephone lines. The name is a contraction of the words **mo**dulate and **dem**odulate, which describe the process of turning data into sounds and back into data again.

Network Two or more computers linked to each other to make it easier for them to share data. These computers may be in the same room or spread out over a wider area. Printers and other devices may also be part of a network.

Because these little graphics represent a way for users to accomplish things on a computer, Windows is referred to as a *graphical user interface* or GUI (pronounced "GOO-ey").

On Your Marks! Get Set! Start Button!

The Start button, shown here, is one of the hot new features of the Windows 95 desktop. The Start button gives you immediate access to all of the applications (and other files) on your PC's hard drive—*automatically.*

It's way cool.

To launch an application with the Start button, just click on the **Start** button. The menu (or one similar) shown in the figure will pop up. When your mouse cursor touches an item with an arrow after it (such as Programs, in the figure) a submenu pops up. Just click on the name of the application you want to launch, and it will start right up.

Mighty menus from little Start buttons grow…

Later on, once you're comfortable with the new features of Windows 95, you can customize what appears in your Start menu. Just select **Taskbar** from the **Settings** submenu on the **Start** menu. You can easily add new items (click **Add**), remove unwanted old items (click **Remove**), or completely juggle the menu's contents around (click **Advanced**). See your Windows 95 manual, or online Help, for details. (It's easy, though.)

To make use of the Start button, desktop icons, and all the other icons used throughout Windows 95, and Works for Windows 95, you need to have some basic mouse skills.

13

Let Your Mouse Do It

This information will probably be more helpful if you're actually at your computer, with the computer turned on, so you can play along.

There are two basic mouse skills you'll use all the time: clicking and dragging.

The Drag

Dragging is just moving the mouse around on your desk (preferably on a mouse pad; it rolls smoother that way). When you do, you'll notice that the little white arrow you saw in the last figure, mostly moves the same way the mouse does.

With a little practice, you can learn to move the mouse so the cursor is pointing at an icon or menu—but forget I mentioned menus, we haven't done them yet (we will shortly). Don't worry about the rules of etiquette either. This is one instance where it *is* polite to point.

For the moment, practice moving the mouse around so the cursor lands in the center of the icon in the upper left corner of your screen, the one called **My Computer**. When you can do that without too much grunting, groaning, and grinding of teeth, move on to the next section.

The Click

Once you have the mouse cursor pointed where you want, to get the icon, or whatever, to do its thing, you need to click. To click, just press the mouse button on the left side of the mouse, once quickly. That's it; that's a click.

If the cursor was pointed at the **My Computer** icon when you did the click, the icon will have turned a dark color. That means the click was successful. It also means that the icon is *selected*. We'll talk more about selecting, or choosing, stuff in later chapters.

You'll usually use a single click in Windows to select an icon, push a button, and to make a selection from a menu (I promise, menus are coming up shortly).

The Drag and the Drop

Now I want you to click on something else—the **My Computer** icon, maybe. This time, when you press the mouse button, don't let go. The icon will stay dark and, if you move the mouse around, you'll see that it *drags* the icon with it.

When you release the mouse button, the cursor releases the icon. That's called *dropping*, for the obvious reason: you just dropped something.

The Double-Click

While selecting an icon can be fun, it isn't exactly *productive*. To get that icon to do a little more, you need to click on it twice quickly. That's called a *double-click*. When you do that successfully, you'll open a window (see the next figure). If, instead of opening a window, the icon only changed color twice, you didn't click quickly enough, or you clicked too quickly. Your PC thought your double-click was two single clicks, or one great big single click. Try it again—practice makes perfect.

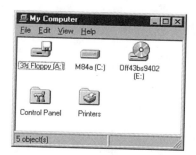

The My Computer window—all that, with only a double-click.

Don't worry about what's what in the window; I'll break it down for you in a moment. The point is, that if you're looking at a window similar to the one shown here, you've mastered the double-click.

Other Assorted Mouse Activities

All the other clicking and dragging you'll do will be combinations of those you've already mastered (you have mastered them, haven't you?).

In some cases, you'll use a *triple-click* (which sounds like a move in gymnastics; "Helga will now attempt a half Mitzi Gaynor with a triple-click finish on the balance beam"). It comes in very handy when editing. We'll explore these fancy-schmancy uses in later chapters, beginning with Chapter 8.

For now, as long as you have that lovely little window open on your screen, let's break it down into its component parts.

15

Anatomy of a Windows Window

In case you've already forgotten what that window looked like, here it comes again. This time, the various parts are labeled for easy identification.

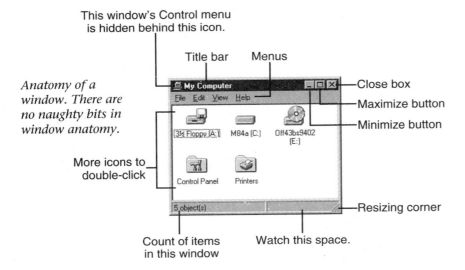

This window's Control menu
is hidden behind this icon.

Title bar   Menus

Anatomy of a window. There are no naughty bits in window anatomy.

Close box
Maximize button
Minimize button

More icons to double-click

Resizing corner

Count of items in this window

Watch this space.

The dark colored bar across the top of the window, where it says **My Computer**, is the title bar. It will contain the name of the icon, folder, or file you've opened.

At either end of the title bar, there are some more icons. To the left, there's a picture of a small computer. That's the same picture as the My Computer icon you double-clicked to open the window. This icon will vary from window to window, and it's a handy way to remember what a window is or does.

If you click on that small icon, a Control menu will drop down from it—you can see what I mean in the next figure. The menu gives you a variety of things you can do with the window (Restore, Move, Size, Minimize, Maximize, and Close). To select a menu item, just click on it. If a menu item is grayed out and hard to read, that menu option isn't available at the moment.

These menu items don't do anything dangerous, so why not just try them out? Just know that the Close command will make the window go away; just double-click on the **My Computer** icon to get it back again.

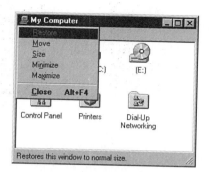

The My Computer window's control menu: what a control freak.

At the opposite end of the title bar, there are three buttons, which duplicate some of the menu commands.

 This is the **Minimize button**. It will shrink the window down to a button in the taskbar. To restore a minimized window, just click on its name in the taskbar, and the window comes back to its original location.

 This is the **Maximize button**. It has the picture of a single window in it. Click on it, and the window will grow to fill your whole screen (that's called *maximized*). It's handy if there are lots of things in the window you need to look at.

 When a window is filling your whole screen, the Maximize button changes to a Restore button, to show two overlapped windows. Click on it now, and the window goes back to its former, small size. This kind of button is called a *toggle* because it switches between two commands, like an On/Off switch.

 The one with the × in it is the Close button. Click this button, and the window closes. To get the window back, you have to double-click on its icon again.

Below the title bar is a row of menus (**File**, **Edit**, **View**, and **Help**). They let you perform some basic tasks on the contents of the window, and I'll explain each in the next section.

Below the menus, there's an open space that (as in the figure) contains icons for the components of your computer, and the Windows control panels.

Double-clicking the floppy icon gives you access to the contents of a disk in that drive. If there's no disk in the drive, you'll get an error message. If the disk in the drive is not formatted, you'll be asked if you want to format it.

If you have more than one floppy drive in your computer, you will have an icon for each.

 This is the icon for a hard drive. Double-clicking this icon will give you a window showing the contents of your hard drive. If you have more than one hard drive, you will have an icon for each hard drive.

 This is the icon for my PC's CD-ROM drive. It gives you access to the contents of a CD-ROM disc. If your computer doesn't have a CD-ROM drive, you won't have this icon.

 The Control Panel icon gives you access to all of Windows 95's customizing features. Here you can toy with the color scheme of your windows and the desktop, and tinker with how your mouse behaves, among other options.

 The Printers folder icon gives you access to any and all printing devices attached to your PC. It may also include a fax modem, if you have one (your computer thinks of faxing like printing).

Naturally, the contents of this window will vary (a little or a lot) depending on your computer's configuration.

Across the bar at the bottom of the window—called the *Status Bar*—there are two indented-looking boxes. The one on the left gives you a count of all the icons in the window.

In the preceding figure, the box on the bottom right is empty because no icon is selected. If you were to click on the icon for your hard drive, the box would show how much free space is left on that drive. In other windows (such as the one that shows the contents of your hard drive), this box will show the amount of space a file takes up on your hard drive or floppy disk. It's a multipurpose box.

If there were more icons than could comfortably fit in a window this size, there would also be a scroll bar at the right side or a scroll bar across the bottom of the window (or sometimes both) to allow you to get at the icons that slipped out of view inside. Don't panic over them. You'll be seeing some, up close and personal—why, *right now!*

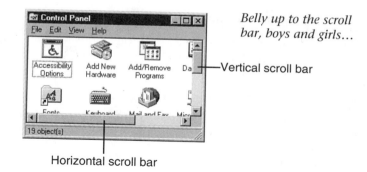

Belly up to the scroll bar, boys and girls...

—Vertical scroll bar

Horizontal scroll bar

Menus Out the Wazoo

The menus you'll find built into most Windows 95 windows are: File, Edit, View, and Help. Let's take a look at each one.

To get at a menu, you can click once on the menu's name, or you can press the **Alt** key, followed by the letter that's underlined in the menu name (F for File, E for Edit, and so on).

File Me!

Two faces of the File menu—its contents vary depending on what you've selected in the window.

As you can see, the File menu is flexible. Its contents change depending on what (if anything) you have selected in the window.

In the File menu on the right, the icon for the floppy drive was selected, so Windows obligingly added commands appropriate to a floppy disk (Copy Disk and Format). In the File menu on the left, a folder has been selected. It isn't a disk, so the disk-specific commands disappear. How convenient.

The File menu commands, in order of appearance:

Open   Opens the icon. If the icon is for a disk or folder, it opens a window displaying its contents. If the icon is for an application, it will launch (start) the application.

Explore   Opens the Windows 95 Explorer (a way to look through all of the files stored on your computer). If you've used an earlier version of Windows, this is the Windows 95 version of the File Manager.

Find   (disk-only option) Will search the selected item for any file by name, date created, or file type.

Copy Disk   (disk-only option) Will make a duplicate copy of a floppy disk in the selected drive.

Format   (disk-only option) Will format a blank floppy disk so your computer can use it. It will also format a hard drive, so *click carefully*.

Create Shortcut   Will create a small icon for a file, folder, or application and place it on your desktop. This is a convenient option for things you use every day—that way you don't have to go searching.

Delete   (file-only option) Will delete the selected file from your disk or hard drive and put it in the Recycle Bin for later disposal.

Rename   (file-only option) Lets you enter a new name for a file or folder.

Properties   Gives you information about the selected item. How much space a file takes up, where it's located on your hard drive, and other useful scoop.

Close   Closes the window.

Edit Me!

The Edit menu.

The Edit menu, oddly enough, contains commands that are handy when editing text and duplicating files. We'll be going over these commands in detail in Chapter 8, so I'm only going to point out the last two in the menu here because they're great time-savers.

Select All   Will select all of the items in the window as though you held down the Ctrl key and clicked on each icon one at a time.

Invert Selection   Will completely reverse the selections you've made in the window. What was selected becomes unselected (deselected? not selected?), and what was not selected becomes selected. Very handy if you want everything except one or two items in a window selected.

Odd Selection Stuff

As I mention in the section on the Select All command, you can select more than one icon by holding down the **Alt** key while you click. Each additional item you click will also be selected.

To select a group of items that are near each other, you can hold down the **Shift** key while you click. Click on the first item in a row of icons, and the last item in the row, and the whole row will be selected. Click on the last icon in the row below the first, and *both* rows will be completely selected. Very cool.

View Me!

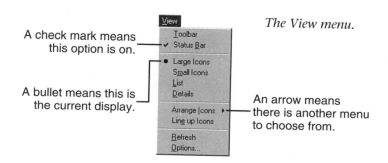

The View menu.

A check mark means this option is on.

A bullet means this is the current display.

An arrow means there is another menu to choose from.

The commands in the View menu let you tinker with how information appears in the window. Instead of long boring explanations, why don't you play around with them after you read these quickie descriptions. You can't hurt anything, and it's more fun.

Toolbar Adds a convenient set of tools below the menus in the current window.

Status Bar Turns the information boxes at the bottom of the window on or off.

Large Icons Uses large icons in the window—easier on the eyes.

Small Icons Uses smaller icons in the window. Harder on the eyes but better for displaying lots of icons.

List Displays the icons in even smaller form, listed in columns.

Details Shows information about each icon when displayed in List view.

Arrange Icons Gives you a number or arrangement options on the pop-up menu.

Line up Icons Makes all the icons in the window jump into order.

Refresh Pours your icons a refreshing beverage. Just kidding. Actually, it makes Windows reread the information that's supposed to be in the window, just in case you added something while it wasn't looking.

Options Gives you a choice between two window options. Try both and see which you like.

Help Me!

The Help menu.

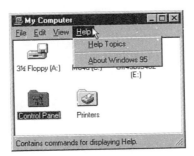

The Help menu gives you immediate access to all the help you might need. This is another menu you should play around with; read through the files because this is cursory coverage of the complex beastie known as Windows 95.

The menu entries shown here will change depending on where you are and what you're doing. As you use Windows and as you try a new thing, I suggest you check out the Help menu first and see what you can learn.

For the Forgetful Like... What Was I Saying?

Don't worry if all this menu business doesn't stick right now. It will.

In the meantime, as long as you have the **Status Bar** turned on (it's in the View menu), whenever your cursor touches a menu name, or item, a brief description will pop up in the Status Bar. You can see what I mean back in the picture of the Help menu.

Closing Windows

That's all we're going to look at in Windows 95 for now. We'll look at other features and functions in later chapters when they're relevant to what we're doing in Works.

However, there's one last thing you should know: when you finish using your computer for the day, *you should not just turn it off.* That's not a good thing to do. Instead, make sure you've saved all of your work in whatever applications you've been using (that's covered in Chapter 5), and then shut down Windows. Here's how:

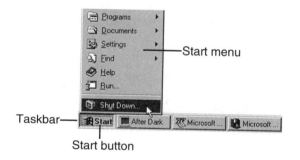

Shutting Windows down for the night.

After you've saved your work, click on the **Start** button at the bottom left corner of your screen (you can see it in the figure here). A menu will pop up.

Click on the **Shut Down** option in the menu. That will give you the following dialog box.

Dialog Box

Sometimes, when you tell your computer to do something, it needs more information to follow your orders. When that happens, a *dialog box* appears on your screen asking for the additional information.

Say "Goodnight,"
Gracie...

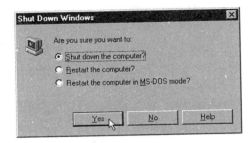

Windows presents you with the dialog box to make sure you really want to shut down. It also gives you the option to restart your computer (go through its startup routine without cutting the power), or restart in MS-DOS mode.

Since, in this example, we want to shut down, make sure that **Shut down the computer?** is the selected option (the circle in front of it has a dot in it, as in the picture), then click on the **Yes** button.

Windows will think about it for a minute and then put up a polite little message telling you it's safe to turn your computer off. When you see that, you can turn off your computer.

The Least You Need to Know

➤ We've barely scratched the surface of Windows 95, so be sure to read your manuals and Help files.

➤ Windows 95 launches automatically every time you start your computer.

➤ You'll use your mouse to click and double-click on menus and icons to get work done.

➤ If you can't remember what menus or menu commands do, the Status Bar will help you out with brief descriptions.

➤ Always shut down Windows (with the **Shut Down** command in the **Start** menu) before cutting the power to your computer. Bad things could happen to your PC if you don't. Trust me.

Chapter 3

Works Gives You "The Works"

In This Chapter

➤ Works helps you get to work

➤ Works' main features

➤ Wizards and other goodies

We all wear a lot of hats. For myself, I write these books, I dabble in professional theater, I volunteer at some not-for-profit organizations, and do desktop publishing, among other things.

You may be a parent, a student, an employee, or a part-time entrepreneur. Additionally, you may have hobbies, be a political or social activist, or any of a million other things.

However many hats you wear, your PC and Microsoft Works can be of help. Works gives you a wide assortment of tools that you can use individually, or together, to tackle many of the chores you need to do while wearing each hat in your wardrobe.

A Typical Works Workday

On any given day, these are the sorts of things I do with my computer:

➤ Check my e-mail (that's "e" as in "electronic" and "mail" as in "letters").

Check This Out...

A Confirmed Online Junkie

I belong to several online services (America Online, CompuServe, and eWorld). I usually include my e-mail address in my books so I can receive feedback from the folks who read them. If you're interested and belong to a service like those mentioned, you can drop me a note on America Online to the screen name **Piv**. From any other service, address it to **piv@aol.com**. If you don't use an online service, you can send me regular mail in care of the publisher—the address is in the front of the book.

➤ Write, write, write. It's my job, after all.

➤ Put together flyers, newsletters, and business cards for self-employed friends.

➤ Do résumés for my actor friends.

➤ Once or twice a month, I update a large database for a local AIDS service organization and generate reports to help them keep the funding-types happy.

➤ Sometimes, I am called upon to do some odd things—such as create fake headlines for newspapers. I did that for a local theater production of "The Midnight Hour." They needed a copy of a Paris newspaper with a particular headline.

All of these things can be done with Works, because Works comes fully packed with tools.

Here's what you get.

Write Up a Storm

Even if it doesn't begin with "It was a dark and stormy night," you can use Works' word processor to write everything from a simple thank-you note to your Aunt Mildred, to the Great American Novel.

A word processor is a software tool that simplifies the editing process, freeing up brainpower for the difficult part of writing: thinking of something to say in an informative, entertaining way.

Works' word processor helps you enter your text, pretty it up, edit (and re-edit, and re-re-edit), and print out a copy so you can share it with others. It also gives you powerful tools to make writing a little easier, including a dictionary to check your spelling, and a thesaurus to help you find just the right word. It won't, however, turn a bad writer into a good one. Take a gander at Works at work on my résumé in the following figure.

Part 2 covers Works' word processor in almost frightening detail.

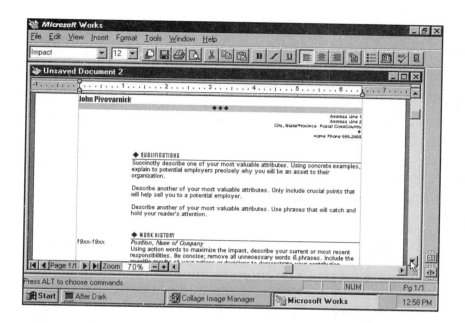

Works' word processor, showing a phony résumé for yours truly.

Crunch Those Numbers

Whether you're trying to balance your own budget, or the Federal budget, it can involve crunching a lot of numbers as quickly as possible.

A *spreadsheet* is a tool that helps you organize and present numerical information in a way that's easy for the reader to understand. Additionally, you can perform mathematical operations (*"Nurse, I asked for a division sign, not a plus." "Sorry doctor."*) on any or all of that numerical information. The following figure shows a Works spreadsheet.

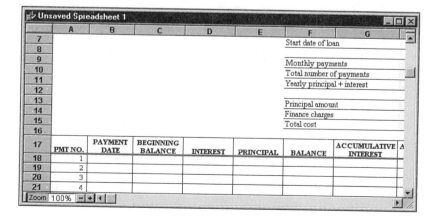

A Works spreadsheet for calculating a loan repayment.

For the mathematically squeamish (like myself), Works for Windows 95 includes Easy Calc, a handy tool to help you put together your equations correctly the first time. Part 3 completely explains the Works spreadsheet.

Data for Days

When I talk about *data*, I don't mean ol' yellow eyes from "Star Trek: The Next Generation." I mean information—just about any kind of information.

A database is a collection of information that, because of how the information is broken down, can be easily searched and sorted for whatever information you need right *now*.

I mentioned that I maintain a database for an organization. It mainly consists of names, addresses, birth dates, and other personal statistics. You can keep a similar database for your family and friends to remind you of birthdays and anniversaries. Or you can, as shown in the following figure, catalog your valuable possessions (there's an *Exorcist* joke there, but I'm choosing to ignore it) in the event of a catastrophe.

A Home Inventory database—a good thing to have for insurance purposes.

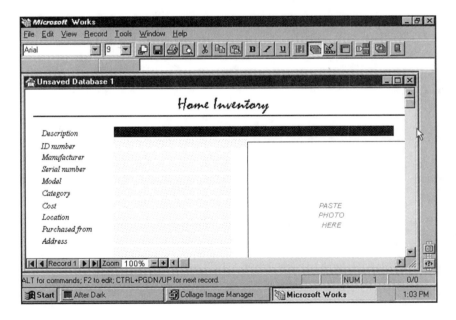

Personally, I've always dreamt of having all of the books I own catalogued in one big database file so I could quickly and easily find reference materials. My brain is such that I can remember gobs of little details and useless information, but things like titles and authors go right out of my head. Still, every month I buy more books, and the more books I buy, the less likely it becomes that I'll actually sit down and catalog them.

Learn about database basics in Part 4. When you get good at it, give me a call. I may have a job for you.

Pretty As a Picture

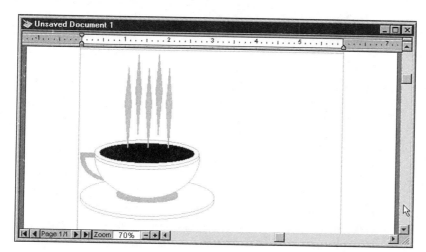

ClipArt in a word processor document—I really need that cup of coffee, too.

Once you've created a document with one of the major Works tools, you can pretty it up with artistic embellishments like the one shown in the preceding figure.

Microsoft Works comes with an assortment of ClipArt (little pictures you can add to your documents), the capability to turn text into art (the WordArt feature), or you can take things you've created yourself, with Works or another application, and plunk them down in your Works documents.

This magical ability to plunk stuff down ("plunk" is a technical term, meaning "to place discreetly") is available because of Works' integration, and its OLE capabilities. OLE is an abbreviation for *object linking and embedding*, and you can read about it in Chapters 22 and 23.

> **Check This Out...**
>
> **Document** Any file you create with Works, or *any* software for that matter: a spreadsheet, a letter, a novel, an address database. They're all documents. It's a term used to distinguish data files from software and system files, since "file" is too generic to be meaningful.

Other Goodies

Works also provides you with communications software, an address book, and tools to make each of the major components easier to use.

The communications features require that your computer has a modem, and you have hooked the modem up to a telephone line. With it, you can contact other computers, electronic bulletin boards, and online information services. Chapter 26 covers computer communications.

A personal address book created with a TaskWizard.

The address book is actually a customized database file you can create with a TaskWizard. You use the address book just like you would a pocket-sized paper one, except you can use this one to add often-used names and addresses (and other information) to your Works documents. Oh, and this one probably won't fit in your pocket—unless you wear some mighty big pants (see Chapter 25).

Wizards, like the TaskWizard you'll use to create your address book(s), are fill-in-the-blank forms that let you take a basic document type (such as an address book) and customize it to your needs. Works holds your hand and walks you through the creation process so it's all simple and painless. You won't even break a sweat.

There are TaskWizards for creating a letterhead or résumé, for printing envelopes and labels, and even some for business and household management. Read Chapter 5 to learn about all of the TaskWizards.

Sample other goodies such as creating charts, graphs, and helpful accessories (such as Easy Text) in chapters devoted to the Works features. For example, check out charts, graphs, and spreadsheets in Chapter 17.

The Least You Need to Know

The *absolute* least, as a matter of fact:

➤ Microsoft Works for Windows 95 is a powerful tool with word processing, spreadsheet, database, and communications capabilities.

➤ You can work with the various components individually or play mix-and-match with them.

➤ For the sake of easy learning, you'll look at each of the major components individually, and then you'll explore the fancy mix-and-match stuff in Part 5.

Chapter 4

Starting from Scratch with Works

In This Chapter

➤ Installing Works

➤ We'll do launch...

➤ The nickel tour

➤ Help!

Since we're taking a whack at all of the Works basics in this section, let's start with something *really* basic: installing Works on your computer. If Works is already installed on your PC, you may talk quietly among yourselves until the rest of the class catches up.

Let's Start at the Very Beginning

Oh, Lordy, now I've got that "Do, a deer" song from "The Sound of Music" stuck in my head. Help me! There are nuns in my head! Must...fight it...must not sing the song...must-not-put-on-*lederhosen*...

Sorry. All better now. Where was I? Oh, yes.

Installing Microsoft Works for Windows 95 is simple. When you purchased Works, you either received the software on a handful of floppy disks or on a CD-ROM disc.

What About Windows 95?

Yes, as I mentioned in the first chapter, you do need to have Windows 95 installed on your PC before you can install Works for Windows 95.

Many folks will already have Windows 95 installed on their computers. If you don't, you'll need to install it. Don't panic—the process is remarkably similar to the one described here. Just follow along with these instructions, using your Windows 95 disks or CD. After you get the Setup program running, follow the instructions on your screen. It's very easy and Microsoft claims it will take from 45–90 minutes to complete, depending on your computer (but my Pentium managed it in fifteen, installing from a CD).

Before you start the installation process, you should save any files you have open and then quit all of your open applications. They could interfere with the installation process.

It's a Setup!

To begin the installation:

1. Insert the first floppy disk (labeled **Setup Disk 1**) in your floppy drive, or insert the Works CD in your CD-ROM drive.

2. Open the **Start** menu and choose **Run** (it's in the lower left-hand corner of the Windows 95 desktop) as shown here. That will open the Run dialog box.

3. In the Run dialog box, type in the drive letter for the drive you just inserted the disk (or disc) in, followed by the word **Setup**.

Selecting Run from the Start menu.

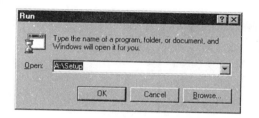

The Run dialog box.

For a floppy disk, it will probably look like this:

A:\Setup

For a CD-ROM drive, it will probably look like this:

D:\Setup

Then click **OK**.

What Drive Is This?

If you aren't sure what letters have been assigned to your drives, you can double-click the **My Computer** icon (as discussed in Chapter 2) to see what drive letters have been set. You could also use the **Browse** button on the Run dialog box to navigate to the setup file in the appropriate drive.

Your PC will churn for a minute while it reads the setup information from the drive. In a moment, you'll see a screen that says **Welcome to the Microsoft Works 4.0 installation program**. After reading the information on the screen, click the **Continue** button to proceed.

Next, you'll be asked to enter your name and organization information (if you'll be using Works at work). If you already have a Microsoft product installed on your PC, this information will already be filled in for you, and you can just click **OK** to continue. If not, enter your name and (if you care to) organization name and then click **OK** to continue.

Setup will show you a screen with your Product ID number. It will look something like: **12345-123-0000000-12345.** You'll need this number if you ever need to call Microsoft's technical support line. You don't need to write it down now; you can get it later by selecting the **About Microsoft Works 4.0** from the Works **Help** menu. Just click **OK** and get on with your life.

Direct Me To Your Directory

Setup assumes you'll want to install Works on your C: drive.

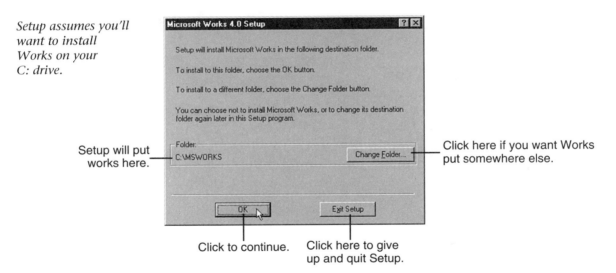

Setup will put works here.

Click here if you want Works put somewhere else.

Click to continue.

Click here to give up and quit Setup.

When the ID number screen goes away, you'll see the preceding dialog box. Works' Setup assumes you want to install Works on your C: drive in a folder (which, in its secret double-life is also known as a directory) called **MSWORKS.** In most cases, that's probably what you do want. If that *is* what you want, click the **OK** button and installation will continue.

If you want to install Works on another drive (if you have another hard disk, say) or you want to change the name of the folder, click on the **Change Folder** button. You'll get the following dialog box.

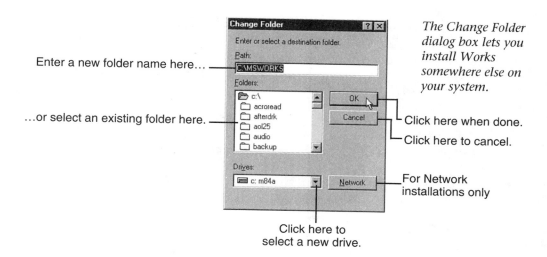

Enter a new folder name here... ─────

...or select an existing folder here. ─────

The Change Folder dialog box lets you install Works somewhere else on your system.

Click here when done.
Click here to cancel.

For Network installations only

Click here to
select a new drive.

Use the Change Folder dialog box to change the drive you're going to install Works on (with the **Drives** pop-up list), or just the name of the folder it will land in (just type in a new folder name preceded by **C:**), or both.

Network Alert!

Unless you *are* the network administrator, don't use the Network button without checking with the person in charge of the network first. You could accidentally booger up the whole network, and that's no way to win friends and influence people.

Click **OK** when you're happy with your changes. You can click **Cancel** if you change your mind and want to go with the **C:\MSWORKS** installation choice.

Works? Or Works Lite?

After you tell the Setup program where you want Works' installed, it will ask you what you want installed with the preceding dialog box.

A **Complete Installation** will install all the files you need to use all of Works' various components. For most folks, this is probably the best choice.

A **Custom Installation** lets you pick and choose what elements of Work's you want to install. Only select this if you know exactly what you do, and do not, want.

Personally, I recommend doing a complete installation. You can always remove elements later by running Works Setup again—a copy of Setup is installed when you install Works. If you insist, you can do a custom installation by clicking on the **Custom Installation** description button. You'll then need to select which components you want installed before you continue.

To do a complete installation, click on the **Complete Installation** button.

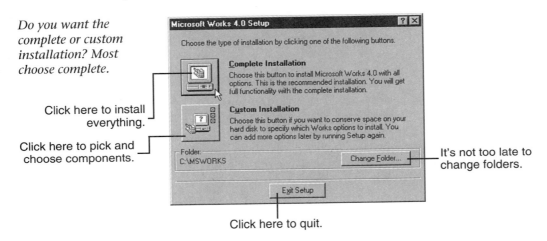

Do you want the complete or custom installation? Most choose complete.

Click here to install everything.

Click here to pick and choose components.

It's not too late to change folders.

Click here to quit.

Taking the Shortcut and Shuffling Floppies

After you choose between Complete or Custom installations, the Setup program will ask if you want to install a shortcut to Works on your desktop.

A shortcut is an icon (like those shown back in Chapter 2) that allows you to launch Works simply by double-clicking on it. It will save you a few steps if you think you'll be using Works all of the time (you won't have to use Windows' Start menu).

If you want the shortcut, click **Yes**. If you don't, click **No**. It's that simple.

With all those decisions out of the way, Setup will begin the installation process. A small thermometer-type display will appear on your screen, showing you the status of the installation. If you're installing from a CD-ROM disc, you can take five and go get yourself a refreshing beverage or something. You won't have anything to do for a few minutes.

If you're installing from floppy disks, stay nearby. Every few minutes or so, the Setup program will ask you to insert the next disk it needs to complete the installation. Just pop out the disk that's in your floppy drive, slip in the requested disk, then click **OK** or press **Enter**. You have about six disks to shuffle through before you're done.

Done!

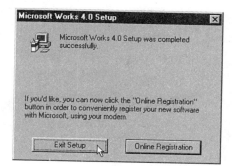

OK or register?

When Setup is finished installing Works on your PC, you'll see this little congratulatory message, which gives you two choices:

➤ You can now quit the Setup program (just click **OK** at the bottom of the dialog box).

➤ Or you can click the **Online Registration** button and register your copy of Works with Microsoft.

In order to use Online Registration, you need to have a modem connected to your PC and a telephone line connected to your modem. If you have both, go ahead. If you don't, exit Setup.

It's important to register your software. That lets Microsoft know you shelled out money for their software, and it gives them your name and address so they can keep you apprised of developments (new version of Works or other new products).

If you choose Online Registration, you'll be asked to fill in some basic information about yourself, and then you can zap it off to Microsoft via your modem. If you can't use Online Registration, there's a registration card in the your software package; just fill it out and mail it in the old-fashioned way.

Launching Works

Launching is just a fancy way of saying "starting up."

You can *launch* Works either by selecting it from the **Start** menu (as shown here), or by using the Works shortcut on your desktop (if you choose the shortcut option during installation). If you had the Setup program drop a Works shortcut on your desktop, just double-click its icon and Works will start right up.

Launching Works
with the Start menu.

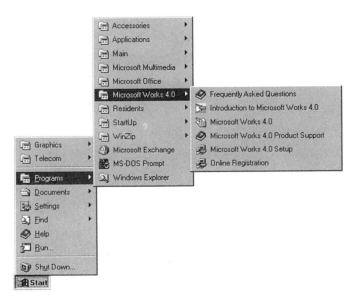

To launch Works with the Start menu (and, *believe* me, it takes a lot less time to actually do this than it takes to explain it):

1. Click on the **Start** button at the lower left corner of your screen.

2. Move the mouse pointer up so it's touching the **Programs** entry on the Start menu. Another menu will pop up.

3. Move the mouse pointer so it's touching the Microsoft Works 4.0 entry in the Programs menu, and yet *another* menu will pop up.

4. Move the mouse pointer so it's touching the Microsoft Works 4.0 entry in that menu, and click. Works will start right up.

The chain of popped-up menus will look something like the preceding figure, but you'll probably have different software installed on your PC; don't let the other different names throw you.

It Keeps Asking for This Bookshelf Thing!

If you have your copy of Works 4.0 on CD, it *may* have also come with Microsoft Bookshelf, a CD-based set of reference books on the same CD. If, when you launch Works, you see a message asking for the Bookshelf CD, you can either pop the Works/Bookshelf CD in your CD-ROM drive (it will be the same one you used to install Works) and click **OK**, or skip the CD and click **Cancel**. Just so you know.

Taking the Nickel Tour

The first time you launch Works, you'll get a little dialog box asking if you want to **see a short demonstration of how to get started with Works.** Click **OK** and take the tour; it's painless, only takes about 10 minutes, and gives you an idea of all the things Works can do for you.

The tour looks a little something like the next figure.

Taking the Introduction to Works tour.

"Help, Jane, stop this crazy thing!"

Go to the next screen

Share the Tour with Other Folks

Check This Out...

If there are others in your home who will be using Works, you can launch the Tour at any time by selecting **Introduction to Microsoft Works 4.0** from the Microsoft Works 4.0 entry in your program listing on the **Start** menu. (You can see it if you sneak a peek back at the picture of the Start menu back in the last section.) Or you can start the tour from the **Help** menu, if Works is already running. More about the Help menu in a moment.

When you finish taking the tour, Works will launch and present you with the Task Launcher.

Your first peek at the
Task Launcher.

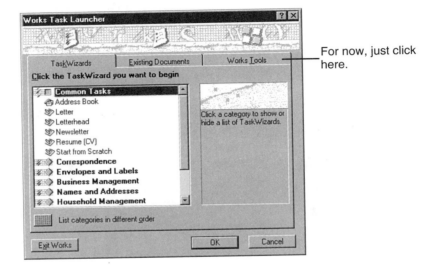

For now, just click
here.

The Task Launcher is where you'll begin every session with Works from here on out. As such, it deserves special attention—it'll get it, too, but not until the next chapter.

For now, just so we can get quickly to the important Help feature, just click on the **Works Tools** tab at the upper right corner of the Task Launcher. That will give you a choice of the four basic food groups—*er*—Works Tools (can you tell I'm hungry?).

Next, click the **Word Processor** button (it's the first one). That will open a blank word processing document.

Help Yourself to Help

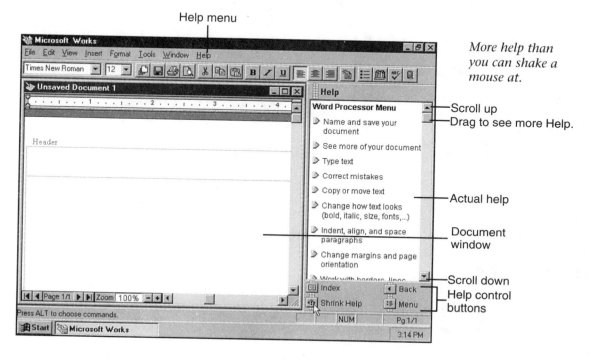

More help than you can shake a mouse at.

Help is just a click away, no matter where you are or what you're doing with Works. If you look at the preceding figure, there are two obvious ways of getting help.

A Helpful Window

The first, and most obvious, is by using the Help window at the right side of the screen. This will display the main help topics for whatever kind of document you're working on at the moment. In the figure, it's help for the word processor. If you'd chosen a spreadsheet, it would be spreadsheet help, and so on.

To see more detailed help, click on the arrow in front of the help topic that interests you. To see more topics, click on the scroll down arrow (labeled in the figure).

The control buttons at the bottom of the Help window will help you navigate through all of the information available. The following list explains what each does, going from top to bottom, and left to right.

Shrink Help collapses this big ol' Help window down to two, teeny-tiny buttons at the bottom right side of your screen: the **Index** and Shrink Help buttons. To return help to full size, click on the **Shrink Help** button again.

This is the **Index** button. It will take you to a complete listing of all the Help topics available, not just the ones for the type of document you're working with.

Clicking on the **Index** button does double duty: it restores the Help window to full size and it calls up the complete index of Help topics.

The **Back** button returns you to the most recent page of Help you were looking at. This is handy if you picked the wrong topic; you can jump right back to where you were.

The **Menu** button takes you all the way back to the Word Processor Menu (as shown in the figure), or whatever menu (Database, and so on) that's appropriate to your document.

A Helpful Menu

The Help menu.

The Help menu, shown here, also gives you access to all the same varieties of help.

Contents   Takes you to the very top of the Help heap, letting you choose from the main Help categories (Word Processor, Spreadsheet, Database, and Communications).

Index   Takes you to the same index of subjects as the Index button, discussed earlier.

Introduction to Works   Runs the Tour you took earlier in the chapter (you did take the tour, didn't you?).

How to use Help   Shows you how to use the Works Help system.

Hide Help   Behaves the same as the Shrink Help button, except it does *not* put the Index or Shrink Help buttons at the bottom of your window. It hides help completely. To get help again, select **Show Help** from the **Help** menu.

Launch Works Forum   You'll only have this one if you opted to install The Microsoft Network (as mentioned in Chapter 2) when you installed Windows 95. This will connect you to The Microsoft Network and take you directly to the Works Forum online.

About Microsoft Works   Shows you copyright information about Works, shows to whom the product is registered and the Product ID number, and lets you look at information about your computer system (the System Info button).

If all that wasn't enough, there's still more help available.

First Time Help

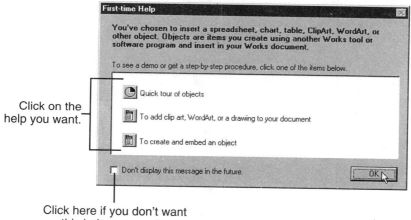

Click on the help you want.

Click here if you don't want this help ever again.

Works is gentle with you when you try something new.

The first time you try to do a new thing (such as insert ClipArt in a word processing document), Works will offer to hold your hand through the process. You can see what I mean in the preceding figure. Just click on the kind of help you want from the list and click **OK**. Works will walk you, step-by-step, through the new thing.

Instant Help Is Gonna Get You

Click

Pop goes the Help box.

Then click on what's
puzzling you.

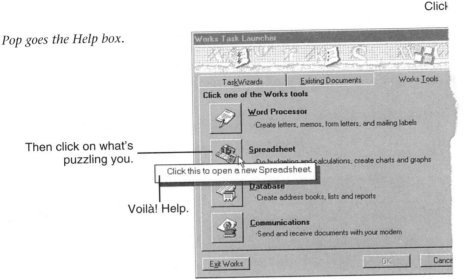

Voilà! Help.

In most of the Works dialog boxes, you'll see a button with a question
the upper right corner. If something in the dialog box puzzles you, cli
(the cursor will acquire a question mark, too), then click on the butto
troubling you. A short and sweet explanation will pop up. Click on th
it go away.

The Least You Need to Know

> ➤ Installing Works is easy—just use the **Run** command in the **Star**

> ➤ You can launch Works by double-clicking its desktop shortcut (i
> option during installation) or by selecting **Microsoft Works 4.0**
> listing on the **Start** menu.

> ➤ Help is available all the time, in a lot of different forms. It will h
> through.

Chapter 5

The BIG Concepts

In This Chapter

➤ Integration explained

➤ Taking wizards to task

➤ The big save—it's better than the big sleep...

➤ Menus and tools

As you may have guessed from the title of this chapter, we're going to take a look at some of the big concepts of Microsoft Works for Windows 95. By "big," I mean the stuff that is central to Works and what it does (such as integration and TaskWizards), things that remain the same no matter which component of Works you happen to be using at the moment, and things you should know how to do before you even *try* to create a document.

Then, in the next chapter, we'll go for a little more detail, building off of these big concepts before we plunge into the main Works components. That's the plan, anyhow.

Start Your Engines!

Since this is a learn-by-doing sort of chapter, it will be more helpful if you read it seated in front of your PC with Works up and running.

If you're skipping around (instead of reading from cover to cover), the explanation for how to launch Works is in Chapter 4. While you do that, I'm going to go freshen up my cup of coffee—back in a minute.

Integration Means Easy Pickin's

Works is made up of four main components: a word processor, a spreadsheet, a database, and a communications application.

You can use each component by itself, but because Works is an *integrated* application, you can also use the components in combination with each other.

One in Every Crowd...

In every group of people, you'll find at least one person who's a little standoffish, the kind who always got a minus sign in the *Plays well with others* box on his report card. In Works, that's the communications package. It's pretty much a loner.

The communications part of Works isn't integrated into the other three—it couldn't be, really. The communications tool isn't there to help you *produce* something, but rather to *accomplish* something.

That will be clearer by the time you reach Chapter 26, the chapter on communications. For now, remember that when I talk about the Works integrated features, I'm not adding communications into the mix. Okay?

The big schmoozer here, the application that mingles well with most of the other components, is the *word processor*. With it, you can include a graphic (such as ClipArt or WordArt), a spreadsheet (or a chart based on a spreadsheet, as shown in the preceding figure), and even information from a database in your word processing document. However, you can also add these elements to spreadsheets and database files.

I think it's best to create the stuff you want to add to your final document *first*, then create the document you want to put them in.

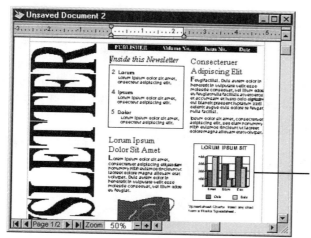

Integration in action.

Spreadsheet data placed in a word processing document

For example: if you want to create a report (with the word processor) that includes a chart from a spreadsheet and data from a database, create the spreadsheet, chart, and the database *first*. When they're ready and waiting, create the word processing document for your report. That way, you can focus your full attention on presenting your ideas and data in your report. You won't have to write, stop to create a chart, write some more, and then create a database. Create the parts, giving each your full attention, and then assemble the whole.

Learn about the details on using Works' integrated features in the sections devoted to the main applications: Chapter 11 for the word processor; Chapter 17 for spreadsheets; Chapter 20 for databases. Fancier integration stuff is covered in Part 5.

Integrate the World

As if Works' internal integration isn't cool enough, Works also allows you to place *objects* from other applications in your Works documents.

Say, for instance, you have a whiz-bang, drop-dead-gorgeous illustration created in a fancy paint program. If your fancy paint program is Microsoft OLE-compatible, you can place your illustration as an object in your Works document.

Object
A document, or part of a document created with another application, that you have prepared for inclusion in a Works document.

Check This Out...

OLE An abbreviation (pronounced "OH-lay," like what gets shouted at bullfights) that stands for Object Linking and Embedding. OLE gives you the ability to place documents created with another, OLE-compatible application, in a Works document, and vice versa.

Contrariwise, you can place a spreadsheet created with Works in a document created with another, OLE-compatible application. The big deal here is this: if *all* of your applications are OLE-compatible, most everything on your PC is *integrated* to some degree. For your amusement and edification, check out OLE in Chapter 23.

We're Off to See the Wizards

TaskWizards, as I mentioned earlier, are the Works feature that create commonly used document types, custom made to your specifications.

Click here to bring TaskWizards to the front.

The Works Task Launcher, with wizards front and center.

Click here to view wizards in this category.

Click here to select the Résumé Wizard.

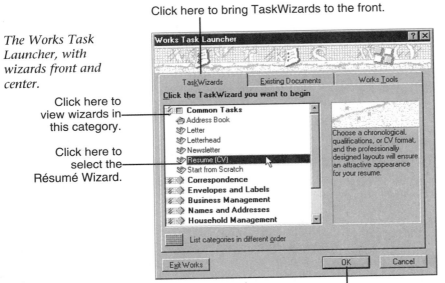

Click here to put the selected wizard to work.

Since TaskWizards are easy and helpful, here's how to use one:

1. To start, make sure the TaskWizards menu is at the front of your Works Task Launcher. If it isn't, click on the **TaskWizards** tab at the top of the Task Launcher.

2. Next, click on the category **Common Tasks** to see its assortment of wizards.

3. For the sake of this example, let's say you want to create a new résumé. Click on the **Resume (CV)** Wizard, as shown in the figure.

4. Click **OK** (or press **Enter**).

The first time you use a TaskWizard, Works will ask you if you're sure you want to use the selected TaskWizard. Since you do, click the button in front of **Yes, run the TaskWizard**.

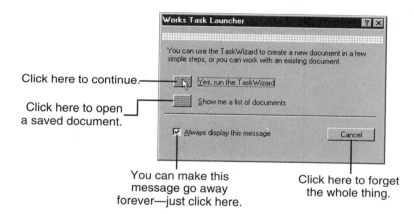

Are you sure you want to do that?

Click here to continue.

Click here to open a saved document.

You can make this message go away forever—just click here.

Click here to forget the whole thing.

Works will think about it for a moment or two, then present you with the following screen. For a résumé, the Wizard gives you three options: Chronological, Qualifications, and Curriculum Vitae. These are three different résumé types. If you click on each, the Wizard will provide you with a brief explanation of the selected résumé. In the next figure, I've selected a Qualifications-type résumé.

Click on the **Qualifications** type résumé, then click **Next** to continue. Works presents you with a list of the customizing options available in the TaskWizard you've selected. In this example, you have four résumé options you may customize: Letterhead (how your name and address are presented); Layout (what the résumé will look like); Headings (what categories you want included in your résumé—they're shown in the next figure); and Entries (the number of jobs you want to list).

The wizard at work.

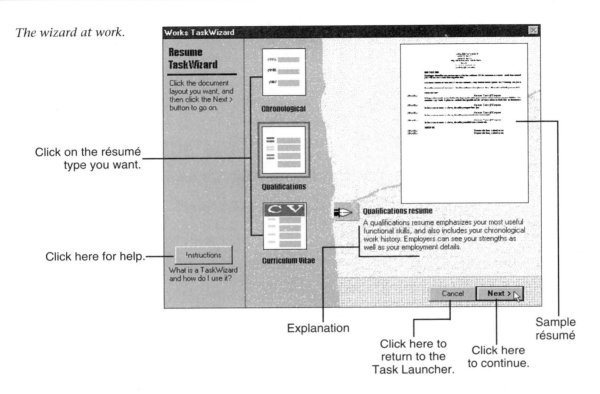

Click on the résumé type you want.

Click here for help.

Explanation

Click here to return to the Task Launcher.

Click here to continue.

Sample résumé

Choose your options...

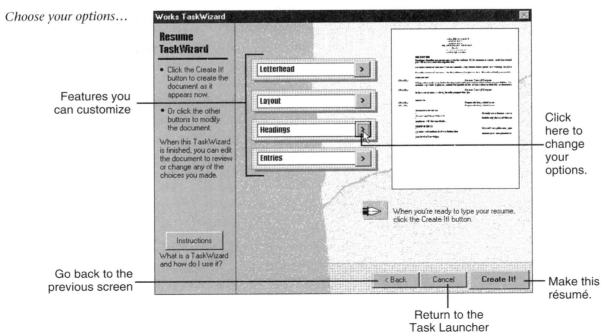

Features you can customize

Click here to change your options.

Go back to the previous screen

Return to the Task Launcher

Make this résumé.

Click here to add an objective heading.

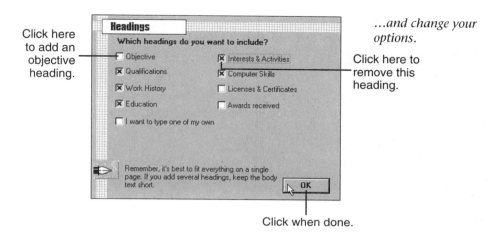

...and change your options.

Click here to remove this heading.

Click when done.

To customize a set of options, click on the arrow to the right of the option you want to tinker with. In the figure, I've selected Headings.

Works selects a few standard headings automatically—the ones with Xs in front of their names. To add more headings, click the box in front of the one(s) you want to add. To remove a heading, click on the X in front of its name and the X will go away—that heading has been removed.

To get an idea of what your résumé will look like, check out the sample résumé at the right of the screen. As you add and remove headings (or other options), the sample shows the changes you've made.

To make the Headings (or other) option dialog box go away, click **OK**. When you're done customizing your options, click the **Create It!** Button.

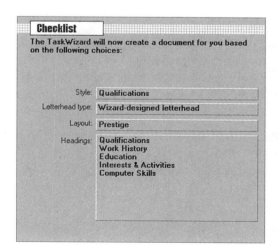

A chance to change your mind.

	F	G

Works will present you with a Checklist (like the one shown here) that s
the choices you've made. If you want to change something, click the **Re**
button, and Works will obligingly take you back to the Wizard so you c
more.

If you're happy with your choices, click the **Create Document** button, tl
amazement as Works automatically creates a résumé to your specificatio
in the following figure, Works even puts descriptive text where you nee
mation about yourself.

*Voilà! A résumé
ready for editing.*

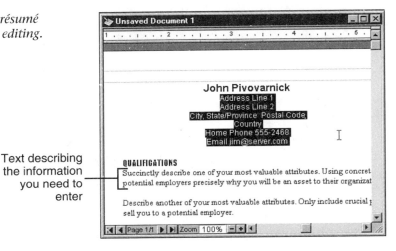

Text describing
the information
you need to
enter

Save Me!

We'll use this résumé file again to talk about entering and editing your o
next chapter. For now, save this file so you'll have it for future sessions.

Saving means telling Works to store a copy of the file you've created on y
or a floppy disk. Saving is important because if you don't save a file, it ex
electronic burps and beeps in your computer's RAM (random-access men
off your computer, or the power goes out, everything stored in RAM sim
never to be seen again—including your résumé, or whatever file you've s

After you save a file, you can open it and work with it again in a few min
days, regardless of how many times you've turned your PC on and off. W
changes to a document, you should save it again, so you have an updatec
stored for future reference.

To save your résumé (or anything, for that matter), select **Save** from the **File** menu. Or you can use the keyboard shortcut **Ctrl+S** (press and hold the **Ctrl** key, **press** the **S** key, and then release both keys). There is another way to save a file—using the toolbar—I'll explain how in a little bit.

The first time you save a file, you'll be asked to give the file a name before your computer can store it on disk. You'll get the Save As dialog box.

Click here to select a new location.

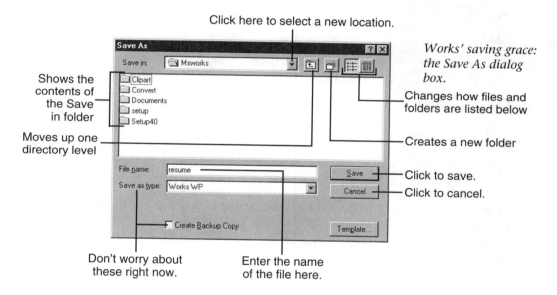

Works' saving grace: the Save As dialog box.

Shows the contents of the Save in folder

Moves up one directory level

Changes how files and folders are listed below

Creates a new folder

Click to save.

Click to cancel.

Don't worry about these right now.

Enter the name of the file here.

Whenever you save anything with Works, Works wants to save it in its own folder on your hard drive. You can see what I mean in the preceding figure. Just below the Save As title bar, there is a box labeled **Save in**, with the **Msworks** folder showing. If that's where you want to save the file, that's swell. If not, you can click on the downward-pointing arrow after the Msworks folder name and select another location (any hard or floppy drive attached to your PC).

The large window at the center of the dialog box displays the contents of the disk or folder that's currently shown in the Save in box. Just double-click on a folder in that window to open it.

If you dig too deeply into the contents of your hard drive (it happens), click on the button with a folder and arrow on it. It will move you up one level. For example, if you're in a folder called Work, that's inside another folder called Arrggh (can you tell I make this stuff up??), that button will move you up one level so the Arrggh folder is the one shown in the Save in box.

If you need to create a new folder inside the current disk or folder, click on the button that has a picture of a file folder and a starburst. That will create a new, untitled folder for you.

Tips for Detail-Oriented Souls

I am a little too organized, I'm told—at least as far as files on my computer are concerned. (Don't ask me about the rest of my life, though, it's a mess.)

I find it's useful to keep a few work folders on my hard drive: one for letters, writing project, graphics, and so on. Inside each, I keep more subfolders for categories. Inside Letters, for instance, there are subfolders for personal, business, and cranky letters I write to Dear Abby and TV talk show hosts (I call that subfolder "venting").

The point is, that if you keep all of your work organized in one central location, you never have to look very far to find it later. It also makes it easy to copy your important work files onto floppy disk for safekeeping. Just a thought.

Once you've navigated to the disk and folder in which you want to save your file, you still need to give your file a name. Type it in the text box called (oddly enough) **File name**. In the figure, I've cleverly named my résumé, **resume**, so I'll know what it is when I stumble on it later.

After you've entered an appropriate name (which, thanks to Windows 95, can be any length and include blank spaces), click on the **Save** button. Works will save your file in the location you selected, with the name you entered.

After the first save, you won't have to do anything extra to save your file. Just select **Save** from the **File** menu, or press **Ctrl+S**, and Works will update the copy stored on your disk without any fuss at all.

At the bottom of the Save As dialog box, there are a few more options (**Save as type**, **Create Backup Copy**, and **Template**). Don't sweat these for now, we'll talk about them later, on a need-to-know basis. The important thing here is that you know how to save a file. Congratulations!

For the moment, close your résumé. To do that, click on the **Close** box—that's the little box at the right of the title bar, the one with the **X** on it. The résumé will go away (I'll show you how to get it back in the next chapter) and you'll be back at the Works Task Launcher.

Works Gives You a Safety Net

If, someday, you're in a hurry to do something else, and you close a document you haven't saved (or saved recently), Works will ask if you want to save the document before it's closed.

If you want to save the document, click **Yes**.

If you don't want to save it, click **No**.

If you'd rather go back and think about it, click **Cancel**, and you'll go back to working on the document. Pretty cool—and very safe.

Creating a New Document

Sometimes, you'll want to do something with Works and there won't be a TaskWizard to automate the job. That's all right; you can do it yourself.

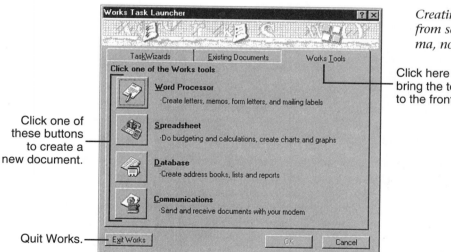

Creating a document from scratch—look, ma, no hands.

Click here to bring the tools to the front.

Click one of these buttons to create a new document.

Quit Works.

To create a new document from scratch, start by clicking on the **Works Tools** tab at the top of the Task Launcher. You can see it in the preceding figure.

Next, click on the **Word Processor** button. Bang! You've created a new word processing document. It's just that simple. If you want another kind of Works document, just click on the button beside the document type you want instead.

As long as you have a blank document up on your screen, let's look at some of the other tools you'll use to produce and beautify your creations.

The Works Menus and Toolbar

Works gives you the right tools for each job.

The preceding figure shows the menus and tools you'll use every time you work with a word processing file. When you're dealing with any other Works document (a database, for instance) they'll be a little different. We'll look at those differences in the appropriate application sections, later on. For now, the big concept here is what the menus and toolbar can do for you.

The Works Menus

Each of the Works menus group related commands together, so they're all there in one handy spot. These menus, and the commands they hold, are how you tell Works what you want done to your documents.

➤ **File**   Contains file-related commands: New, Open, Save, Print, and the like.

➤ **Edit**   Contains your editorial tools: Cut, Copy, Paste, and others. We'll be using these in the next chapter. The thing to remember about the Edit menu is that you usually need to *select* something in your document to use these commands—they need something to work on.

➤ **View**   Controls how things appear on your screen, and what things appear there. You'll use this menu to view and hide the toolbar and rulers, change how your document appears (Normal vs. Page Layout modes), and more. Most of these are toggle commands, and most of them don't affect your document. Play with them at your discretion.

➤ **Insert**   Contains the commands for plunking things into your document—everything from the date and time, to ClipArt, WordArt, and files from other applications. We'll use this menu a lot, especially in Chapters 22 and 23.

➤ **Format**   Contains the commands that affect the appearance of your documents, both on the screen and on the printed page. Here's where you control your fonts and font size. It's also where you set things such as margins and tabs.

➤ **Tools** Contains the fancy-shmancy tools that make working with Works a joy: spell-checking, and access to a thesaurus, among others.

➤ **Window** Controls your document windows, letting you arrange or switch between them, easily. You can also split a long document into two screens so you can see both the beginning and end of the same file at once. Very handy.

➤ **Help** Contains all the varieties of assistance (I just used the thesaurus, could you tell?) built into Works. Since we looked at it in the last chapter, I won't say much more about it.

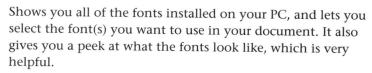

Font Generic word for a digital typeface. A font is a complete set of letters, numbers, punctuation, and commonly used symbols (what you find on your keyboard). The differences between fonts, visually, are how the letters are drawn: thick or thin, slanted or not, and so on. Fonts are identified by names that usually tell you nothing about what the font looks like.

The Toolbar

Belly up to the toolbar, boys, fonts are on me. Sorry. I've been watching too many Westerns, lately.

The toolbar duplicates many of the most frequently used commands from Works' menus. Instead of having to select them from a menu, you can just click on a button in the toolbar and save yourself some time. Here's what each does:

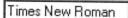 Shows you all of the fonts installed on your PC, and lets you select the font(s) you want to use in your document. It also gives you a peek at what the fonts look like, which is very helpful.

 Shows you the font sizes you have to choose from.

 Calls up the Works Task Launcher, which is handy if you need to create a new document when you're in the middle of another. It happens.

 Save button—it's the same as selecting Save from the File menu.

 Sends the current document to your printer.

 Shows you, on your monitor, what your document will look like when it prints out.

Same as the Cut command in the Edit menu. Removes selected item (text or graphics) from your document and stores it in Windows' Clipboard so you can use it elsewhere.

Same as the Copy command in the Edit menu. Copies selected item (text or graphics) from your document and stores it in Windows' clipboard so you can use it elsewhere.

Same as the Paste command in the Edit menu. Takes whatever you have stored in the Clipboard and drops it in your document.

Turns selected text **boldface**.

Italicizes the selected text.

Underlines the selected text.

Left alignment gives a smooth edge on the left side of the page (just like on the page you're reading).

Center alignment puts the middle of each line on the middle of your page like this.

Right alignment gives your text a smooth edge down the right side of the page.

The remaining buttons on the toolbar in the figure are peculiar to Works' word processing module. The database and spreadsheet toolbars have their own peculiarities. We'll look at all these peculiar things when we look at each application.

The Least You Need to Know

The aim of this chapter was to get you thinking about some of the big concepts behind Microsoft Works, and the features and commands you'll use whenever you use Works. You don't have to hang on to any of it for dear life—well, except that Save thing. That you should hang onto—it's a keeper.

The rest will be covered again, in more detail, in the context of a particular Works application. The next time you see the font name list or an alignment button, I expect you to think, "Oh, yeah. I remember seeing that."

Chapter 6

Works: Beyond the Basics (Sounds Like A Movie of the Week...)

In This Chapter

➤ Open sez me!

➤ Putting text in its place

➤ Text fixer-uppers

➤ Quit it!

Previously on "NYPD Blue..."

Sorry. I meant, "In the last chapter."

In the last chapter, we created new documents (both with a TaskWizard and from scratch), saved one, and took a brief introductory glance at Works' menus and toolbar. In this chapter, we're going to play around with a document: add text, tinker with it, and generally make it pretty.

To start, we need to open a saved file—so your PC should be turned on, and Works should be running.

Open Up. It's the Law!

It *is* a law, sort of: you have to open a file to work with it. You can open a saved file, either with Works' **Task Launcher**, or with the **Open** command in the **File** menu.

Using the Task Launcher

As you've seen, when you start Works, the Task Launcher is the first thing you see—Works logically assumes that you want to *do* something.

Any time after you launch Works, you can call up the Task Launcher by clicking on the **Task Launcher** button in the toolbar (it's the one with the three, multi-colored pages on it).

However you get there, when the Task Launcher is on your screen, click on the **Existing Documents** tab. The Task Launcher will show you this dialog box.

Opening a file you've saved.

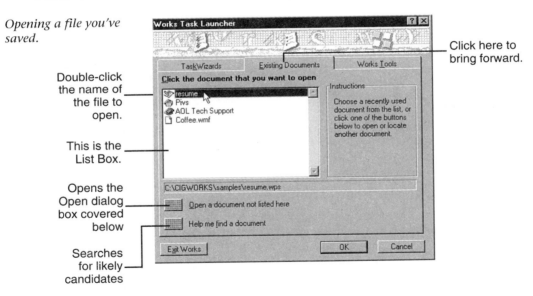

Now, the Task Launcher's Existing Documents dialog box is *very* obliging. It keeps a list of files you've worked with recently, no matter where you've saved them, so you can open them with a few clicks of your mouse.

Locate the name of the file you want to open in the list box (you may have to scroll a little to see all of the file names, if you've been creating a lot of files). For the purposes of this chapter, find the résumé you saved in the previous chapter.

If The File You Want Isn't Listed...

If, by some chance, the file you want isn't shown in the list box of existing document, click on the **Open a document not listed here** button. It will give you the regular Open dialog box described in the next section.

Click on the file name and then click **OK**. The energy-economical (ahem, lazy, like myself) can simply double-click the file name. Either way, Works will open the file p.d.q.

Using the Open Command

The Open command works very much the same as the Save command (covered in the previous chapter), except in the opposite direction. Where Save asks you where you want to store a copy of your open file, Open asks you to locate the stored file you want to open. The dialog boxes even look similar. Why, here's one now!

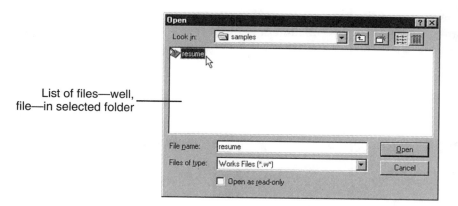

List of files—well, file—in selected folder

Open Sarsaparilla?
Open Saskatchewan?
Open Sesame.

The Open dialog box is not as obliging as the Task Launcher. It doesn't keep track of the files you've created and saved, so you need to tell it where the file is you want to open. (Which is why I suggest keeping all your documents organized in one central location—you won't lose any brain cells trying to remember where you put stuff.)

Navigating to the file is easy enough, though. You get the same set of navigational tools we used to save your résumé in the previous chapter. When you locate the file, click on the file name to select it, and then click **Open**, or just double-click on the file name. Whichever you choose, the file will open.

Opening More Than One File

There may come a time when you're in a working frenzy. (Really, it could happen.) You'll be whipping through work so fast, you'll look like a Stephen Speilberg special effect. You may want to have one or more documents open at the same time. It's easy. Just repeat the process for each file you want opened.

Why Work with Multiple Documents?

Keeping two or more documents open at the same time can save you time and energy.

When writing, I usually have the chapter I'm working on, *and* the glossary, open at the same time. That way, when I add a geeky definition to a chapter, I can just copy and paste it into the glossary. It saves much searching and retyping later. Did I mention that I'm lazy?

You may also produce documents that rely on a lot of standard information (contracts, leases, press releases). If you keep often-used information in a file, then you, too, can copy and paste it into a new document without retyping. Read about Copy and Paste later in this chapter.

With two or more windows open on your desktop, you can switch between them with either of two methods.

Use the Window Menu

Swapping document windows with the Window menu.

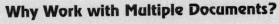

If you leave your documents full-sized (not minimized), you can switch between open windows by selecting them from the Window menu as previously shown.

Works automatically adds each document you open to the bottom of the Window menu. A check mark marks the window that's active (that is foremost on your screen—the one you're working with).

To bring another window front and center, just select it from the **Window** menu. It will jump to the front, ready to serve you.

Which Window Is Which?

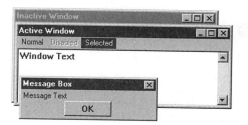

A field guide to windows, active and inactive.

Works, and all Windows applications, let you have multiple windows open. Things can get a little messy and confusing when windows pile up. You could have a hard time telling which window is which.

The document window that is foremost on your screen, the one you're working with, is usually (but not always) the active window. You can also tell it's the active window because its title bar is a vibrant color (*what* color depends on the color scheme you've selected in Windows' Display Control Panel).

A document window that you have moved to the background is *inactive*, because you can't do anything with it. Normally, an inactive window's title bar will turn gray (or a grayish color, also depending on your chosen color scheme). To activate an inactive window, just click on any part of it, or select its name from the Window menu.

Managing Windows: A Minimalist Approach

You can also keep track of your windows by *minimizing* them when they're not in use. To minimize an inactive document window, make it the active window by clicking on it, or selecting its name from the **Window** menu. Next, click on its **Minimize** button; that's the one with the line across the bottom, at the window's upper right corner.

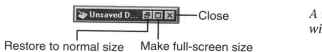

Close — A minimized window.

Restore to normal size   Make full-screen size

The window will shrink down to a teeny-tiny title bar with three buttons on it, as shown above. If you minimize two or more windows, they'll line up across the bottom of your screen.

When you need the window back, full-sized, click on either of the buttons with window-icons (labeled in the figure) and the window will spring back.

To make a minimized window go away, click the **Close** button (**X**), and the window will close.

Playing with Windows

Don't feel compelled to commit to one of these management schemes now. Commitment is a scary thing, especially to us guys.

While you're learning your way around Works, play around with multiple windows. Minimize, leave them open and stacked up, or do both. Eventually, you'll develop a personal strategy that works for you. These are just options.

Entering Text

Hi! Remember me?

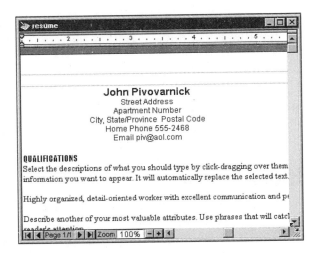

When last we saw our trusty résumé, it looked a little something like this figure. It has your name at the top, but the rest of the information is bogus—just dummied out text to show what the final product will look like. If you give *this* résumé to a potential employer, she'll think you're a goof.

Let's make this sucker look more like a real résumé by entering text.

Start by moving your mouse so the arrow cursor moves over the text in your résumé. You'll notice that as soon as the arrow touches the "page" it turns into something that looks like a fancy capital **I**. Strangely enough, that is an I-beam cursor.

Cursors! Foiled Again!

You'll discover, as we move through Works' components that there are a number of cursors you'll be using. You'll get to know them soon enough, so don't sweat the details. The big thing to know about cursors is this: you always get the cursor appropriate to what the cursor is pointing at.

If you point at a menu, or other clickable thing, you get the arrow cursor. When you point at text, you get the I-beam. When you work with a spreadsheet, you'll get this chunky plus-sign cursor. The different cursors are a visual clue to what actions are appropriate at the moment. Life should be so clear cut.

To find out what the I-beam cursor does, place it anywhere in the résumé and click once. You'll see that it has deposited a blinking vertical line. That's called the insertion point because, where ever the insertion point is, that's where what you type is inserted. Try it and see.

That's basically how you enter text. Point where you want the text to go. Click. Then type—type anything, I won't peek.

With a blank document, your text will start at the top of the screen and work its way down the page. In a document that already has text in it, the new text will magically push existing text ahead of it.

Overstrike Mode

There is another way to insert text. This one's a little destructive: overstrike mode.

To get into overstrike mode, press the **Insert** key on your keyboard (on a typical PC keyboard, it's the top left button in the little clutch of six buttons above the arrow keys). When you do, the letters **OVR** will appear at the bottom of your Works window, like this.

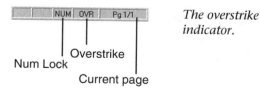

The overstrike indicator.

NUM's the Word

The abbreviation NUM you see in the figure shows that the Num Lock key (upper left button of your keyboard's numerical keypad) has been pressed. Num Lock is short for Number Lock.

When you press the Num Lock key, you can use the keypad to enter numbers into your documents. When the Num Lock key isn't pressed, those keys function as a second set of arrow and Page Up/Page Down keys.

OVR stands for overstrike. That means that when you place your cursor in your document, and begin to type, the existing text is not pushed along to accommodate the new. It's eradicated, typed over, erased, gone bye-bye.

Be careful in Overstrike mode. If you get carried away typing a new thought, you could wipe out part of your document you didn't intend to erase—at least, that's what I do. I don't care for Overstrike mode for just that reason.

Okay—at this point, we have a beaucoup bogus résumé with some extra practice typing thrown in for good measure. Let's clean it up and hone our editing skills at the same time.

The Unkindest Cut of All: Editing

You have no idea how many jokes I throw into these books—nun jokes, fart jokes, jokes about nuns farting—that are cut by my ruthless editors. (Really Ruth-less. There isn't a Ruth among them.) They have this quaint notion that useful information is better than a good Sr. Mary Mayonnaise joke. Go figure.

Editing is a dirty job, but someone's got to do it. Here are some skills you'll need to do your own editing.

Inserting New Text

Didn't we just do that? Yes, we did. You can add a missing word, phrase, or paragraph(s) to your work: click once where you want to insert the new material and begin to type. It's that simple.

Selecting Text

To edit your work, you need to know how to *select* text. When you select text, it becomes *highlighted* (turns white on a black background as shown in the following figure) so you can tell what you've selected.

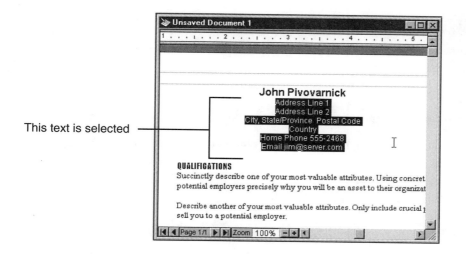

Some selected text.

This text is selected

There are several ways to select text in Works:

➤ Double-click on a word and you select that word.

➤ Click in the margin, to the left of a line of text (the I-beam cursor will turn back to a right-pointing arrow), and you'll select the whole line.

➤ Double-click in the margin, to the left of a paragraph, and you'll select the whole paragraph.

➤ Click on **Select All** in the **Edit** menu to select every bit of text in your document.

If what you need to select isn't just a word, line, or paragraph, you can select any amount of text by click-dragging over it. Here's how:

Move the I-beam cursor so it's at the beginning of the text you want to select. Press and hold the mouse button. Slide the mouse until you have selected all the text you want. Release the mouse button.

Once you select some text, you can do a number of editorial-type things to it.

Deleting Text

If you just want the selected text to go the heck away, you can hit your **Delete** or **Backspace** key, and those words are outta there. It's much faster than deleting a word one letter at a time.

In case you didn't know, the Delete key will erase the next character in front (to the right) of the cursor. The Backspace key will delete the character behind (to the left of) the cursor. Check it out.

Replacing Text

If you begin to type while text is selected—a word, line, or whatever—what you type completely replaces the selected text.

I Didn't Mean It! Bring It Back!

If you accidentally replace or delete selected text—I do this all the time— you can get it back.

As soon as you realize you've done it, *take your hands off of the keyboard*. With your mouse, click on the **Edit** menu. Then click **Undo Editing**. Works will restore the accidentally deleted text.

While the Undo command is a fabulous thing, it will only undo the very last thing you did. It won't fix something you did two or ten steps ago, just the very last thing. Sometimes (depending on what you just did), the Undo command will fade out and the scary words **Cannot Undo** will appear there. Consider that a warning as well as an explanation.

In our résumé, each heading is followed by a few short paragraphs (Qualifications, for example, has two). To replace them with actual information about yourself, you would double-click in the left margin beside the first paragraph under Qualifications. That will select the whole paragraph.

While selected, type: **Nine years experience managing academic retail stores.** (Actually, your résumé will work better for you if you type your own qualifications, but this is just an example.)

Repeat the process for the other paragraphs under each heading, typing in information about yourself that matches the description in the paragraph you are replacing.

At the top of the page, under your name, click once in the left margin beside each line, and replace the text with your actual address and telephone information.

When you finish, you should have a firm grasp of this selecting/replacing thing, and a fair-to-good résumé to boot. If you *still* don't care for your résumé, read about more advanced editing skills in Chapter 8.

Save Me II

Since you've made some pretty substantial changes to your résumé, you should save it again; that way, you will store the current version on your hard drive. To save a file, select

Save from the **File** menu. Since you're updating a file that you have already saved and named, you don't have to do anything else.

Prettying Up

Works' Resume TaskWizard originally let you choose a basic combination of fonts (type-faces) for your résumé. Now that you have the whole thing done, you may not care for your initial choices. The fonts may look unappealing, or the type may be too large or small for your taste. You can easily fix that.

Changing Fonts

Since the name and address, headings, and information paragraphs are each in a different font, it will be easier to see them one at a time.

Click-drag over your name and address at the top of the résumé to select it. While selected, click on the down arrow to the right of the **Font Name** in the toolbar (shown here). Scroll through the list of fonts until you find the one you want to use, and then click on the name of the font. Poof! Your name and address appear in the new font.

The toolbar's Font menu lets you see what your fonts look like before you use them.

Repeat the process for each of the headings (Qualifications, Work History, and so on.). Then repeat the process again for each of the informational paragraphs. Your résumé has been completely refonted.

Size Matters

Well, in fonts anyway. A rule of thumb for résumés is that they shouldn't be longer than one page. If you have a little bit more, or less, than a full page, you can adjust your résumé a little by changing the size of your fonts. Here's how.

Again, it will be easier to work with your name, address, the headings, and the information paragraphs separately.

Select the text you want to resize. The font and size menus in the toolbar will change to display the name of the font and the size used in the selected text (if you have selected more than one font and/or size, the display(s) will go blank).

A sizable Size menu.

Point Font sizes are measured in *points*, from an old typesetting term. One point (abbreviated pt.) equals about 1/72 of an inch. A 72 pt. letter would be about an inch tall.

Click the **Font Size**. It will look like the one in the preceding figure. If your résumé is too short (doesn't fill one page), click the next larger point size (the numbers go up; 12 is larger than 10). If your résumé is too long (more than one page), click the next smaller point size.

Be careful when making fonts smaller; anything under 10 or 12 *points* will be difficult to read, especially in a long document. Chapter 10 contains more detailed tips for selecting and using.

Save Me III

If you're happy with the font changes you made, you should save your résumé again before proceeding. (You remember how, don't you? I mean, we just did it a couple of pages ago.)

A Peek Before Printing

Your résumé won't do you much good trapped on your PC. In order to circulate it, you'll need to print out at least *one* copy.

Before you commit your résumé to paper, you can take a sneak peek at it by clicking on the **Print Preview** button in the toolbar (the page with the magnifying glass), or by selecting **Print Preview** from the **File** menu. You'll get a small preview of your résumé, like the one shown here.

Print Preview gives you a chance to eyeball your document for obvious wrongness (a résumé that lands on two pages, for example) before you waste ink and paper printing it out.

Need a better look? Click the **Zoom In** button at the right of the screen, and you'll get a closer look.

What your document will look like on paper   Page number you're looking at

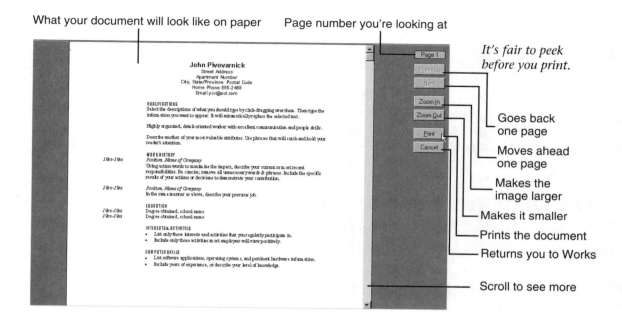

It's fair to peek before you print.

Goes back one page

Moves ahead one page

Makes the image larger

Makes it smaller

Prints the document

Returns you to Works

Scroll to see more

If your résumé looks good, you can click **Print** to send it to your printer. Otherwise, you can click **Cancel**, and you'll be back in the word processor where you can make any changes you'd like.

About Printing

You can also print your documents by selecting **Print** from the **File** menu.

Naturally, printing requires that you have a printer hooked up to your PC, with the appropriate driver software installed. If you don't know what that means but have printed things before, you shouldn't have a problem printing from Works. Each of the main sections here, contain tips for printing the various flavors of Works documents.

If you don't have a printer installed, consult your Windows 95 and printer manuals for instructions on how to hook it up and install the appropriate software.

I Quit!

Now that you've produced an actual document, you'll probably want to take a break (although you may have already taken several—it's not like I'm watching you).

If you're done with Works for now, shut it down. You can:

1. Click the **Close** box (**X**) in the upper right corner of your monitor. It's on the title bar that says **Microsoft Works**.

2. Select **Exit Works** from the **File** menu.

3. If the Task Launcher is open, click the **Exit Works** button in the lower left corner.

Whichever method you choose, Works will shut down. If you have a document open that you haven't saved recently, Works will ask if you want to save it. Clicking the **Yes** button will save the document before Works shuts down. Clicking the **No** button will exit Works without saving the document (dangerous, unless you know you didn't make any changes to your document, or you've made changes you don't want to keep). Clicking **Cancel** will stop Works from shutting down and let you continue to work with the document.

The Least You Need to Know

You learned some skills in this chapter that you'll use all of the time. With a little practice, they'll all become second nature to you.

➤ You can open an existing document either by selecting it from the **Task Launcher**'s **Existing Documents** list or by using the **Open** command in the **File** menu.

➤ Entering text is as simple as: Point where you want the text to go; click and then type.

➤ There are several ways to select text in your documents: double-click a word, click in the left margin to select a line, or double-click in the left margin to select a whole paragraph.

➤ Whatever you type will replace selected text if you are in Overtype mode.

➤ The **Undo** command (in the **Edit** menu) will undo the very last thing you did, but *only* that thing.

➤ You can change fonts and font sizes by selecting text and then using the font and size pop-ups in the Works toolbar.

➤ Save your file after you make changes you want to keep. Save often.

➤ **Print Preview** can save you time and paper.

Part 2
Works' Word Processor—Getting Your Word's Worth

Hey, now that you have the big picture of what Works is and does, let's zero in on each of Works' main components. In Part 2, you'll learn to do just about everything you can do with the word processor: write a novel or a shopping list, create an impressive newsletter, or just write a simple thank-you note.

We'll start with a look at how word processing differs from typing, and what Typing 101 habits you need to break to be an effective word processor. That's Chapter 7. Afterward, you'll hone your editing skills (Chapter 8), get the lowdown on layout and formatting (Chapters 9 and 10), and then you can get fancy with Chapter 11.

All in all, this part will give you the skills to turn out word processing documents that will melt in your mouth, not in your printer. Something like that.

Processing, Not Typing

In This Chapter

➤ No more white-out products!

➤ Write now, spell later

➤ Don't touch that Return key—yet

➤ Rules that were made to be broken

I learned to type back in high school, during the post-Beatles, pre-disco '70s. The '70s were also PPC, pre-personal computer, so we're talking actual typing on IBM Selectric typewriters. I didn't even *see* a desktop computer until the early '80s. Man, I'm getting old.

I've always considered taking those two semesters of typing one of the smartest moves I ever made. Really. I mean, think about how much typing I do these days. I'm sorry, not typing, *word processing*. There is a difference. Their goals may be the same (getting words neatly on paper), and the techniques may be similar (you still have to tippy-tap those keys, one at a time), but beyond that they are very different.

Some of the habits that made you look like a very professional typist will make you look like a very sloppy word processor. Break 'em.

Typos Begone!

Back in them thar' typewriter days, if you misspelled a word while typing, you had two choices:

1. Tear up the page and start over.

2. Remove the mistake with an eraser, or some white-out product, and type over it. Wait! There were *three* options! (Nobody expects the Spanish Inquisition.)

3. Just type over it, and let legibility be damned.

With word processing, you can just *change* it, either manually (by deleting the stupid spelling, and typing in the correct one), or automatically (by using a spelling checker like the one built-in to Works). Larger changes (whole paragraphs, say) are much more painless, too.

Editing Without Retyping

With typing, when you wanted to edit your work, you'd go through the typed pages with a pen or pencil and write in all the corrections and changes you wanted to make; then you'd go back and retype the whole bloody thing, incorporating the changes.

You always retyped more carefully the second time around, because you didn't want to have to type it a third time—but you usually wound up typing it again anyway, at least a page or two.

With a word processor, you can make major, major changes, not just simply, but undetectably. You can replace clunky paragraphs with lovely, lilting ones. You can juggle paragraphs around to improve sense and structure. You can change every occurrence of an overused word (like "stuff," which I use *waaayyy* too often) by having your word processor search for it.

When my editor gets my pages, she has no idea if I cranked this stuff (see?) out in one sitting, or if I agonized over it for draft after draft. (Don't ask. I won't tell.)

The ease of editing with a word processor is a double-edged sword. On the one hand, it's very easy to make changes. On the other hand, it's *so* easy to make changes, you may never stop tinkering with your work. You could spend the rest of your days fine-tuning a paragraph, phrase, or word.

At some point, you have to learn to let go.

Another Quarter Heard From...

*There is never finality in the display terminal's screen, but an irresponsible whimsicality, as words, sentences, and paragraphs are negated at the touch of a key. The significance of the past, as expressed in the manuscript by a deleted word or an inserted correction, is annulled in idle gusts of electronic massacre.**

Alexander Cockburn, Anglo-Irish journalist. "Pull the Plug," in *Mother Jones* (Boulder, 11 Nov. 1986; repr. in *Corruptions of Empire*, pt. 2, 1988), on his preference for typewriters over word processors.

Many modern authors (Harlan Ellison, for one) eschew the use of computers as writing tools because they make for lazy writers. That's probably true. No computer or software will make you (or me) a better writer—they're just tools, after all, and no substitute for discipline and a well-learned craft.

Keep in mind as you go that learning to use a word processor is not at all the same as learning to structure a sentence, build a plot or argument, or breathe life into a character. Learning to process words is the same as learning to bang a nail. It's a skill, nothing more. Learning to write is taking that skill of nail-banging, and using it to build a cathedral (or, in the case of this book, a nice, simple little log cabin).

*Taken from Microsoft Bookshelf 1994. *The Columbia Dictionary of Quotations* is licensed from Columbia University Press. Copyright 1993 by Columbia University Press. All rights reserved.

Typing Habits You Should Break (And Why You Should Break Them)

It's been so long since I've actually used a typewriter, I had to think long and hard about this section. I'd broken my habits so well, I couldn't remember them.

Don't Double Space at the End of Each Sentence

It took a long time for me to break my thumb of the habit of hitting the Spacebar twice at the end of a sentence, but the practice is really unnecessary when word processing. Here's why.

Typewriters typed by striking the paper with metal keys. Each letter was on a key of the same size, so each letter (yes, and each blank space) took up the same amount of space on the page. A lowercase "i" took the same space as a capital "Q."

To help the eye distinguish the space between words, from the space between entire sentences, typists double-spaced at the end of each sentence.

Computers, however, place each letter proportionally, that is, a lowercase "i" takes only the space it needs, and a capital "Q" does the same. That makes the extra space at the end of a sentence unnecessary.

Typed versus word-processed.

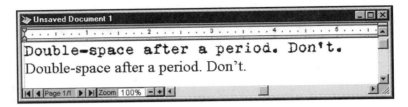

Double-space after a period. Don't.

Computer Type Can Be a Space Hog, Too!

Most computer fonts are proportional, as discussed here. Each letter only gets the amount of space it needs. However, there are *some* fonts that mimic the spacing of typewriters (like the font used in the top line of the figure). These are called *monospaced fonts* (for "one space") because each letter takes up a set amount of space whether it needs it or not. Courier, a standard Windows font, is a monospaced font.

Shameless Self-Promotion

The font in the preceding figure, the one that looks like actual typewriter type, was designed by Susan Townsend of Hot Metal Type. About a dozen of her very cool fonts are on the CD-ROM disc that's included with *The Complete Idiot's Guide to CD-ROM, 2nd Edition*.

Don't Indent Five Spaces at the Start of Paragraphs!

The indent at the beginning of a new paragraph was another visual clue to help readers follow along with your writing.

It's still a good idea to indent (if it's appropriate) at the beginning of a new paragraph, but don't indent by hitting the Spacebar five (or however many) times. It goes back to that monospace/proportional thing again.

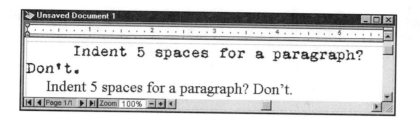

With monospaced typewriters (and apologies to Gertrude Stein), a space is a space is a space. Five spaces at the beginning of one paragraph take up the same space as any other set of five spaces. You get that nice, even, left margin with matching indentations at the beginning of each paragraph.

With proportional type on a computer, five spaces with one font is *not* the same size as five spaces in another. You can see what I mean in the figure. Not at all pretty and very annoying for the eye to follow as you read.

Instead of indenting five spaces, you can set Works to automatically indent the same amount of space (half an inch, say) every time you start a new paragraph. The indentations then match no matter what fonts you use (see what I mean in the next figure).

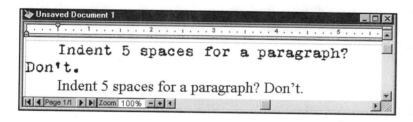

Much prettier.

You set the indent, along with other paragraph formatting, by selecting **Paragraph** from the **Format** menu. You'll tinker with indents and other settings in Chapter 9. Speaking of starting a new paragraph...

Lay Off the Enter Key, Why Don'tcha?

When typing, you needed to hit the return key every time you typed to the right edge of the page, otherwise you'd type right off the paper and onto the platen. A little bell even went off to remind you. (That used to be the biggest pain in the butt for me. My brain always wrote faster than my fingers could type, and I'd never get that spiffy, razor-sharp right margin that really great typists seemed to get without breaking a sweat or hyphenating a word.)

Well, stop it.

With word processing, when you reach the end of a line, the cursor will automatically jump to the beginning of the next line as long as you keep typing. That's called *word-wrapping*. The sentence will wrap around to the next line. If you're midword when you hit the end of the line, Works will either carry the whole word down to the next line or automatically hyphenate a longer word so you still retain a nice right margin.

Some Typing Habits You Should Keep

Far be it from me to chuck your typing lessons completely out the window. The actual act of typing on a computer keyboard is essentially the same as typing on a typewriter. Many of your old typing habits still apply. For example:

➤ The keyboard layout for letters and numbers are still the same. If you were a touch-typist before, you still can be with your computer. You just have to deal with a few extra keys.

➤ Your mother and typing teacher were right: posture is important. Sit up straight. Rest your feet on the floor in front of you. Your wrists should be held parallel to (not resting on) the desk. The correct posture will keep you from getting tired too fast and keep you from developing neck, back, and wrist troubles.

➤ I don't know about you, but my typing teacher was always yelling at me to use tab stops to get nice columns of information when typing tabular data, not millions of spaces. You still should.

Works' word processor *will* create a table for you, and do columns, but sometimes it isn't appropriate. Sometimes, you just have to set and use tabs. I tend to use them most when I'm doing theatrical-type résumés for friends, where much of the information falls into columns for roles played, the name of the play, the theater, directors, and so on. Chapter 9 tells you how to tab to your heart's delight.

Some Typing Habits I've Never Been Able to Break

These aren't necessarily good things, or bad things—just things I haven't been able to retrain myself to stop doing.

For instance, even though it's perfectly simple to correct a typo like "freind" by moving the cursor back and swapping the "i" and "e," I don't do it. I backspace, deleting the word back to the mistake. Then I retype the rest of the word.

Why? I don't know. Probably because I used to have one of those correcting typewriters that would back up one character at a time and slap correcting film over the mistyped word. With typing, you'd need to erase a word back to your mistake, especially if it involved adding another letter or two. You don't need to do that with a word processor, but I can't stop myself. Muscle memory is a terrible thing to overcome.

Also, I can't edit on-screen. I need to print out my pages and go through them with a pen and physically write my changes on them. To me, there's just something about hand-correcting my pages on paper. It's a horrible waste of power, paper, and ink, but I can't seem to get the same personal satisfaction from editing on-screen. I don't feel as if I've written anything if I don't have a sheaf of papers in my hand. It's probably something I should talk to my therapist about—but that's not your problem.

The Least You Need to Know

Oh, Toto, we're not using a typewriter anymore!

➤ Forget about double-spacing at the end of each sentence.

➤ Don't indent your paragraphs manually with spaces.

➤ Don't hit the Enter/Return key at the end of each line you type.

➤ You should *still* use your **Tab** key when typing columns of information. It looks much better than inches of spaces, and it's easier to do.

➤ Concentrate on breaking the typing habits that affect how your documents look (such as those in this list). The ones that affect how you work (like my editing on paper and overdeleting typos) will come with time. Or not.

Chapter 8

Editorial Skills

In This Chapter

➤ Cutting, copying, and pasting

➤ Drag 'til you drop

➤ Search and replace mission

➤ Find a synonym or check your smelling—uh, *spelling*

Way back in Chapter 6, we played around with some of the basic editorial skills you'll be using as you learn to work with Works. This chapter here hopes to build off those skills, putting some more powerful tools at your disposal. Oddly enough, most of the things that follow are done through the Works Edit menu.

You may, if you're at your PC, follow along using the résumé we created as your plaything. Many of the skills, tips, and tricks you'll pick up here will also work with Works' database, spreadsheet, and communications modules, so pay close attention. You're learning for four (which may not be as much fun as *eating for two*, but it is less fattening).

The Selection Process: A Quick Brush-Up

In case you've suffered a case of brain-drain since Chapter 6, these are the basic text-selection methods, in brief:

➤ Double-click a word and you select that word.

➤ Click in the margin, to the left of a line of text, and you'll select the whole line.

➤ Double-click in the margin, to the left of a paragraph, and you select the whole paragraph.

➤ Click on **Select All** in the **Edit** menu to select every bit of text in your document.

➤ You can also use the ever-popular click-drag. Move the I-beam cursor so it's at the beginning of the text you want to select. Press and hold the mouse button. Slide the mouse until you select the text you want. Release the mouse button.

More Things to Do with Selected Text

Now, it's lovely to be able to select a chunk of text and, just by typing, replace it with a *better* chunk of text. However, sometimes what you've written is peachy-keen, and all you want to do is *move* it to another spot in your document, or to another document.

The figure on the left shows how the Edit menu looks without text selected in your document. The one on the right shows how it looks with text selected in your document. See the difference?

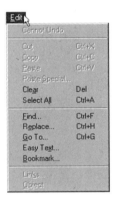

You can do that, and more, with the help of the Edit menu. You'll notice, looking at the two figures, that selecting text in your document activates several options in the Edit menu. Let's take a look at them.

Cut!

The *Cut* command (Ctrl+X) removes the selected text from your document and places it in the Windows *Clipboard* for later use. This is handy in cases where the text is fine but you want to place it somewhere else in the document. (To place the text, you use the *Paste* command. That's coming up in a moment.)

Clipboard

A bit of your computer's memory that Windows uses to temporarily store information that you have cut or copied from documents. The Clipboard can only hold one item at a time. You can paste that item into the same Works document, a different Works document, or a document created with another Windows application entirely.

Copy, Anyone?

The *Copy* command (Ctrl+C) copies the selected text (leaving the original text in your document) and places the copy in the Windows Clipboard for later use.

Copying is useful if you repeat yourself—you know, say the same thing over and over in the course of a document. It may be an important phrase, for instance, that you're discussing in a school report (Hamlet's "There is nothing good or bad but thinking makes it so" comes to mind), or your name and address in a letter, or dozens of other repeatable information. To place the text copy, you use the Paste command.

Paste Me! Paste Me!

The *Paste* command (Ctrl+V) takes the text that you have copied/cut to the Clipboard and places it in your document at the insertion point.

To try it out:

➤ Select some text in your résumé.

➤ Use the **Copy** command as previously described.

➤ Move your cursor and click once to place the insertion point somewhere else in your résumé.

➤ Select **Paste** from the **Edit** menu. *Et voilà*; the text you copied appears in its new home.

Techno Talk

A Clipboard Alert!

The Clipboard is a handy tool, but it isn't all-powerful. It can only hold one thing at a time. If you copy something to the Clipboard and use it, then copy something else, the first thing is no longer in the Clipboard.

Paste Special

(Sounds like a "blue-light special" at K-Mart: *"Attention shoppers—we have an unadvertised Paste Special in aisle six...."*)

Not only can you paste text in your Works documents, but with the Paste Special command, you can also paste paragraph and font formatting onto other paragraphs.

Say, for example, you've been slaving away on your résumé, changing the fonts (as discussed in Chapters 6 and 10) and paragraph options (Chapter 9) until one paragraph is practically perfect in every way, just like Mary Poppins.

Instead of having to remember what you did to make that paragraph perfect, you can simply copy and paste your special formatting onto other paragraphs. Here's how:

1. Select the perfect paragraph.

2. Select **Copy** from the **Edit** menu.

3. Select the text of the paragraph you want to reformat.

4. Select **Paste Special** from the **Edit** menu. The dialog box shown here will appear.

The very special, Paste Special dialog box.

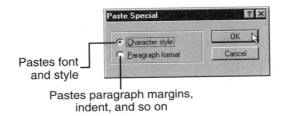

Pastes font and style

Pastes paragraph margins, indent, and so on

If you select **Character style** (as in the figure) and click **OK**, the selected text will change so that the font, font size, and style (bold, italic, and so on) will be exactly the same as the practically perfect paragraph.

If you click on **Paragraph format** instead, the selected text will now have the same margins, indentations, tabs, and other paragraph-related formatting as the practically perfect paragraph you copied it from.

That's a great big time-saver, since you only have to format a paragraph once, and then you can apply that formatting to the rest of your document with a few clicks of your mouse.

Select It All, Then Clear It All

The Select All command (Ctrl+A) selects all of the text in your document. You can then perform huge feats of editing on it. Speaking of huge feats (mine are size 13) of editing, you can get rid of piles of pesky unwanted text, easily, too.

The Clear command (Del) deletes the selected text without sending it to the Windows Clipboard. Kiss that text good-bye. If you accidentally clear text (or something else) from your document, you can retrieve it if you use the Undo command immediately.

Drag-and-Drop Editing: An Easier Way to Move Your Words Around

When you're writing something, do you often find yourself juggling words, sentences, or paragraphs around trying to find the best way to present your information? I do, and how.

After a heavy juggling session, selecting, cutting, and pasting for hours, it can get bloody tedious. There's an easier way, called *drag-and-drop* editing. It works like this:

➤ Select some text: a word, sentence, paragraph, or whatever.

➤ Point at the selected text with the cursor. Magically, you'll see the I-beam cursor turn into an arrow. The bottom of the arrow will be dangling the word **drag**.

➤ Click on the selected text and hold down your mouse button. The word **drag** at the bottom of the cursor will change to the word **move**.

➤ Still pressing the mouse button, move the cursor so the insertion point is where you want the selected text to land.

➤ Release the mouse button.

Word will move the selected text from its old location to wherever your mouse was pointing when you released the mouse button.

Don't like the new location? Select **Undo** from the **Edit** menu and your text will pop back to its old location.

Try it out. It's very cool, lots of fun, and very convenient.

Lost And Find

I've mentioned it before: I have a problem with the word "stuff." I'm told (by some) that I use it too often. If I think something I'm writing is too stuffed with "stuffs," I can use the Works' *Find* command to check it out.

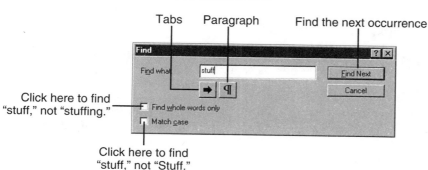

Tabs   Paragraph   Find the next occurrence

Click here to find "stuff," not "stuffing."

Click here to find "stuff," not "Stuff."

Looking for "stuff" in all the right places.

To start, select **Find** from the **Edit** menu. That will call up the dialog box shown here. Type the word(s) you want to find in the **Find what** text box (where **stuff** is entered in the figure). If you want to be sure you only find the word "stuff" and not "stuffing" or "Puffinstuff," click on **Find whole words only**.

If you want to be sure you only find the word "stuff" and not "Stuff," click on **Match case**.

Techno Talk

Finding Invisible Stuff

There are two buttons below the Find what box in the Find dialog box. Clicking the one with the arrow will add the symbol for a Tab marker in the Find what box. Clicking on the one with the backward "P" on it will add the symbol for a carriage return in the Find what box. You can use these to find the ends of paragraphs, stray tabs, or words that you only use before/after tabs or carriage returns. I don't use them often, myself, but you may find them useful.

After you've restricted the search as much, or as little, as you like, click **Find Next** and Works will search along from the insertion point until it finds the word "stuff." When it does, it will highlight it.

If you care to, at this point, you can close the Find dialog, and change the found word to another, delete it, or do anything you want to it. When you're ready to move on to the next "stuff," just select **Find** from the **Edit** menu, and repeat the process. The Find dialog keeps the information you entered, so you won't have to enter "stuff" or anything else again unless you want to change settings.

In a case like my own sad "stuff" abuse, you'd want to find most of the "stuffs" in a document and change them to a variety of other words to break that repetitiveness.

However, sometimes you're writing and you want to change every occurrence of a word to another word—a one-for-one trade. You can do it with the Replace command.

Please Replace Me, Let Me Go...

True story: once I was writing this novel, and I kept changing the main character's name. First he was Jack, then he was Nick, then he was Ned, then he was Jack again. (Who says it's only a woman's prerogative to change her mind?)

Once upon a time, that kind of indecision could mean hours and hours spent retyping, but not anymore. Now it's as simple as selecting **Replace** from the Works **Edit** menu.

When you select **Replace** from the **Edit** menu, you get a dialog like the one shown here. If you look at it, you'll notice that it's almost exactly the same as the Find dialog, with one big difference: the Replace dialog also has a text box where you can enter what you want to replace each occurrence of, well, whatever it is you're looking for.

Lets you pick and choose
what you replace

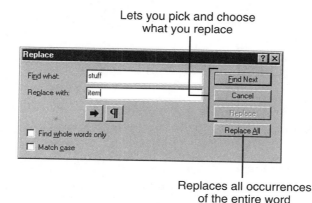

We're on a search and replace mission here.

Replaces all occurrences
of the entire word

In our example earlier (that "stuff" stuff), if I'd wanted to replace every other occurrence of the word "stuff" with the word "item," I'd enter the word "stuff" in the Find what box. Then I'd enter the replacement word ("item" in the figure) in the Replace with box.

To replace the first "stuff," click **Find Next**. Works will search for "stuff" and highlight it, when it finds it. To replace "stuff" with "item," click the **Replace** button. Then you can repeat the process, starting with the **Find Next** button, picking and choosing which "stuffs" you want to replace and which you want to leave alone.

In cases where you *know* you want to replace every single solitary occurrence of a word, like the name of that cranky Jack/Ned/Nick fellow I mentioned, you can use the **Replace All** button instead.

When you use the **Replace All** button, you should be careful to select Find whole words only and/or Match case, as appropriate. It will keep Works from turning "turkey **stuff**ing" into "turkey **item**ing." Which would you rather eat?

A Lazy Trick: Replace Unwanted Junk with Nothing!

If you regularly offend your own sensibilities (as I often do), you can search for an overused or badly used adjective or other grammar gremlin (the very earth seems to tremble at the thought) and replace it with nothing. Enter **very** in the Find What box. In the Replace With box, don't enter anything. Click **Find Next** (to be sure you really want to eliminate each one) and **Replace** at will.

Check Yourself

I don't know about y'all, but my typing skills are such that—well, let's be honest—I stink. Sure, I can touch-type, but my brain usually races so far ahead of my fingers that I accidentally omit little details. Like vowels.

I'm one of those people, too, who will stare at a word like "occurrence" for hours because "It doesn't look right" (too many double consonants, if you ask me). At the same time, I absolutely hate to break the flow of my writing to actually go look something up in a dictionary (I have an *Oxford English Dictionary* with about three inches of dust on it).

The advent of spelling checkers has made my writing life an absolute pleasure. You can use the Works spelling checker three ways: to check the spelling of a single word, a number of words, or your whole document.

A Pickled Peck of Personal Preferences
Before I go and check my spelling, I've made it a habit to save my work first. After I've checked my spelling, I save my file again. It's just an anal-retentive thing I do. You do what you want; I won't be upset.

Checking Your Spelling

To check the spelling of a single word, just double-click on the word to select it. Next, select **Spelling** from the **Tools** menu.

To check the spelling of a line, paragraph, or more, select the block of text you want to check, by the appropriate method (there's a quick review of them at the top of this chapter). Next, select **Spelling** from the **Tools menu.**

To check the spelling in your whole document, don't select any text. Just select **Spelling** from the **Tools** menu, and Works will check the spelling of each and every word in your document.

Save Yourself Some Clicks!

To start the spelling checker, you can also click the spelling button on the Works toolbar; it's the one with a check mark and the letters ABC on it. It works the same as if you select **Spelling** from the **Tools** menu.

Whether you're checking a word, line, or whole document, when Works comes across a word it doesn't recognize, it will show it to you in a dialog box like this one.

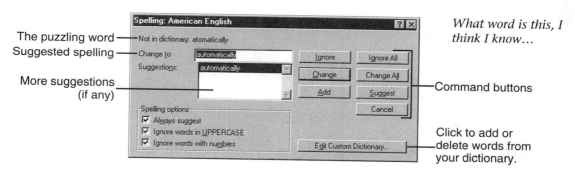

What word is this, I think I know...

The puzzling word
Suggested spelling
More suggestions (if any)
Command buttons
Click to add or delete words from your dictionary.

Just because a word gets brought to your attention, it doesn't mean it's misspelled. It's just not in the Works dictionary. That's why Works shows you each word and asks you what you want to do with it.

In the preceding figure, Works has identified a misspelled word and is offering the correct spelling. To change the word to the correct spelling, just click **Change**.

If you suspect that you've misspelled the word consistently throughout your document, you can click **Change All**, and Works will change every occurrence of that boo-boo spelling.

Sometimes, Works will point out a word that you spelled correctly—the word just isn't in the dictionary. You can deal with it a couple of ways:

➤ Click the **Ignore** button. Works will ignore the word and proceed on its merry way. If it runs into the word again, it will bring it to your attention—*again.*

➤ Click the **Ignore All** button. Works will ignore this word through the rest of your document.

➤ Click the **Add** button. Works will add this word to your Custom Dictionary, and you'll only be asked when about it when you actually misspell it.

I, personally, prefer to use the **Add** option. It saves a lot of time down the road. If you're more together about your word usage than I am, you can add a pile of words to your custom dictionary in one sitting.

Techno Talk

A Weird to the Wise...

Even though spelling checkers are great, wonderful, fabulous things, they are entirely idiotic.

If, by some chance, you typed the word "weird" instead of "word," but spelled it correctly, a spelling checker won't even bat an eye at it. It will let you use it, no matter how stupid it makes you look. Think about it: they're, their, there; its, it's; hare, hair, heir...

Bottom line: check your spelling, but then check your spelling checker. Also proofread your documents the old fashioned way, by reading them. It's the only way you can be absolutely certain you're using the right word the right way.

Editing Your Custom Dictionary

Adding words to your own, custom dictionary.

Enter new words here. ———

Yes, sometimes I misspell my own name. ———

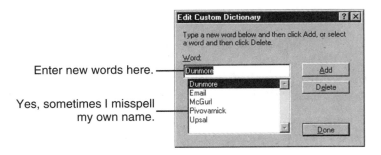

To add your favorite words to your custom dictionary, click on the **Edit Custom Dictionary** button at the bottom of the Spelling dialog box. That will bring up the preceding dialog box.

Type the word you want to add in the text box labeled Word. Make sure it's spelled correctly (you might want to have a real dictionary at hand), then click **Add**. Works will add the word to the list in the display box below.

To delete a word from your custom dictionary (if you find out you've spelled it wrong), scroll through the display box until you find the word you want to delete. Click on the word to select it. Then click **Delete**.

When you finish tinkering with your dictionary, click **Done**. Those words will never trouble you again, unless you misspell them in a document.

Other Spelling Options

At the lower left corner of the Spelling dialog, there are three options you can change however you like.

➤ **Always suggest**   With this option turned on, Works will always suggest alternate spellings to words it can't figure out. If you turn it off (by clicking on the check mark in front of it), you'll have to click the **Suggest** button if you want Works to provide alternate spellings.

➤ **Ignore words in UPPERCASE**   With this option turned on, Works will not check the spelling of words typed in ALL CAPITAL LETTERS. It's handy if you work for, say, a government agency and get tired of telling Works to ignore acronyms like HUD, CIA, FBI, and the like.

➤ **Ignore words with numbers**   With this option on, Works will not check the spelling of words that contain numbers. This is handy if you find yourself referring to file names (Memo12, Resume03), or other word/number combinations, in your documents.

Try them out and see which options work best for the kind of writing you do.

I Need A Synonym for Cinnamon

In addition to checking your spelling, Works can also help you overcome that horrible word-on-the-tip-of-my-tongue syndrome where you sort of know the word you want, but can't quite think of the exact word.

To use the thesaurus, double-click on a word in your document that's similar in meaning to the word you're looking for. Then select **Thesaurus** from the **Tools** menu. You'll get a Thesaurus dialog box like the one shown in the following figure.

Since I seem to have a "stuff" fixation in this chapter, that's the word I selected, and it's the word that shows up in the box labeled Looked up in the dialog box. Below it are the three Meanings: substance (noun), as in, "What's this stuff it's made of?"; nonsense (noun), as in "Stop talking all that stuff"; and fill (verb), as in "Stuff the turkey."

Click on the meaning you meant (how you're using the word), and the right side of the dialog box will show you some synonyms.

Click on the synonym you want to use (it will jump up to the text box labeled Replace with synonym) and then click the **Replace** button. The word you selected in your document will be replaced with the word you've selected in the thesaurus dialog box.

If you can't find just the right word on your first go-round, select a word that's closer to what you mean in the synonym list. Then click **Look Up**. The thesaurus will go through its song and dance again, this time using the new word.

The thesaurus at work.

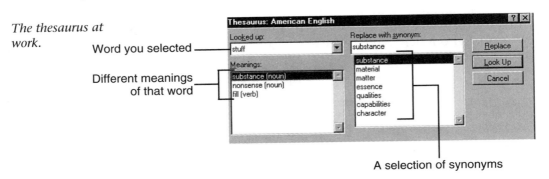

Word you selected

Different meanings of that word

A selection of synonyms

You can repeat the process as often as you like, zeroing in on exactly the right word. At any time, you can go back to a word you've already looked up by selecting its name from the Looked up list; just click on the text box and the list will pop up.

When in Doubt, Save As

Paranoia being what it is, sometimes you can go through a document revising, reformatting, and editing until you're blue in the face. All along the way, you may suspect that you aren't really improving the document, or (the horror, the horror) actually making things worse.

If you're in one of those self-doubting moods, one of the best things you can do is use the **Save As** command in the **File** menu.

Where the regular Save command updates the existing copy of your file on your disk, the Save As command creates a *new* copy of the file with a new name. Your behind is covered because you have your original document (sad as you may think it is) and your revised document (good, bad, or indifferent) saved to disk.

When your mind is clearer, and your ego is a little stronger, you can look at both documents and decide which is better for your needs.

Save As works exactly the same as a first time save (detailed in Chapter 5). To save a copy of your revised document with a different name, select **Save As** from the **File** menu. You'll get the Save As dialog shown here.

Since the original file (in the figure, anyway) was called **resume**, I've cleverly named the revised version **resume02** (simply by adding the **02** to the end of the file name) so I'll know it's the second version of my résumé.

You, of course, can use any naming or numbering scheme that helps you remember what your files are. Since Windows 95 allows long file names, you can even name your file **resume second version** if you want.

Techno Talk

You Have to Give It a New Name You have to assign the new copy of your file a new name, as described here. If you don't, Works will write over the old file, defeating the point of the Save As command.

There is a safety net, though. Works will ask you if it's okay to overwrite the file with the same name, before it actually does it. You can click **No** and change the name before it's too late.

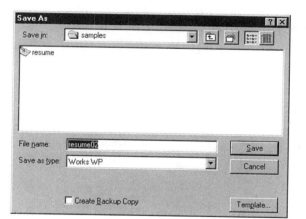

Hedge your bets with the Save As command.

Save As will come in handy again in later chapters, particularly Chapter 11 (saving files as a template) and 23 (saving files for use with other applications).

The Least You Need to Know

These editing skills will serve you well for as long as you're using Works for Windows 95—and even with other Windows 95 applications, too.

It's all pretty important, but the *really* important things you need to remember are:

➤ The various ways to select text, because you can't use most of the Edit menu if you haven't selected text first.

➤ Cutting text removes it from your document and places it in the Windows Clipboard.

➤ Copying text leaves the original in place and puts a copy in the Clipboard.

➤ The Clipboard can only hold one item at a time. When you cut or copy a new thing to the Clipboard, it completely replaces whatever was there before.

➤ Cutting text removes it from your document, period.

➤ The Paste command places a copy of whatever is in the Clipboard in your document, at the insertion point.

➤ Find and Replace let you search for and replace words, phrases, and even formatting (such as tabs and carriage returns).

➤ If you're uncertain about the changes you've made, save your revised document with a different name, using the **Save As** command to save it in a separate file with a different name. That way you'll have the best of both worlds.

Chapter 9

Fun with Paragraphs

In This Chapter

➤ Marginal margins

➤ The space between the lines

➤ An indent-ity crisis

➤ Tabs and bullets: a love story

One of the things you'll discover as you use and learn more about Microsoft Works (or any computer application) is that you'll develop your own style of working. You'll probably develop a few quirks, too.

For example: some folks I know can't be bothered prettying up their documents as they write them. Worrying about how it looks, they say, interferes with figuring out what it should say. These people write, write, write, and when they're satisfied with the content, tackle the appearance.

Others pretty things up as they go. They already have an idea (before they start writing) of how the final document will look, so it's no big deal for them to format while writing.

I fall into this last category, if you care. One of my own personal quirks is that I need to create these elaborate title pages for my other writing (plays and such), before I even begin to tackle the project itself. Why? I have no idea. (Gee, John, thanks for sharing.)

In this chapter and the next, we're going to look at some basic formatting techniques: margins, spacing, fonts, and the like. We'll put them to some traditional, and not-so traditional uses, and explain the whys and wherefores.

After we're done, you can make up your own mind about how you want to work—tinkering with format while you write, or after.

Marginalia

"Marginalia" actually refers to the notes people write in the margins of books and manuscripts, however I'm stretching the definition to include the little details about creating those margins.

Margins are the white spaces that surround text on the printed page. Traditionally, margins are set at about an inch at the top, bottom, and sides of the page (based on the size of the paper you're using, and its orientation—both are covered in Chapter 11). That's pretty standard. Works' *default* margin settings are 1-inch at the top and bottom of the page, and 1.25-inches left and right.

Default

Default refers to software settings, not placing blame (the accident was default of the other driver). Default settings are the way your software is set up right out of the box. Default may also refer to standard options (such as margins) that Works assumes you want to use unless you tell it otherwise.

Sometimes, you may want your margins a little larger, or smaller. If you're writing a report that's going to be bound (put in a binder, for example) you may want to increase the left margin to 1.5-inches, or so, to accommodate the binding.

Sometimes, too, you may want to change the margins of just a paragraph or two within your document—here I'm thinking of term papers, where you use quoted material set off from the main text like this:

> *"That's a great deal to make one word mean," Alice said in a thoughtful tone.*

> *"When I make a word do a lot of work like that," said Humpty Dumpty, "I always pay it extra."*

It's easy to adjust your margins, so they're either smaller or larger.

Setting Your Margins

To set the margins for an entire document (if you don't want to use the Works default settings), the document should be open—but you knew that already, didn't you?

Next, select **Page Setup** from the **File** menu. That will give you the Page Setup dialog box shown here. If the margin options aren't foremost in the dialog box when it opens, just click on **Margins** tab to bring them front and center.

Click to
accept

Previews
what your
page will
look like

Set your
margins
here.

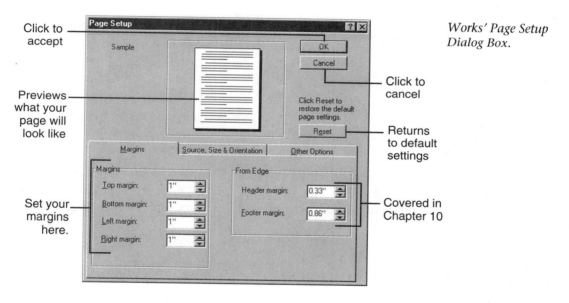

*Works' Page Setup
Dialog Box.*

Click to
cancel

Returns
to default
settings

Covered in
Chapter 10

To change the margin settings, double-click in the text box after the appropriate margin (Top, Bottom, Left, or Right), and type in the new size in decimal form (you know: 1.25" is the same as 1¼").

Alternatively, you can click on the teeny-tiny up and down arrows to the right of the text box. Each click will change the margin by a tenth (.1) of an inch.

You can see how your new margins will look, as you're adjusting them, by checking out the dialog box's sample page. When you're satisfied with the margins, click **OK**. You'll see your document again, with its brand spanking new margins.

This works whether the margins are for a document that you're formatting after writing, or for a new blank document. Every page of the document will have the new margins.

Changing Paragraph Margins

Control those margins…

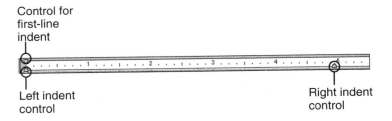

When, in the course of human events, you decide you need to change the margins for just a portion of your document, you don't even need to call up the dialog box. You can do it using the ruler at the top of your document window (previously shown).

(This is actually a margin trick using Works' indent controls. Don't let the appearance of the word "indent" here throw you for a loop. Paragraph "margins" is a misnomer. They're actually a variety of indents. Indents are covered as a species later in this chapter. Just call me Margaret Mead.)

It's as easy as 1-2-3:

1. Click on the paragraph you want to change, to place the cursor in it.

2. Click-and-drag the left indent control (it's labeled in the preceding figure), and move it to its new position.

3. Finally, adjust the right indent control (also indicated in the figure), and you're done.

You'll notice, when you try this, that only the margins of the paragraph that holds the cursor actually change. If you want to change the margins of two or more consecutive paragraphs (as shown in the next figure), you need to select them. You can change several, scattered paragraphs by changing the margins of one, and then using the **Paste Special** command as discussed in the last chapter.

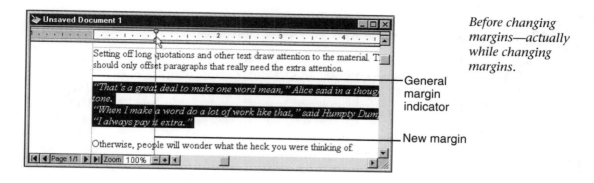

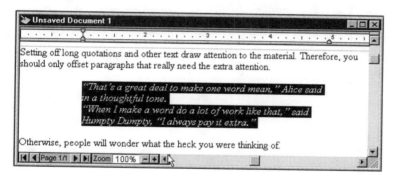

Before changing margins—actually while changing margins.

After the change (which sounds like a book about menopause).

You can also achieve the same effect (indenting a quotation block) using indents, discussed a little later in this chapter.

Spacing Out

I'm sorry, what was I talking about? Oh, the space between lines (not the space between my ears).

The space between each line of text, and between paragraphs, is important. Too little space, and the reader's eye has trouble distinguishing between one line and the next, making it difficult to read. Too much space, and it's also difficult to read—and it wastes a lot of paper.

A Painless Factoid You May Find Useful

Typists know that the amount of space between lines is called *spacing*, however some computer applications borrow their terms from the language of typesetting, where that space between lines is called *leading*. It comes from the days when type was set by hand, one letter at a time, and each line of type was separated by one or more strips of lead.

The common line spacings.

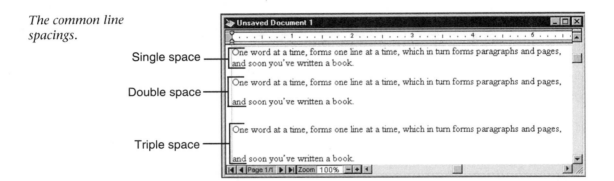

Single space
Double space
Triple space

The most common line spacings are single, double, and triple space. Single spaced text (like what you're reading now) has no blank lines between each line of type. Double-spaced type has one blank line, and triple-spaced has two. That makes perfect sense, doesn't it?

For letters and other short documents, single spacing is fine. You should double-space longer documents such as reports and other homework-like stuff so your readers have somewhere to make notes and correct your spelling and grammar.

Triple spacing is used in only a few cases I can think of—it doesn't mean there aren't more uses, just that I don't know them. One is speech writing: triple-spaced text (in a large-ish font) is easier to read, especially when you must look up at your audience, and then find your place again in your text.

The other use for triple-spacing may not even be valid anymore. When I took journalism in college, we were taught to write our stories triple-spaced to make it easier for the editor to edit, and the typesetter to set the story in type. Nowadays, with editors doing their editing on computers and honest-to-goodness typesetters a vanishing breed, who knows if that's still standard operating procedure?

Setting the Spacing for a Whole Document

When you create a new word processing document with Works, the default line spacing is single-spaced. If that's what you want, type away.

If you want another line spacing, select **Paragraph** from the **Format** menu. The Format Paragraph dialog box will appear and looks like the one shown here. If the Spacing options aren't foremost when the dialog box opens, click on **Spacing** tab to bring them to the front.

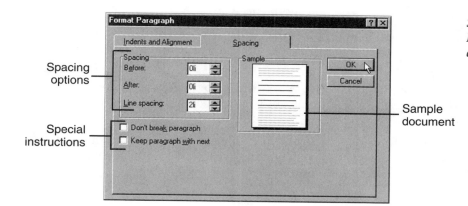

Spacing out in the Format Paragraph dialog box.

You have three spacing options, as you can see in the figure. In order of appearance, they are:

➤ **Before** Sets the number of blank lines Works will insert in your document before each new paragraph.

➤ **After** Sets the number of blank lines Works will insert in your document after each paragraph.

➤ **Line spacing** Sets the number of blank lines Works will insert between each line of type.

The Before and After options replace the touch-typists' instinct to automatically do a second carriage return at the end of each paragraph. They're an either/or proposition. If you have Works insert extra space before your paragraphs, there's no need (none that I can think of, anyhow) to have extra space after your paragraphs, too.

I use these paragraph spacing options when I'm writing a single-spaced document and I'm not indenting the first line of each paragraph. Then I put an extra line after each paragraph, to make the letter easier to read. You, however, may do whatever you like. We'll talk about indents in a bit.

To change any of the three spacing settings, you can double-click in the text box after the appropriate setting and type in the number of lines you'd like. You may also use the up- and down-arrows, one click adds or subtracts one line from the setting.

Those Special Instructions

The "Special Instructions" I alluded to in the figure are, in my experience, rarely used. In fact, I've never used them, but you should know what they are and do, in case the need arises.

If you click on **Don't break paragraph**, Works will end your pages early to keep from splitting a paragraph over two pages—even if it means you wind up with a lot of half-blank pages in your document.

If you click **Keep paragraph with next**, Works will keep the two selected paragraphs together on the same page—even if it means you wind up with a lot of half-blank pages.

You should not apply these options to an entire document, only to specific paragraphs. If you apply them to a whole document, you'll waste so much paper a spotted owl will poop on your head for punishment.

As always, the sample display will give you a little preview of your changes.

When you're happy with the spacing options, click **OK** and you'll be back at your document, and it will be all spaced out (*like, wow, man—like, totally*).

To Change Spacing for a Paragraph or Two

The procedure is exactly the same as above, except you need to place the cursor in the paragraph you want to change. If you want to change consecutive paragraphs, you should select them (with the double-click or click-drag in the margin trick) before you change the spacing.

To change the spacing on a few paragraphs that aren't consecutive, you can do one and then use the **Paste Special** command as discussed in the last chapter.

In-nie And Out-ie Indents

Use indents (or *indentations* if you insist on the $2 word) to indicate the beginning of a new paragraph. It's another one of those things that help make your writing easier to read. I mentioned them briefly back in Chapter 7, explaining how you should break the habit of indenting with your Spacebar.

You can also use indents to set off a paragraph of text, like we did earlier with that quotation from *Through The Looking Glass*.

To set your indents, select **Paragraph** from the **Format** menu. The Format Paragraph dialog box will appear, and look something like the one shown here. If the Indents and Alignment options aren't foremost when the dialog opens (and they won't be, since we were fiddling with spacing just now), click on the **Indents and Alignment** tab to bring them to the front.

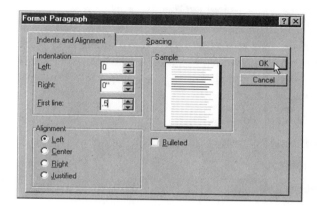

Indenting and aligning.

As with spacing earlier, you can apply indents to your entire document, or individual paragraphs. Your three indentation options are Left, Right, and First line. The text boxes work the same as the ones we've been using all along, so you already know you can type in a number or use the arrows to adjust by tenths of an inch.

The Left and Right options will indent every line of text the amount indicated, in addition to whatever margins you've set. In other words: if you set 1-inch margins and then indent an inch with the Left and Right options, your text will be two inches away from the edge of the page. Got that?

The First line option indents the first line of your paragraphs the amount indicated (in the figure it's half an inch).

You can also do a funky thing called a *hanging indent* where the first line of each paragraph is indented outward, extending beyond the rest of the paragraph. Or would that be "out-dented?" Whatever.

Indentation flavors: normal and hanging.

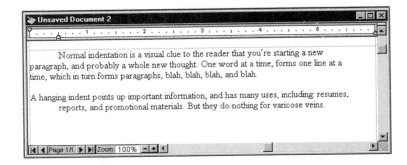

You can see what a hanging indent looks like in the figure here. They're useful for bulleted lists (more on those in a moment), résumés, and other documents where you want the reader to be able to quickly pick out the most important concepts. Here's how to create a paragraph with a hanging indent:

1. Select the paragraph(s) you want to dangle

2. Select **Paragraph** from the **Format** menu.

3. Set the Left indentation to .5".

4. If you care to, or need to, you can set the Right indent to .5" as well. (I think it looks better with both sides indented—just a personal preference.)

5. Set the First line indentation to -.5" (yes, that is a negative number).

6. Click **OK**.

Bada-bing bada-boom, you have a lovely hanging indent—which sounds like a sleazy pick-up line. I may have to try it sometime. You can get the same effects by tinkering with the margin and indent controllers in the document ruler, just like we did back in the "Marginalia" section.

As long as the Indents and Alignment portion of the Format Paragraph dialog box is handy, we may as well look at alignment, too.

Madonna: Justify My Paragraph

Alignment (also called *paragraph justification*) means how your text lands on the page. There are four Alignment kinds, as follows:

Left alignment is typical. It gives you a nice crisp line of text down the left side of your page, with a raggedy looking right side.

Center alignment is unusual for lots of text, but common for titles and headings. It centers each line of text on the page giving you ragged right and left sides.

Right alignment is also unusual for lots of text. It's the opposite of Left alignment. The right side is razor sharp, and the left is raggedy.

Justified alignments are very crisp and professional looking. It gives you razor sharp right and left edges, but text in the middle can wind up kind of gap-toothed looking from the random spaces Works adds to force lines to the margins.

Most of your writing will be aligned left, or justified, with the occasional title or headline centered, or right-justified, on the page. That's the standard, the norm, and there isn't much we can do about it until the alignment revolution comes... and don't hold your breath waiting for it.

Don't close the Format Paragraph dialog box just yet. We're going to talk about...

Love and Bullets

Not the "kiss-kiss, bang-bang" sort. We're talking about bulleted lists, which I love (if you haven't noticed) and use often. There are a number of uses for bulleted lists in a document, for example:

➤ Lists of things to do.

➤ Highlight important information in a concise, easy-to-read manner.

➤ As a way to group unrelated, but important, statements together without wasting a paragraph of explanation on each.

To create a bulleted list, first make sure that each point you want to bullet is a paragraph unto itself. Next, select all the paragraphs (there should be at least three—less than that hardly seems worth the effort). Then, click the bulleted list button on the tool bar. It's the one with the (*duh*) bulleted list on it.

Works will fudge the first line indent (to a negative number) to make it a hanging indent, and add a bullet to the beginning of each paragraph as shown here.

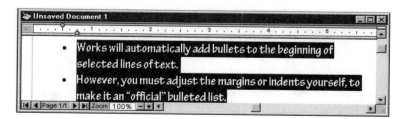

A beautifully bulleted list, if I do say so myself.

Bullets and Other Special Characters

Bullets (➤) and other special characters (like copyright and trademark symbols) are part of most Windows fonts. You can use them anytime you like by pressing special key combinations. For example, you can add a bullet on your own by pressing and holding the **Alt** key while you type **0183**.

Those combinations can be a pain in the butt to remember. Fortunately, you can set Works to use one of a dozen or so bullets automatically, by selecting it from the Format Bullets dialog—just select **Bullets** from the **Format** menu. Click the bullet you want to use, and click **OK**. You can also turn the hanging indent option on or off by clicking in the check box labeled **Hanging indent**.

For bullets not listed in the Format Bullet dialog box, and other special characters, you can use the Windows Character Map accessory to view and use any font's special characters. You'll find Character Map in the Accessories folder (under Programs) in the Start menu.

The Tab Stops Here

Tab stops are a handy thing. They're little markers in the ruler, placed at half-inch intervals (these are the default tabs; we'll set other ones, too).

When you press your keyboard's Tab key, your cursor jumps magically to the next tab stop, so you don't have to sit there pounding the Spacebar.

A fancy list, done with tab stops.

Tab stop ——

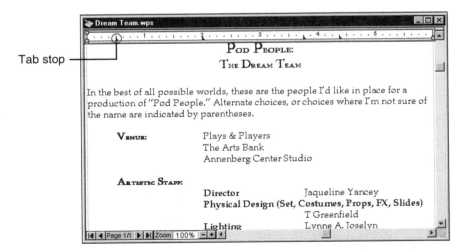

Tabs are good for creating lists with multiple columns, such as the one shown here. You'll notice that each of the columns precisely aligns with a tab stop in the ruler at the top of the figure.

Tabs make creating columns so painless; I can't tell you how painless it is. You'll have to try for yourself.

Setting Tabs

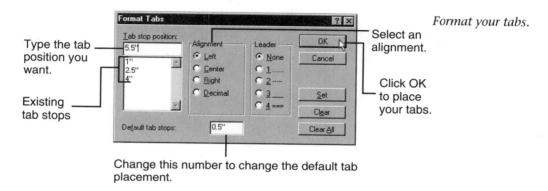

Format your tabs.

Type the tab position you want.

Existing tab stops

Change this number to change the default tab placement.

Select an alignment.

Click OK to place your tabs.

You may never need to set tabs of your own, what with the default tabs at every half inch; they may be enough for you. If you do need to set up some special tabs, there are two ways to do it.

If you're the precise type, like me (not!), and know exactly where you want your tabs to go, you can set them with the Format Tabs dialog box. To use it, select **Tabs** from the **Format** menu.

Type in the position of the tab stop you want to place in the Tab stop position box (where it says **5.5"** in the figure). Then click **Set**. Works will add the tab stop to the list in the scroll box. Repeat the process until you've added all the tabs you want or need.

To remove a tab stop, click on the tab stop in the scroll box that you want to delete; click **Clear**. That tab is history.

To remove all of your tab stops, click **Clear All** and they're all history.

You can also specify the alignment of your tab stops—just as you can align text. You can align the text at a tab so it's set to the Left, Center, or Right, which is nice for making your columns easy to read. You can also select Decimal alignment, which is great for columns of figures. They'll line up around the decimal point like this:

$ 10.95

5.95

10,036.25

To align a tab, just click on the tab you want to format. Then click on the Alignment option you want to use.

Tab stops that have different alignments look different when displayed in your document ruler. They look like those shown here, in case you run into a strange tab some night.

A field-guide to tab stops.

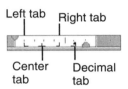

You can also set a *leader*, which is just a string of characters before whatever you type at the tab stop—that's how they get those perfect sets of dots between the chapter number and title in the table of contents of books, like this:

Chapter One......................*In Which Doris Gets Her Oats*

The tab stop to the left of "Chapter One" has no leader specified. The tab to the left of *"In Which Doris Gets Her Oats"* has a dotted leader. Leaders make it easy for the reader to read across several columns, without her eye accidentally skipping to another line.

To give a tab a leader, just click on the tab you want to format, to select it. Then click on the **Leader** you want to use.

The Lazy Way to Set Tabs

This is my own personal favorite. The lazy way to set a tab in your documents is to simply click on the ruler wherever you want a tab stop. Works will plunk a basic, left-aligned tab down right where you clicked.

If you need to do any fancy formatting with your tabs, just double-click on the tab you want to format, and you'll open the Format Tabs dialog box shown earlier.

With the Format Tabs dialog box open, you can format any or all of the tabs you have going in your document as previously described.

Moving Tabs

Sometimes, when setting tabs, you just make a bad guess about how much room you'll need. I do it all of the time. To adjust a tab stop (and all the text it affects), do this:

1. Select the paragraph(s) that are affected by the tab.
2. Click-drag the tab to its new position.
3. Release the mouse button.

It's that simple. You can make any tab-related change (adding a leader, say, or changing alignment) the same way. Just make sure you select the affected text before changing the tab's format.

To delete a tab the lazy way: click-drag the tab right off of the ruler, and release the mouse button. Poof. It's gone.

Just for fun, try creating some columns of information in a word processing document and playing around with the various tab settings. Pretty soon, you'll have those tabs jumping through hoops for you.

A Sneaky Editing Trick

Windows 95 gives your right mouse button special powers. Check it out:

Select some text. While selected, click on it using the *right* mouse button. Magically, a shortcut menu will pop up that includes portions of both the Edit and Format menus—including the cut and paste commands, and paragraph formatting options—saving you time and energy while prettying up your documents.

The Least You Need to Know

We covered some formatting basics in this chapter: margins, spacing, alignment, and tabs. If you don't want or need to do more than write simple, single-spaced letters, with no bulleted lists or quotations, using the Works default settings, you don't need to remember any of this. Really, you don't.

However, if you want to create some effective, fancy, and professional-looking docu-ments, you may use these features every day. Only you know what kind(s) of document formatting you'll be doing. So, the least you need to know is that this is Chapter 9, and it covers basic document formatting. It'll be here when you need it.

Format This!

In This Chapter

➤ Miss Format America speaks

➤ Confessions of a font addict

➤ Attention getters

➤ Breaking pages

I feel vaguely dishonest writing about fonts and formatting when the most exciting layout I get to do with these manuscripts is the occasional tab and (if I'm lucky) some bold-italic in a chapter title. Yippee.

That won't stop me, however, because the rest of the time I'm a formatting fool.

Formatting is taking your plain, vanilla document and spicing it up with some fancy margins, fonts, and other typographic effects—most of which are done with the Works toolbar, or the Format menu. Think of it as the "bathing suit competition," because it's where you get to show your stuff.

"What Formatting Means to Me"

Document formatting is a pretty ephemeral subject to discuss because a lot of it hinges on questions of taste: what you find pleasing to the eye, versus what someone else finds pleasing.

One of the hardest lessons I ever learned was not to argue about questions of taste (or *aesthetics*, as the highbrows like to say) because there is no right and wrong. What you like is right for you, what I like is right for me, and what everybody else likes is right for them.

This chapter presents some very general guidelines that will help you begin, but nothing I say here is set in stone. At some point, you'll need, or want, to break one or two of these so called rules, and that's *okay*. Let your taste be your guide.

Start easy, take it slow, and soon you'll develop a strong sense of what looks good to you, and what doesn't. It's no guarantee that anyone else will appreciate it, but you'll have pleased yourself—and that's okay, because you're good enough, you're smart enough, and gosh darnit, people like you.

Take It Easy with Easy Formats

One of the easiest ways to learn the ins and outs of formatting is by using Works' pre-defined set of formats called *Easy Formats*.

Using an Easy Format

To use an easy format, select the text you want to tinker with—it's simplest to work with whole paragraphs. With your paragraph selected, click on **Easy Formats** in the **Format** menu. This dialog box will pop up.

Easy does it, with Easy Formats.

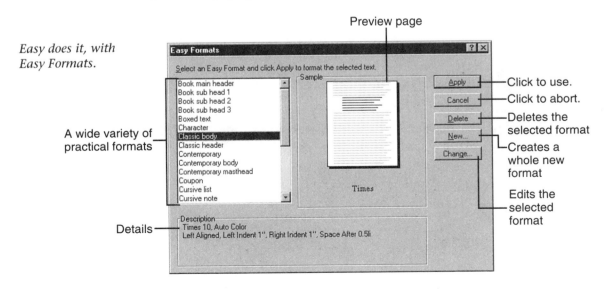

114

The list box on the left side of the dialog box gives a large number of predefined formats you can apply to your own document. To use a style, just click on the style's name in the list, and then click **Apply**. Works will reformat the paragraph to the selected Easy Format's specifications (you can read the specs in the Description box and see a sneak preview in the Sample page display).

Techno Talk

A Kick in the Head(er)

Don't let the use of the word header in the Easy Format dialog box confuse you. There are two kinds of headers you'll run into while using Works.

In this case, header means a heading, or title, for a section of your document. Sub header is another heading that is below the previous heading (the actual term is "inferior," but that sounds so judgmental). For example, the headers in this chapter are:

Chapter 10

That's the main header, similar to the Book Main Header format in the Easy Formats dialog box. Under that heading is the Chapter Title:

Format *This!*

That's on a par with the Book sub head 1 format in the Easy Formats dialog box. With the "In This Chapter" being a Book sub head 2.

You can use these headers to give readers a clue to the structure and relative importance of each section of your writing.

The *other* sort of headers (found under the Edit menu) are simple lines of text that Works can automatically place across the top (header) or bottom (footer) of every page of your document. You can use these to identify the document, the author, and usually include a page number. The how-to on these headers is coming up later in this chapter.

Unfortunately, they're both called *headers*; don't let it throw you.

Rather than run through the whole list of Easy Formats, which would be pretty boring for all concerned, why not just dash off a nonsense paragraph in a new, blank word processing document and then apply a few random formats to it yourself. You'll see, up close and personal, what Easy Formats are and do. And you can't hurt anything, so go nuts with them—it's time to learn by playing.

Changing an Easy Format

While you're playing with the Easy Formats, finding out what they'll do for you, you may find one that's *almost* exactly what you need for one of your projects—but only almost. You can easily edit the format so it's *exactly* the one you need. Here's how:

1. Select **Easy Formats** from the **Format** menu.

2. Click on the name of the format you want to alter.

3. Click **Change**. The dialog box shown here will open.

Changing Easy Formats is easy...are easy...no, is easy.

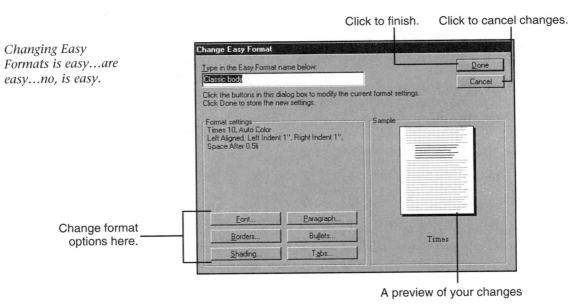

Click to finish. Click to cancel changes.

Change format options here.

A preview of your changes

4. You can make changes to the font used, paragraph format, bullets, and tab stops. You can also change or add borders and shading (more about those next chapter, but I won't tell if you play with them now).

5. When you finish, click **Done**, and Works will save your changes.

Be aware that the changes you make with the Change Easy Formats dialog box replaces the original format. If you want to keep the original format, you need to create a new format rather than change an existing one.

Creating New Easy Formats

The simplest way to create a new Easy Format (for me, at least) is to format a single paragraph so it's just the way I want it. You can start by formatting a paragraph with an existing Easy Format. Then you can alter the paragraph some more, so it's exactly what you need.

When your paragraph is perfect (or close enough for government work), select the paragraph.

Next, select **Easy Formats** from the **Format** menu, and then click **New**. The New Easy Format dialog box will appear (looks kinda familiar, doesn't it?).

Type in a new name.

Works picks up the format of the selected paragraph.

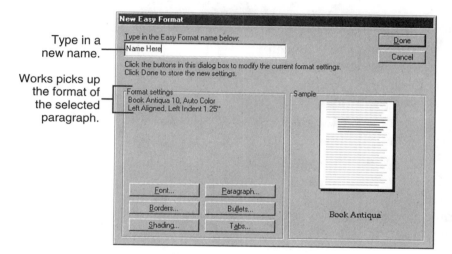

A New Easy Format—it really is easy!

The dialog box is exactly the same as the Change Easy Format dialog box, except for one thing: there's no name assigned to the format, since it's brand-new. Type a name in the text box at the top of the screen (don't give it a name that's already been assigned to another Easy Format, though).

You can, if you care to, use any of the six format setting buttons at the bottom of the dialog box to fine-tune your new format.

When you finish tinkering, click **Done**; Works will save your Easy Format and add it to the list in the Easy Formats dialog box, and you'll never need to create that format from scratch again.

Confessions of a Font Addict

I admit it: I am a font addict. I love fonts—the stranger, the better. I have more fonts than any human being should be allowed to have. That's just me.

I also love font *theory*, if you will: the history and traditional uses of the different kinds of fonts. This section is a brief introduction to that font theory. It is, by no means, exhaustive—that would be a book by itself—but it does give you enough information to start.

Font Varieties

A font sampler—almost a smorgasbord.

Basically, there are three types (pardon the pun) of font: text, headline, and novelty (though it's probably more politically correct to say "specialty") fonts. There are samples of each in the preceding figure.

There's another kind of font that keeps getting shuttled between categories (at least in *my* mind) and those are script fonts. Script fonts are designed to look like fancy handwriting, or calligraphy. You'll see them, most often, on formal invitations—just look at any wedding announcement you've received. I say they're specialty fonts because they're of limited use. Others will disagree, and that's okay. It's that taste thing again.

Fonts for Text

Text fonts are appropriate to long-ish (say, three pages or longer) documents, because they help the eye recognize the shapes of letters and words, and therefore are easier to read.

Most fonts that are appropriate for text are *serif* fonts, that is, letters that have the little tales and curlicues that make them easier to identify quickly. The text of this book is set in a serif font.

I Shot the Serif—Headlines and Signs

Sans serif fonts don't have those tails and curlicues (sans serif is actually Middle English for "without tails"). They're rather Spartan-looking; the chapter and section names in this book are set in a sans serif font.

Sans serif fonts are odd: on the one hand, they're not very easy to read at small sizes, for a long document. On the other hand, they're very good for headlines, and almost every traffic sign in the world is done with a sans serif font.

The difference is readability versus legibility. Serif fonts are very readable: you can look at them for hours without hurting yourself. Sans serif fonts are very legible: it's very easy to pick out letters and words, but only for very short bits of text, such as *Next Exit 6 miles* or *Attorney General Resigns in Shame*.

Because of their legibility, most TV shows and movies also use sans serif fonts for the credits, since they scroll by so quickly.

It's a Novelty

Novelty and/or specialty fonts (including script) have an appeal based only on their uniqueness. By definition, these unique fonts are hard to read for long stretches. The letters are so fractured, stylized, or surrounded with frou-frou that you'd go nuts trying to read more than a dozen words or so.

Novelty fonts are good to establish a mood, or an effect. Scary, blood-drippy fonts are great for saying "Boo!" on a Halloween card, but you wouldn't want to read a 400-page book with them.

Generally, use novelty fonts for headlines and other short text. Keep their use to a minimum, since they'll keep folks from actually reading what you have to say.

Edith, You Dingbat

A *dingbat* is a kind of specialty font. Instead of being made up of the usual assortment of letters, numbers, and punctuation marks, a dingbat font is composed entirely of symbols, like this:

★✤ ★✹ ★✪○✳ ✳▲ ✪▢✳■

That actually spells out "Hi my name is John," but in dingbats. These are appropriate any time you need to draw attention to a list of items (as alternate bullets) or just to add a touch of class or whimsy to a headline. They can also be practical: writing a survey for your church group? Why draw all those check boxes by hand? Use a dingbat.

Trying Fonts on for Size

Way back in Chapter 6, we looked at using the toolbar to change the font and style of text in your documents. It involved selecting the text, selecting the font from the font menu, selecting the font size from the size menu, and, finally, clicking on a style button or two (you remember: **bold**, *italic*, and underline). That's a lot of menu and button clicking.

With the **Font and Style** option under the **Format** menu, you can do all of those changes in one easy dialog box.

To begin, select the text you want to re-font. Then select **Font and Style** from the **Format** menu. You'll get the Format Font and Style dialog box shown here.

Fonting with style and panache.

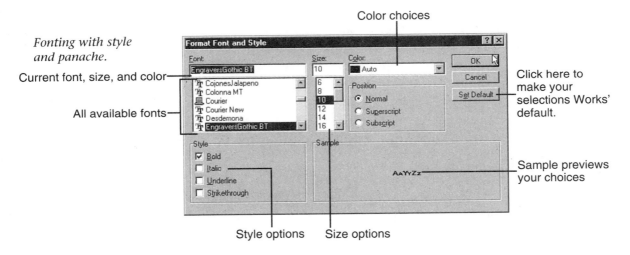

Color choices

Current font, size, and color

All available fonts

Click here to make your selections Works' default.

Sample previews your choices

Style options   Size options

The **Format Font and Style** dialog box lets you choose from all of the fonts you have installed in Windows on your PC. To change the selected text to another font, just click on it in the list box (you may have to scroll a bit to see all of your fonts). You select a new font size the same way.

If you're working on, say, the second draft of a document, you may want to make revised text a color, so it stands out from the sea of black-on-white letters. (You might also add color for a desktop publishing project, too, like those in the next chapter—but you need a color printer to have them still be in color when you print them out.)

To change the color of the selected text, click on the **Color** drop-down list and select your new color from the menu.

In the Style box, you can choose one or more styles to apply to selected text (though why you'd use Strikethrough is beyond me—I've never found a use for it). Just click on the style(s) you want.

In the Position box, you can make the selected text sit above (Superscript) or below (Subscript) the rest of the line of text. It's handy for flagging footnotes with a˙ or if you type extensive math formulae or chemical stuff like H_2O.

You can check to see what your tinkering will look like in the Sample box at the bottom of the dialog box.

If you want the font and style you've chosen to be the basic font and style for all of your documents, you can make it so (I felt like Captain Picard for a second there). Just click on the **Set Default** button, and it will become Works' default font and style.

When you finish tinkering, click **OK** and the selected text in your document will transform before your eyes.

Headings, Subheadings, and Captions

Headings, subheadings, and captions are bits of text that require a little, teeny-tiny bit of special handling. As I mentioned earlier, you can always use an Easy Format, but in case you want to do them on your own here are the "rules."

Head This Way

A heading, like the title of a chapter, should be larger than the main text. If your text is 12-points, you can make your heading 16- or 18- points. (Remember what "point" means? It's back in chapter 6.)

To stand out, you can use a different font than the main text (a sans serif headline font, or even a novelty font if it isn't too annoying—but that's a question of personal taste again). You can make it bold or italic, or even bold italic, if it helps.

Under Your Head

Subheadings, to indicate that they're beneath (sub) the main heading in terms of your document's structure, should be smaller, but in the same font. You can add variation by using a different style for each level of subhead.

If you trace the headings and subheadings through this section, you'll see what I mean.

Subheads Are Tough to Keep Track Of...

Or maybe I'm just a goof. If I don't indicate, somehow, what kind of subheading I'm supposed to be using, I always goof it up. When I'm writing, I actually include the level in the heading, like this:

(A)Chapter 10

(B)Format *This!*

(C)In This Chapter

That way I can tell, just by looking, what level the last heading was, and what sort the next one should be. Of course, the A, B, and C usually get edited out before you see it, but it works.

Caption

A caption is a little bit of explanatory text that goes under a photo, illustration, or other doodad you might stick in your documents.

Where headings are meant to attract attention, captions aren't. They should be in a small (say 9-points or so), serif or sans serif font (but nothing novelty, or hard to read—9-points is tiny), preferably the same as your headline font. If your headline font is a novelty number, use your text font, or something simple (like Arial) so it's unobtrusive but easy to read.

We'll caption some samples in the next chapter.

Headers, Footers, and Footnotes

These *headers* are the other kind: the information that appears across the top (head) of every page of your document. There are headers at the top of many pages in this book, identifying the Part you're reading, the chapter you're reading, and the page you're on.

Footers are the same sort of thing but appear at the foot (bottom) of the page.

You use them to identify your work (homework, for instance), title a report, and automatically number your pages. Headers and footers, generally, are an either/or proposition. If you use a header, don't use a footer, and vice versa. Otherwise, your page will get too cluttered and your reader won't be able to tell what's important.

Getting a Header

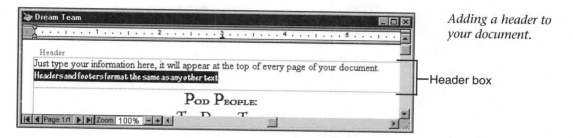

Adding a header to your document.

—Header box

To place a header in your document, select **Header** from the **View** menu. Your cursor will jump to the header at the top of whatever page you're working with (as shown here). Just type in the information you want displayed (your name, perhaps, and the name of your project).

If you want to add the page number to your header, select **Page Number** from the **Insert** menu. You can also add the **Date and Time** or **Document Name** (the name you gave the file when you saved it) by selecting those options from the **Insert** menu as well.

Techno Talk

Inserting Stuff Elsewhere

You aren't limited to using these insertion commands in headers and footers. You can use them pretty much anywhere, in any Works document. Just place the insertion point (by clicking once) wherever you want the information to appear, and choose the appropriate item from the **Insert** menu. Works will graciously oblige you.

You can format header text the same as any other text with Works, so coordinate the font, style, and font size (the same or smaller than your regular text) with the rest of your document.

My Left Footer

To place a *footer* in your document, select **Footer** from the **View** menu. Your cursor will jump to the bottom of whatever page you're working with. Proceed as previously described. Should you, or any member of your IM force, be captured, I will disavow any knowledge of your actions.

Footnote Notes

Footnotes used to be the bane of my existence, back in the bad old typewriter days. The pain! The retyping! The re-retyping! (The exclamation points!) What a pain in the hind-quarters! What a breeze they are with Microsoft Works!

To add a footnote to your document, leave the cursor at the end of the quotation, or whatever you're noting. Select **Footnote** from the **Insert** menu. A spiffy little dialog box will appear, as shown here.

Yeah, insert this footnote, buddy...

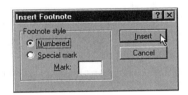

Select the footnote style: **Numbered**, for papers with a lot of notes; **Special mark** if you'll only have one or two. If you're using a special mark, type the special mark you want to use (an asterisk (*), say) in the box labeled Mark.

Next, click **Insert**. Works will draw in that obnoxious little dividing line, number/mark your note, and place the cursor where you need to type your reference (check out the next figure). If you're using numbers, Works will even keep track of them for you—no more having two footnote number 7s. Just type your note, format it, and forget it.

A fabulous pre-fab footnote. How easy, how Levittown.

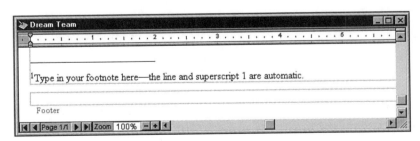

Some Formatting Rules of Thumb

These aren't "I'm gonna have to write you a ticket, you've got too many fonts on that page" rules, just some general guidelines. Most of these fall under the KISS rule of design: Keep It Simple, Stupid. It's a rule I try to live by, but you (as always) can do whatever you like. (What am I, your mother?)

➤ Try to keep your documents to two or three fonts.

➤ Contrast your headline and text fonts for maximum effect. For example, use a heavy-looking sans serif font for headlines and a lighter-looking serif font for your text.

➤ Get variety by using bold and italic variations.

➤ Try to keep to one special element (like clip art or a graph, like we'll be doing in the next chapter) per page. A well-placed illustration has more impact when it's the only one on the page.

➤ Formatting is meant to help the reader read, understand, and enjoy your document. Complex layouts with multiple fonts and gobs of graphics work against that noble goal.

➤ Enjoy yourself. Formatting is fun.

Breaking Pages and Other Niceties

Sometimes, especially when you're writing an important report or paper, you want everything to be perfect. I, personally, have never gotten that obsessed with things, but I know folks who are. More power to them.

The Broken Page

In a case where you're ending a major section of a book or paper, you may want the next section to start at the top of a new page. That's easy. Insert a page break.

A page break says to Works, I don't care if this page isn't full, start a new one. And Works does.

To insert a page break click (to place your cursor) where you want to end your page. Next (I bet you know what I'm going to say), select **Page Break** from the **Insert** menu. Poof, you have broken your page.

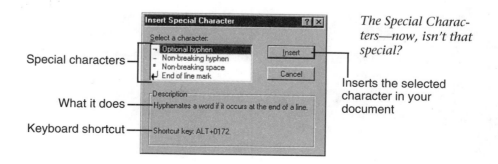

Special characters

What it does

Keyboard shortcut

The Special Characters—now, isn't that special?

Inserts the selected character in your document

Other Special Goodies

To get a look at the other special things you can use to get your pages just right, select **Special Character** from the **Insert** menu. The previous dialog box will appear.

You have four special characters to choose from:

➤ Optional hyphen   Place an optional hyphen in a word and Works will hyphenate it only when the word is at the end of a line.

➤ Non-breaking hyphen   Keeps hyphenated words (such as non-breaking) together on the same line, even if it means extra empty space at the end of the previous line.

➤ Non-breaking space   Keeps the two words at either side of the space together on the same line, even if it means extra empty space at the end of the previous line.

➤ End of line mark   Starts a new line of text without starting a new paragraph (like this)
so you can do some funky formatting things.

My guess is that you won't need these special characters much in the course of everyday writing, but they may come in handy sometime, and you should know what they are, just in case.

The Least You Need to Know

Now, don't go all ashy in the face over this header, footer, footnote, and other special formatting stuff. Works' Easy Formats will probably do you just fine for most uses. If you get cranky over creating a footnote with Works, you've never done one manually, with a typewriter. Trust me, this computerized formatting is a piece of cake in comparison. You kids today are just spoiled, that's all. Why, when I was in school, we had to walk twelve miles through the snow just to ask how to *type* a footnote... sorry. I turned into my grandfather for a second, there.

➤ Formatting is the process of beautifying your Works projects and covers everything from margins and indents to fonts and styles.

➤ Easy Formats (under the Format menu) are a simple way to explore many of Works' formatting options.

➤ The Font and Style dialog box (also under the **Format** menu), gives you one-stop font and style shopping.

➤ Some special text (headings, subheadings, captions, page headers and footers) require a little special handling, but not much.

Chapter 11

Getting Fancy-Shmancy: Works as a Page Layout Tool

In This Chapter

➤ What's your orientation?

➤ Working With columns

➤ Eye-catching color

➤ Adding ClipArt and WordArt

While Microsoft Works isn't as powerful a design tool as, say, Microsoft Publisher or Aldus Pagemaker, you can (with a little patience and a willingness to tinker) use Works to create some impressive desktop publishing documents.

Need It in a Hurry? Use a Wizard!

If you don't have the time or inclination to play around with the desktop publishing power that's built into Works, there are several TaskWizards designed to help you create a few common documents.

You can create a Certificate, naming your Dad as *The Best Dad in the World;* a newsletter explaining all the family gossip and goings-on; a brochure advertising your yard sale; and flyers you can post around the neighborhood looking for that runaway pussycat.

Desktop Publishing

You can literally publish from the top of your desk. Personal computers, software, and other hardware, have made it possible for common folks like you and me to design, edit, print, and duplicate professional-looking documents without resorting to typesetters, printers, and all the old-fashioned headaches and hassles of printing. Desktop publishing software is also sometimes referred to as *page layout software*.

As with all TaskWizards, these will hold your hand and let you choose from a variety of custom options you can use. Then Works will create the document and have it ready for you to edit and fill in with your information.

You read about the details on using a TaskWizard back in Chapter 5. This chapter doesn't use a TaskWizard because, frankly, they're *too* easy (like that's a problem). Instead, we're going to take a new, blank, untitled word processing document (so if you want to play along, take a moment to get one set up with Works), and turn it into a lovely, folded pamphlet-brochure kind of thing. Chapter 5 explains how to create a new word processing document, if you're reading random chapters.

What's Your Page Orientation?

Page orientation is the direction in which words and images appear on the printed page.

There are two page orientations: *portrait* and *landscape*. Portrait orientation is the way most folks think of a sheet of paper. That is, with an 8 1/2-by-11-inch page, it is taller than it is wide. Landscape orientation, with an 8 1/2-by-11-inch page, is *wider* than it is tall.

Portrait is the page orientation you'll probably use most of the time. Reports, letters, and other documents are generally in portrait orientation. Portrait is also the Works default page orientation, so you need only worry about changing a document's orientation when you want landscape.

Landscape orientation is good for creating brochures, booklets, and pamphlets. (It's also handy for printing out some spreadsheets and database reports, but we'll talk about that in the appropriate chapters, later.)

For the sake of playing around with the Works page layout powers, we'll create a pamphlet/brochure on a regular, letter-sized (8 1/2-by-11-inch) sheet of paper in landscape orientation.

To start, select **Page Setup** from the **File** menu. That will bring up the dialog box shown below. If the Source, Size & Orientation options aren't foremost on the dialog (as shown in the figure), just click on the **Source, Size & Orientation** tab and it will jump to the front.

Sample page

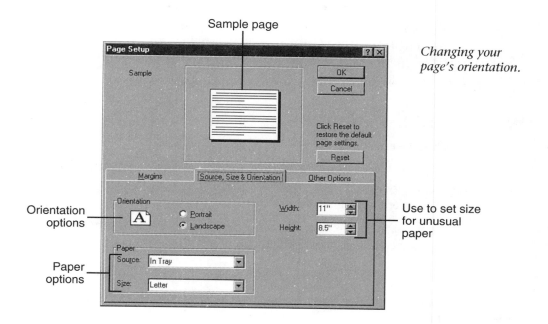

Changing your page's orientation.

Orientation options

Paper options

Use to set size for unusual paper

To change the orientation from portrait to landscape, click on the word **Landscape** in the Orientation options box. That's all there is to it.

When your orientation is set, click **OK** and we'll continue.

Changing Paper Size

For our example, we'll use regular letter-sized (8.5-by-11 inches) paper. In the future, you may want to use legal-sized paper (8.5-by-14 inches), and you need to let Works know it has more paper to work with.

To select another, standard paper size, click on the **Size** pop-up menu in the Paper options box. Select the appropriate paper size from the menu.

If you're using an unusual size of paper, you can manually enter the paper size by typing the Width and Height in the appropriate boxes (labeled in the figure).

Margins Revisited

While standard margins for letters and reports are about 1-inch all the way around (as we saw in Chapter 9), they can be as small as your printer can handle for desktop publishing projects. (Check your printer's manual for details on its margin needs.) You change your page margins with the Margins tab of the Page Setup dialog box. For this particular project, I'm going to set them to a half-inch (0.5") all the way around (top, bottom, left, and right). Details on how to change margins are back in Chapter 9, as well, if you've forgotten how to do it.

Doric or Ironic Columns

Man, Greek architecture jokes. I need a vacation. Or a nap.

Columns in a word processing document look pretty much the same as columns you'll see every day in your local newspaper. To Works, they're just a matter of fooling around with your document's margin settings.

Works can automatically break your document into two or more columns. To do it, select **Columns** from the **Format** menu. The dialog shown here will pop right up.

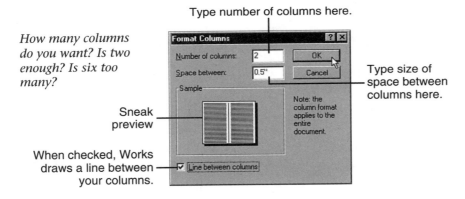

Type number of columns here.

How many columns do you want? Is two enough? Is six too many?

Sneak preview

When checked, Works draws a line between your columns.

Type size of space between columns here.

For this sample document, since we're creating the front and back covers of a booklet, two columns are plenty. Type **2** in the Number of columns box.

The Space between option sets how much blank space Works will leave between the columns. The default is half an inch (as shown in the figure) and that will be fine for this example, and many desktop publishing chores. If, however, you want to change the space between columns later, just type the decimal version of the measurement in the Space between box—.5 for half an inch, .25 for a quarter-inch, and so on.

At the bottom of the dialog, there's a check box called Line between columns. If you check the box (as in the figure), Works will draw a line between each of your columns. It's a good idea, because it helps a reader's eye keep to one column while reading. For our example, it's good because it gives us a guideline to help us fold our pamphlet. If you ever want to eliminate the line(s), just click on the check box and make the check mark go away. Click **OK** and you're ready to roll.

Staying Within the Lines

When you're working with columns in a Works document, it's pretty much the same as working with a regular page without columns, but with one difference.

With columns, you *have* to start typing in the first column. Then, as you type, and the first column fills, your text moves into the second column (and so on, if you're using more than two columns). So will your pictures, charts, graphs, and anything else you plug into your document.

That's the only drawback to using Works for page layout, and it's only a challenge/ annoying (choose one) if you've used a dedicated page layout package like those mentioned earlier.

With special page layout software, you can place text in a specific spot, and it stays put— the same with pictures and other embellishments. You can also control what text flows into which column, but that's one of the reasons page layout software is expensive. It's finely tuned to the needs of layout professionals.

Works won't do that, and there's no reason to grouse about it, since it's relatively easy to cope with. To me, the simplest way to deal with Works' drawback as a page layout tool is to *plan ahead*. Figure out what's most important to you in your document: words or pictures. Decide where you want things to land (on which page, or in which column). Enter your text. Drop in your graphic elements (WordArt, ClipArt, charts, or whatever— more on those in a moment). Then tinker with sizes, spacing, and fonts until the elements end up where you want them.

Techno Talk

blah blah blah bla h bl b

Dummy, Dummy, Dummy...

That's a strategy, I'm not calling you a name. The easiest way to make the choices discussed in this section (about placement of text and graphics) is to create a *dummy* document. Using blank paper, assemble a model of what you want the final product to look like: the same number of pages, folded in the same place (if you're folding) with columns, text, and graphic blocks penciled in, and the pages numbered in the proper order.

It gives you a tangible goal, and it will help you sort out some confusing things like why a brochure's back cover is actually the first thing on the page (it's all in the folding, don't'cha know).

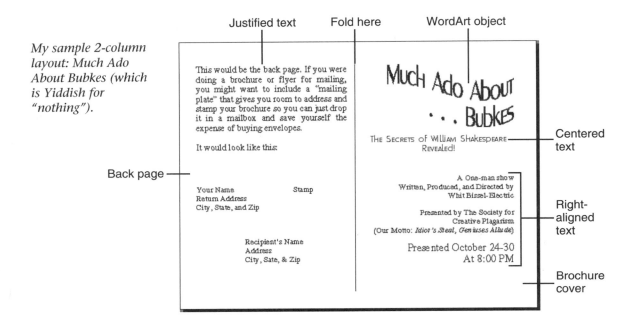

My sample 2-column layout: Much Ado About Bubkes (which is Yiddish for "nothing").

For example, these are the steps I took to get my sample page looking the way it does (I also saved my document after each step, so nothing horrifying would happen).

1. I created the blank, landscape page as previously described.

2. I created the "Much Ado About Bubkes" WordArt. (Creating WordArt and other art is covered in Chapter 22.)

3. I began entering text in *front* of the WordArt, until the title was positioned at the top of the second column.

4. I entered the subtitle and other text *after* the WordArt.

5. I tinkered with font size and spaces between paragraphs to make sure everything stayed in the correct column.

Borders and Color Draw Attention

To paraphrase George Orwell, some elements are created more equal than others (there's a reference that'll get you scurrying to your high school paperback collection).

Some elements can use some extra tinkering to get them the attention they deserve from your readers.

Putting a Border Around Text

In the last figure, you can see I've added what's known as an *address plate*, which is an area set aside in a document to hold a mailing label, stamp, and your return mailing address in the typical envelope-type arrangement.

It's acceptable the way it is in the figure, but it will stand out (and make the Postal Service happy) if we put a border around it. Here's how to do it.

First, select the text you want to put a border around. Then select **Borders and Shading** from the **Format** menu. The following dialog box will open. If the Borders panel isn't foremost, just click on its tab to bring it to the front.

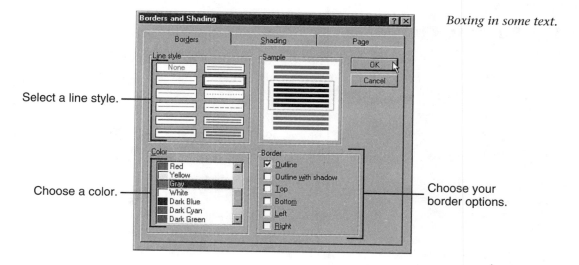

Boxing in some text.

Select a line style.

Choose a color.

Choose your border options.

First, click on the style of line you want to use (there are a dozen choices). Then, if you care to, you can make the line a color—just click on the color you want in the Color list box. Then select the border options.

There are a half dozen border options to choose from. Outline puts a box around the selected text. Outline with shadow puts a box around the selected text, and adds a shadow behind and below the box. A very nice effect, but use it sparingly.

The last four border options give you parts of a box (lines, really) at the Top, Bottom, Left, and Right of the selected text, so you can build whatever portion of a box you want. As always, you can get an idea of what the final product will look like by checking out the sample page in the dialog box. When you're happy with your border options, click **OK**.

Text in a box.

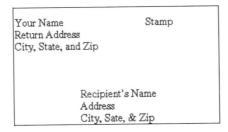

For my mailing plate, I chose the simple black border shown here. That's perfect for a mailing address because you don't want any extra stuff getting in the way of the Post Office reading the address and delivering your mail. You can get fancier, though.

110 Boxes in the Shade

To draw more attention to text in a box, you can add shading. Shading (to your computer) is just an arrangement of dots that turns a plain white area into shades of gray (or other colors).

To begin, select the text you want to alter. If you care to, you can follow the preceding steps for placing a box around it, but you don't have to. Click on the **Shading** tab in the Borders and Shading dialog box. That will bring up the following shading options.

You can create some ***Dark Shadows*** *(ooh, scary).*

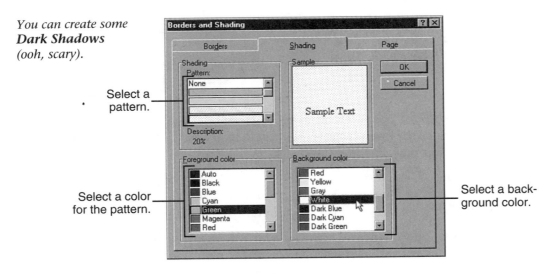

First, select the shading pattern you want to use. I tend to avoid the darker shadings (like the one just after the None option) unless I make the shading a very light color; otherwise it can distort the text behind it.

Next, select the **Foreground color** you want—that's the color the shading pattern will be.

Finally, select the **Background color** you want—that's the color that appears behind the shading pattern. I usually leave the background plain white—I'm boring that way. You can do whatever you want.

Beware of the Ugly

Be careful: If you choose, say, an electric green for your foreground color, and, oh, a mondo red for your background color, you could do your eyes a mischief. Avoid pain; avoid color clashes.

As always (are you tired of me saying this yet?), you can get an idea of what the final product will look like by checking out the sample page in the dialog box. When you like your shading, click **OK** and Works will apply it to the selected text in your document. Play around with the various shading and border options. They're fun (I think).

Slap a Border on a Whole Page

If dressing up mere paragraphs isn't enough for you, you can add a border to the first, or every page in your document.

The process is similar to putting a border around text, except you don't have to select any text first. Instead, just select **Borders and Shading** from the **Format** menu. The following dialog box will open. If the Page panel isn't foremost, just click on its tab to bring it to the front.

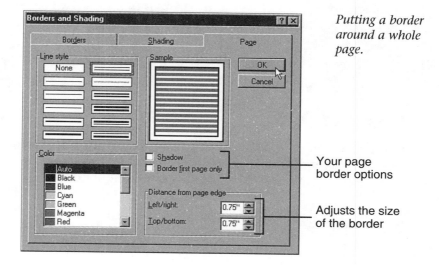

Putting a border around a whole page.

Your page border options

Adjusts the size of the border

The line options remain the same. Click on the Line style you want to use. If you want the border in color, select a color from the Color list.

With the Page border, you only have two options (the border is automatically a box). You can select Shadow, to have a drop shadow beneath the border. You can select **Border first page only**, to only put the border on the first page of your document. Or you can choose both.

You can also tinker with how far from the edge of your page the border will be, with the Distance from page edge box at the bottom right of the dialog box.

As a general rule of thumb, the border should be set a little bit closer (say, .25") to the edge of the page than your margins (that way you won't run into the problem of your border and text running into each other, or worse, hiding each other). That means if you have .5" margins all the way around, your border should be set at .25–.45" from the edge of the page—if your printer can handle that large a print area. Check your printer's manual for details.

Otherwise, you may have to set larger margins to accommodate a whole-page border. You'll need to experiment to see what works for you and your printer. You can also shade the whole page but that may make your text very hard to read.

Rule of Thumb

Not that it has anything to do with Works or desktop publishing, but I just recently learned where the expression *rule of thumb* came from, and I thought I'd share. It seems that in about the 16th century, there was a law on the books in England that allowed husbands to beat their wives, as long as the stick was "no thicker than his thumb." It was known as the "rule of thumb."

Funny how such an everyday, harmless expression could develop out of such an ugly, despicable thing. I flinch every time I say it now. Thanks for letting me share.

Add a Spot of Color

Spot color is actually a technical term for using teeny-tiny bits of color (even gray) on an otherwise black-and-white page. Typically, you'll find spot color applied to the first letter of an important paragraph, or to the bullets in front of lists of important information.

You Don't Need a Color Printer

Really, you don't need a color printer to get the eye-catching benefits of spot color. You can use a black-and-white printer to accent things with shades of gray—either as the selected color or the gray equivalent of other colors.

You can also cheat and use an open face, or outlined font (where the characters aren't solid black) for your initial capital letters and bullets; then carefully color them in with a magic marker. It's tedious, but you can do it.

To use spot color, select the text you want to colorize (you little Ted Turner, you). Then select **Font and Style** from the **Format** menu. The Format Font and Style dialog box will appear.

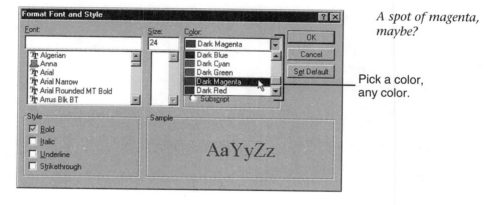

A spot of magenta, maybe?

Pick a color, any color.

To make that letter or bullet stand out, you might want to make it **bold**, and a little larger than the rest of your text. Then select your color from the pop-up menu and click **OK**.

Add Some Art

You can easily add some of Works' prepared ClipArt to your document with a few clicks of your mouse. You can also fine-tune its placement and how text flows around the picture.

Insert a Clip

To start, click to place the cursor where you want to add a piece of art. Next, select **ClipArt** from the **Insert** menu. That will open up the Microsoft ClipArt Gallery shown here.

A rogue's gallery of ClipArt.

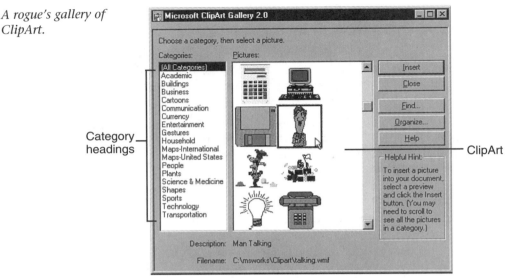

Click on a category to display the pictures in that category (or select **All Categories** to see all the pictures at once). Click on the picture you want, to select it. Click **Insert** and Works will drop a copy of the selected picture in your document where you placed the cursor.

You can place the picture on the left, right, or center of the column (or page) by using the left, right, and center buttons on the Toolbar. They work the same for pictures as they do for text.

Resizing a Clip

The picture you chose may not be the size you want or need when it appears in your document. You can resize it, easily enough.

There are two ways to resize ClipArt in your documents. The first is a "best guess" method; the second is very precise.

Techno Talk

Scale (-ing)
A really techno-geeky way of saying "resize" a picture. Use it. It will make you sound *soooo* smart at cocktail parties, or wherever geeks collide.

To resize a picture to a best-guess size, click on the picture to select it. A box will appear around the ClipArt with little boxes at each corner and in the center of each side. These are dragging, or resizing, handles.

To resize (or *scale*) the picture, click-drag on the appropriate *handle*. If you want to make the picture wider, drag one of the handles on the right or left side. If you want the picture to be taller, drag a handle on the top or bottom. If you want it to be both wider and taller, drag one of the handles in the corners. When the picture is the size you want, release the mouse button, and your picture will appear resized.

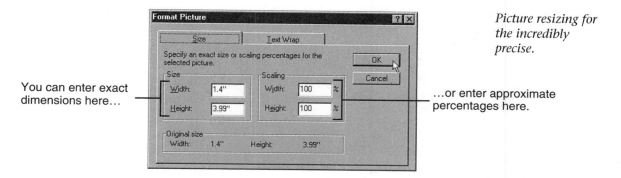

Picture resizing for the incredibly precise.

You can enter exact dimensions here…

…or enter approximate percentages here.

The precise way of resizing a picture is to select **Picture** from the **Format** menu. That will bring up the preceding dialog box shown. If the Size options aren't showing, just click on the **Size** tab to bring them forward.

You can enter the exact dimensions you want the picture to be in the Size box. Or you can guess and enter a percentage larger or smaller in the Scaling box. For instance, if you want the picture twice as large, enter **200%** in the Width and Height boxes. For another instance, if you want the picture at half the original size, enter **50%** in the Width and Height boxes.

Beware of the Distortion Effect!

That sounds like a warning from an episode of *Mystery Science Theater 3000*, but it's a legitimate concern. When scaling by percentages, as described here, you don't have to enter the same percentage in the Width and Height boxes.

However, if you don't, you run the risk of seriously distorting your ClipArt. It will seem as if you're looking at it in a fun house mirror. Try it, and you'll see what I mean.

This percentage business is very simple if you remember that the original picture size is 100%. Then, you can make it larger or smaller by adding or subtracting the appropriate percentage.

Wrapping Text Around a Clip

Once your clip is the size you want, and in the position you want, you can then tell Works how to deal with the text near the picture. You do this with the Format Picture dialog box, using its Text Wrap options.

Wrap that rascally text.

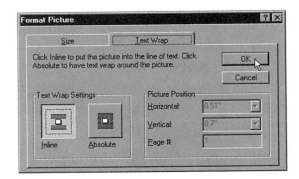

To bring the Text Wrap options to the front, click on the **Text Wrap** tab. If you've closed the Format Picture dialog box, you can select **Text Wrap** from the **Format** menu.

Either way, you have two text flow options. Inline text wrap places text above and below the object, as space allows. Absolute text wrap also places text on either side of the object (also as space allows). Click the option you want.

If you select **Absolute** text wrap, you can use the Picture Position box to (again) precisely place the picture on the page. Just type in the measurement of how far you want the picture placed from the top (Vertical) and left (Horizontal) edges of your paper. You can even specify the exact page where you want the ClipArt (in the Page # box).

Add a Chart or Table

Much of what you can do to format a bit of ClipArt, you can do to a chart or graph (created with Works' spreadsheet).

You don't really know what charts and graphs are yet, or why you'd want to add one to your documents, so let me just say that you can insert charts and graphs into a word processing document. I'll tell you how in Chapter 23 after I've explained what charts and graphs are, and how to create them in the first place.

You can also use information from a database in a word processing document. You can send out chain letters (this letter has traveled around the world nine times…), and create your own junk mail (You may already have won $10,000,000!). Check out Chapter 24.

A Gussying Up Review

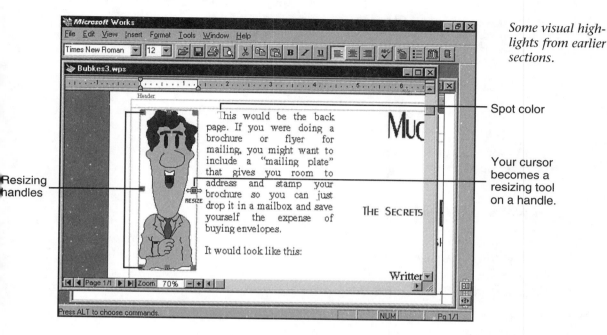

Some visual highlights from earlier sections.

The screenshot above just recaps some of the things you can do to your Works documents to dress them up (*and* take them out—which is more than you can do with me). Here's a bit of ClipArt, showing the resizing handles (and the resize cursor). And here's some spot color with the big T at the top of the paragraph.

Layout Tips and Tricks

My biggest trick is creating a dummied-out version of the final product before I even sit down at the computer (as described in the "Dummy, Dummy, Dummy" sidebar, earlier in this chapter).

That saves me so much time and energy; I can't recommend it enough. Otherwise, I let a few simple principles govern my desktop publishing projects, *viz.*:

➤ KISS: Keep It Simple, Stupid. I try to limit myself to two fonts and one graphic element (boxed text, ClipArt, WordArt, and so on) per page.

➤ The Bauhaus rule also applies: *less is more*. Don't underestimate the effect of a well-placed line or bit of fancy type on the page. You may not need any other embellishment with it.

141

➤ Enter your text first, and then place your graphic elements where you want them in relation to the text. Then tinker with resizing and formatting things so they fall where you want them on the page.

➤ Add color last. Your document may go through so many changes; the colored bits will move around, shift, and become generally annoying. Finish your document so all the important elements are where you want them; then add spots of color if you want.

➤ If you do add color, add one color, and be consistent. If you colorize a bulleted list, colorize all of your bulleted lists.

➤ Don't be afraid to play, experiment, and have fun. If you create a really ugly thing, so what? You can always fix it later.

The Least You Need to Know

The tips here will help you use Works as an occasional page layout program. If you find yourself using Works for page layout (newsletters, brochures, and other fancy things), more than three or four times a month, and you keep wishing it could do this or that, or even just keep up with you, think about investing in an actual page layout program.

Works is great at what it does, but an actual desktop publishing application does all this, plus more, with more precise control over your design elements.

Think about it; it couldn't hurt.

Part 3
Spreadsheets: Dollars and Sense

This section of the book explains the Works spreadsheet module—that about says it all, really. You'll learn what a spreadsheet is and how to create one; some new spreadsheet terms, such as columns, rows, formulas; and how to turn your spreadsheet information into charts and graphs.

You'll also discover that many of the skills you learned working your way through the Works word processor translate nicely to spreadsheets (and even databases in Part 4) so you're already ahead of the game.

So why not dig out a stack of bills, a checkbook that needs balancing, or tax receipts and lets get busy making some sense of those cents (unless your finances are like mine, in which case it's scents—because they stink).

Chapter 12

Spreadsheets Explained

In This Chapter

➤ New terms just for spreadsheets

➤ Special spreadsheet tools in the toolbar

➤ Selecting spreadsheet stuff

A *spreadsheet* is a valuable tool that can help you organize and present a lot of numerical information in a way that's easy for folks to understand.

You can also perform mathematical operations on the numbers in the spreadsheet, you know: add, subtract, multiply, divide, and even more complex operations. Oops, I used the "M" word: math. Ack! Ack! Now, just because there's math involved, don't start with that "I'm no accountant" whine. You don't have to be an accountant to effectively use a spreadsheet.

You can create spreadsheets for:

➤ Monthly budgets

➤ Itemizing deductibles for your taxes

➤ Tracking profits and losses for a business

➤ Charting sales by the week, month, or year

➤ And more! (Hey, it's hard to make anything math-related sound like fun.)

Some Special Spreadsheet Info

The parts of a simple, blank spreadsheet.

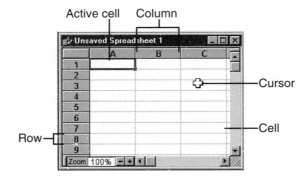

Like most new computer junk, there's some special vocabulary for spreadsheets. It will be good for you to at least see some of it before we start, so let's get it out of the way.

In the preceding figure, you see a portion of a basic, run-of-the-mill, everyday spreadsheet with its parts labeled. It isn't at all fancy (we'll talk about dressing up a spreadsheet in Chapter 16) because the frills just disguise the basic parts.

Those basic parts are:

Row   A horizontal (side to side) line of cells, like rows in a theater. You identify rows by numbers.

Column   A vertical line of cells, like the columns that hold up the roof over your front porch. You identify columns by letters.

Cell   The basic unit of a spreadsheet designed to hold one piece of information. In the light gray grid, each rectangle is a cell. You identify cells by the letter of the column they are in, followed by the number of the row (also like theater seats). The cell with the box around it in the figure (the active cell), is cell A1.

Active cell   A thicker box for easy identification surrounds the active cell. This is the cell you can enter data in, or edit existing data.

There are some other spreadsheet-related terms, but we'll talk about those on a need-to-know basis. These four are the basic building blocks of a spreadsheet, like the four basic food groups.

By the way, that big, chunky-looking plus sign is the cursor you'll use most often with a spreadsheet. It's your selection tool. We'll talk more about selecting cells, rows, and columns shortly.

Spreadsheet Tools

Formula bar ⎡—The current cell's name

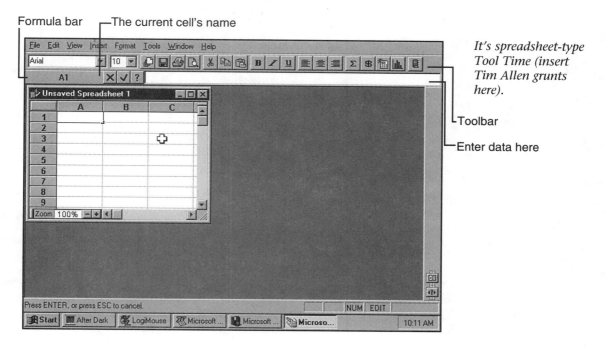

It's spreadsheet-type Tool Time (insert Tim Allen grunts here).

└Toolbar

└Enter data here

As I mentioned early on, Works' toolbar is pretty consistent: it's always there when you want it, and most of the tools remain the same (you can see what I mean in the preceding figure).

However, specialized applications (such as the spreadsheet) require some specialized tools. Works adds a few buttons to the toolbar to make working with spreadsheets easier, and it gives you a second toolbar (called the formula bar) to help you work out your math.

The Toolbar

We've seen and used, oh, the first fifteen tools on the toolbar already (unless you've been skipping around, reading random chapters). Check out the preceding figure, in case your memory needs jogging.

The buttons below are the new ones, for spreadsheets only:

 Σ	**AutoSum button**	Since one of the most common things done with spreadsheets is to add a row or column of figures, the AutoSum button will do that for you automatically. (There's more on using AutoSum in Chapter 14.)
 $	**Currency button**	Since you often use spreadsheets to follow money matters, the Currency button is a quick way to format your figures as money; that is, with dollar signs ($) and two decimal places ($0.00) for cents.
	**Easy Calc button**	Some spreadsheets aspire to more than simple addition and subtraction. The Easy Calc button helps you create formulas (mathematical instructions) to do more complex math on the figures in your spreadsheet. (There's more on using Easy Calc in Chapter 14.)
	**New Chart button**	A click of the New Chart button will take the numbers from your spreadsheet and help you turn them into a graphical representation—like those pie- and bar-charts they're so fond of using on C-SPAN. Creating meaningful charts is an art form, so they have a chapter all their own: Chapter 17.

The Formula Bar

As I mentioned earlier, a *formula* is a set of mathematical instructions that tells your spreadsheet what to do with some (or all) of the information you've entered.

The Formula Bar simplifies the process of creating and entering those formulas. The Formula Bar politely identifies the active cell or a selected range (group) of cells by putting their IDs in the first portion of the bar (where it says A1 in the figure).

Next, there's a set of three useful buttons:

Cancel button — When you click this button, Works will delete the contents of the selected cell(s). If you're in the process of replacing an old formula, it deletes the new formula and leaves the old one untouched.

Enter button — A button shortcut to keep you from having to reach for the Enter key all the time. When you click the Enter button, just like when you press Enter, Works looks your formula over and tells you if it finds any bogus logic.

Help button — Need I say more? Yeah, I guess I do. Help is available all of the time in the spreadsheet module, just as it was with the word processor. The Help button is one way to get at all that good information.

The remainder of the Formula Bar is a big ol' text entry box where you can type in your numbers and formulas, and then edit them. That's all covered in Chapter 13.

Sister Margo's Mystic Math Symbols

One of the more confusing aspects of using a spreadsheet's mathematical functions is that keyboards don't have all of the usual math symbols on them. Other symbols are substituted.

The symbols you know, and have on your keyboard, are:

+ Plus sign

- Minus sign

= Equals sign

The ones you *don't* have (and their substitute players), are:

÷ Division sign, instead use /

× Multiplication sign, instead use *

Other, more advanced math functions become abbreviations. For example, if you want to add a column of numbers together, instead of using a lot of plus signs, you can use the command SUM, which means add all this stuff together.

We'll look at these abbreviated functions in more detail in Chapter 14—so don't break out in a math sweat just yet.

You Can Pick a Cell, And You Can Pick a Row...

Selecting stuff in a spreadsheet is simple. To select a single cell, just click on it.

To select a whole row, click on the row's number (at the left of the sheet).

To select a whole column, click on the column's letter (at the top of the sheet).

To select a *range* of cells (two or more adjacent cells), click on the first cell and hold down your mouse button. Then drag the mouse until the cursor is touching the last cell you want in the range, and release the button. You can see a range of cells in the following figure.

First cell in range

Selecting a range of cells.

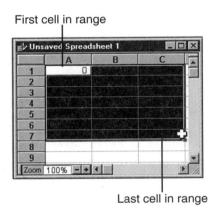

Last cell in range

In the figure, the range of cells starts with cell A1, and ends with cell C7. In spreadsheet speak, that range is **A1:C7**. The colon (:) means "through," so if you were saying A1:C7 out loud, you'd say: "I selected the range of cells, A1 through C7."

You'll also notice, in the figure, that selected cells turn black (to show that you selected them) except for the *active cell*. The active cell is still the only one into which you can manually enter data. (However, you can copy information from, and paste into a range of cells. I'll show you how and why in Chapter 15.)

You Can Use TaskWizards to Create a New Spreadsheet

As always, Works tries its best to get you started with new projects. The TaskWizards portion of the Task Launcher (covered back in Chapter 5), contains several spreadsheet wizards that may or may not meet your needs. They include:

Schedule	Organize your life, classes, and work.
Mortgage/Loan analysis	For the mathematically squeamish who want to know what a 6.9% fixed-interest rate means in dollars and cents.
Grade Book	Keep a running total on your students' test scores, and average grades automatically.
Bids	A spreadsheet to estimate job costs (labor and material) for yourself or your customers.
Quotations	Generate a form you can use to send customers price quotes for your goods and services.
Employee time sheet	Tired of figuring out an employee's hours worked? Use this handy spreadsheet.

For the sake of learning to create a spreadsheet from scratch, we won't use any of the TaskWizards—we'll do it ourselves. The TaskWizards make things just a little too easy to use as a learning tool.

If you want to see the TaskWizards in action, play around with them and enjoy.

Before You Start a New Spreadsheet

A new, blank, do-it-yourself spreadsheet can be a little intimidating to see. Before you start one on your own (even if you're just playing around), you should think about what you want the final product to look like.

What information will the spreadsheet contain? If it's a budget, for example, will it be weekly, monthly, annual, or a combination (such as an annual budget broken down by months)?

The kind of information, and how it's broken down, will limit/expand what you'll be able to do with the finished spreadsheet.

If you want to examine, say, your investment portfolio in minute detail, you might want to break things down by individual investments under categories like Stocks, Bonds, CDs, Municipal Funds, and the like.

Here's the point: your final product will often dictate how the spreadsheet needs to be set up, so think about the end result before you even begin. It will save you a lot of editing and juggling of information later on. Trust me.

After You Start a New Spreadsheet

Right after you start a new spreadsheet, even before you've entered any information in it, you should save the file to your hard drive. (See Chapter 5 for the scoop on saving.)

Afterward, you should save the file every few minutes. Losing data is a pain in the butt under any circumstances, but losing numerical data is a double pain because it's harder to enter (for me, at least) than words. I don't relish the thought of having to enter it all again—I probably didn't want to do it in the first place.

Save early, save often, and don't forget to call your folks.

The Least You Need to Know

Spreadsheets aren't just for accountants; they're good for anyone who needs to keep track of numerical information. The few tidbits that follow will help you keep your cool as you begin to explore this strange new world (that has such formulas in it).

➤ The basic component of a spreadsheet is a cell. You identify cells by combining the letter of the column they're in with the number of the row they're in (A1, C17, and so on).

➤ Selecting cells in a spreadsheet is simple. One click on a cell selects it, making it the active cell (the one you can work with).

➤ Several selected cells (sailed silently out to sea), together, form a range. You can identify a range of cells by the first and last cells (as in the example A1:C7, earlier).

➤ Think about what you want your spreadsheet to be when it grows up, before you even create it. Preplanning will save you work down the road.

➤ Save your files early and often. You don't want to have to retype all those numbers, do you?

Chapter 13

Spreadsheets 101

In This Chapter

➤ Planning a spreadsheet

➤ Starting a new sheet

➤ Entering information

➤ Labels, labels, labels

I admit it: I'm a goof. I don't do nearly the amount of record keeping and financial planning that I should. I don't do monthly budgets and all that good stuff. I live from check to check.

Mainly, I use spreadsheets for figuring out how much work-related junk I can deduct from my taxes—and I probably wouldn't do *that* much if I didn't have to write about spreadsheet programs two or three times a year.

Don't let this happen to you. Don't turn into a financial idiot like me.

You can use Works' spreadsheet to do all the spiffy things I don't. Calculate your total worth, plan for your retirement or major purchases (such as a car or a home), and much, much more.

A spreadsheet can also help you on the job, if you have to deal with a lot of numbers from time to time (in a small business, say), or if you have to fiddle with small sets of numbers all of the time (like teachers and their grade books, or students and their grades).

This chapter builds off the basics covered in Chapter 12. If you're skipping around as you read, you should read Chapter 12 before you continue this one.

Have a Plan

I've found that the most important part of starting a new spreadsheet is the brain work you do before you sit down at your computer. It's like that corny business saying (the one so popular with insurance salespeople): Nobody plans to fail; they just fail to plan. It's only corny because it's true.

Before you begin a spreadsheet, sit down and think about it. What information do you need to present? Keep in mind how spreadsheets display and use information (in cells, rows, and columns). What sort of data will fall logically into columns? What information will logically make up a row?

Techno Talk

Son of "Dummy, Dummy, Dummy..."

In Chapter 11, I suggested that you dummy out your desktop publishing projects before you actually sit down at your PC. I'm going to suggest the same for spreadsheets (and I'll probably do it again when we get to databases).

Fool around with your numerical data on scrap paper before you begin work. Figure out how you want it to look, what information will go where, and anticipate the mathematical operations you'll want to perform. That will give you a big head start when you actually begin to enter the information in your spreadsheet.

Let's use the example of a spreadsheet to organize and total tax deductions. The IRS has established certain broad categories for the deductions you may take. For a writer, like myself, they typically include: office equipment, office supplies, telephone charges, and postage, among others.

Expenses tend to trickle in, one or two receipts at a time (but still faster than income). An individual receipt (which is your *proof* of expense, so practice saying *"May I have a receipt, please?"*) may be for several items that fall into two or more different expense categories (like office supplies and office equipment).

The deduction categories make good spreadsheet columns (it's easy to total each category if it's in a column). Receipts, because they itemize a single purchase, make good rows (multiple purchases items can be kept in one row, and still be broken down by category). You also need a column for the date for each receipt and another to briefly describe what each receipt is for.

Finally, the math. With this sort of spreadsheet, the most complicated math you'll do is addition and, maybe, some subtraction (to deduct expenses from your income, and see how much is left after a deductible shopping spree—I don't do that; it depresses me).

With a general idea of what you want to put in your spreadsheet and how you want to arrange it, now you can fire up your PC, Works, and...

Start a New Spreadsheet

Click here to start.

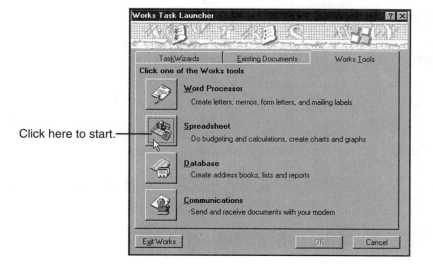

Using the Works Task Launcher to create a new spreadsheet.

To create a new Works spreadsheet, use the Task Launcher. If the Works Tools aren't front and center (as they are in the preceding figure), click on the **Works Tools** tab, and they'll jump to the front—if we could get them to jump to the left, and take a step to the right, we could do "The Time Warp."

Next, click on the **Spreadsheet** button. Works will chug and churn and create a new blank spreadsheet all ready for you to enter your information.

Stick a Label on It

Before I do anything else with a spreadsheet, I slap labels on all of the columns. Since I dummied out a copy of what I want my spreadsheet to look like (with column names penciled in and everything), it's just a question of copying them from my planning copy.

The first label I'd type is **Date** in cell A1. (Remember how cells are identified? It's explained in Chapter 12 if you don't.) To do that, click on cell **A1** to select it. Then type: **Date**.

As you type, the word **Date** will appear in two spots on the spreadsheet: in the selected cell, and also in the text entry part of the Formula Bar. When you finish typing, press **Enter**.

Repeat the process in the first cell of each column (B1, C1, D1, and so on), using these labels: **Description**, **Office**, **Supply**, **Phone**, **Dues/Subs** (for professional memberships, such as union dues and subscriptions), **Research**, **Charity**, **Travel**, **Entertainment**, **Insurance**, **Medical**, and **Totals**.

Feel free to substitute your own category labels, as you may have different expenses (writers get to deduct some bizarre things). Press **Enter** after each entry.

When you finish, your spreadsheet will look something like the one shown in the following figure (only bigger). You'll need to scroll to the right to see all of the column headings. Furthermore, some of the labels (such as **Description**), are more than 10 characters long, and won't fit in their cells properly. Don't worry about it right now. Chapter 16 explains how to fix that, along with other ways to pretty up a spreadsheet.

A spreadsheet, nicely labeled.

	A	B	C	D	E	F	G	H
1	DATE	DESCRIPTIO	OFFICE	SUPPLY	POSTAGE	PHONE	DUES/SUBS	RESEAR
2								
3								

95Expenses — Zoom 100%

Check This Out...

Easy Tip for the Lazy

Instead of pressing enter after you type each entry in a spreadsheet, hit your **Tab** key. That will not only complete your last typed entry, but also select the next cell to the right, so you can continue typing without having to select the next cell. All those seconds you'll save will really add up.

Right now you should congratulate yourself. You've not only *labeled* your spreadsheet's columns, you've also learned how to enter data in a spreadsheet, too. That's fabulous, but there is a little more you need to know.

Before we get to some nitty-gritty data entry details, go ahead and save your sample spreadsheet. It's the same process as saving any Works file (covered back in Chapter 5). Remember my motto: Save early, save often (because it often saves your butt).

Entering Information: Some Nitty-Gritty Details

You can enter any sort of information into a spreadsheet that you can type on a key-board: words, numbers, and even combinations of letters, symbols, and numbers (*alpha-numeric data* is the hoity-toity way of saying it). A date (such as 7/7/95) is alphanumeric because it includes numbers and symbols (the slash marks).

Works will take a stab at figuring out what sort of information you're entering. For example, click on one of the labels you entered in the spreadsheet, and you'll notice that Works has altered it a little. Since it's a word, Works adds a double quotation mark (") in front of it. The " won't show up in your spreadsheet, on-screen, or when you print it. You'll only see it in the Formula Bar. It's just a reminder that this is a word, and Works probably won't have to do anything special with it.

Works automatically tags any entry that begins with a letter as text, using that double quotation mark. Numbers (when we get around to entering some) aren't preceded by anything—no quotation mark, nothing.

Formulas (also when we get around to them) are preceded by an equal sign (=). That tells Works the entry is an instruction, not data to be tinkered with, or text to be ignored. However, Works doesn't add the = automatically, you have to do that.

Formulas are alphanumeric. They include a word or abbreviation (for example, SUM tells Works to add things together) followed by cell IDs. Chapter 14 completely covers formulas and the magic that they do.

The point of all this is to tell you that since Works assumes that any entry that begins with a letter is text it should ignore, and that all formulas begin with letters, you need to enter an equal sign at the beginning of each formula you enter, otherwise Works will ignore it as text. Whew!

You don't have to worry about plain text, or numbers, or even most alphanumerics (dates and such), only formulas. Formulas start with an equal sign (=). Got that? Formulas start with an equal sign (=). I'll remind you again when we get to the chapter on formulas.

Enter Those Receipts!

Some nicely deduct-ible receipts.

If you have your own receipts to play with, feel free to use those (or just make some up), otherwise you can use mine (shown here)—but *I* get to take the deductions.

Nice and Easy

The receipt on the right is a simple one for $15.95 worth of postage, no multiple categories.

To enter the receipt:

1. Click on cell **A2** to select it.

2. Type in the receipt's date (3/21/95).

3. Press **Tab** to move to cell **B2** (the next cell in the row).

4. Type the description of the receipt: **Postage**.

5. Press **Tab** three times to move to cell **E2** under the heading **Postage**.

6. Type: **15.95**

Entered in our spreadsheet, it would look like the following figure.

	A	B	C	D	E	PH
1	DATE	DESCRIPTION	OFFICE	SUPPLY	POSTAGE	
2	03/21/95	Postage			15.95	

95Expenses — Zoom 100%

From receipt to deduction with a few mouse clicks and some typing.

It's lovely, but there's one thing wrong. The 15.95 isn't in correct currency format—there isn't a dollar sign ($) in front of it.

There are two ways to fix that. The hard way is to go back and reselect the cell and manually add a dollar sign. Too tedious. The easy way is to go back and reselect the cell, and click on the **Currency** button in the toolbar (it's the one with the $ on it). Your cell automatically converts to currency format.

More Tips for the Energy Efficient (Lazy)

You can convert a pile of cells to currency format with two clicks of your mouse. Click or click-drag to select the cells you want converted to dollar format (the how-to on selecting columns, rows, and cells is in Chapter 12). Then click on the **Currency** button. They'll all be in currency format, and you may never need to type a $ again—well, not in a spreadsheet, anyhow.

A Little Complicated: Multiple Categories on the Same Receipt

But only a *little* complicated. The receipt shown on the left in the figure at the top of this section has *two* items on it: a $29.99 desk lamp (office equipment) and a $24.99 ink cartridge for my printer (office supply).

Enter each in the third row of the spreadsheet. The date on the receipt is 6/2/95. As a description, I'd put something like "Lamp/ink refill" just so an IRS auditor wouldn't have to ask, "What's this deduction for?"

	A	B	C	D	E	F
1	DATE	DESCRIPTION	OFFICE	SUPPLY	POSTAGE	PHONE
2	03/21/95	Postage			$15.95	
3	06/02/95	Lamp/ink refill	$29.99	$24.99		
4						
5						
6						
7						

95Expenses.wks — Zoom 100%

More deductibles, and MORE (mwah-hah-hah)...

When you finish, the spreadsheet will look something like the one shown here—don't forget to change the dollar entries to currency format, like I did.

Carry on Entering Data

You can continue the exercise with as many real (or imaginary) receipts as you care to—just don't try to use the imaginary ones on your taxes.

Even with only these two receipts, however, you can see how helpful such a spreadsheet would be, come tax time. If you updated your expense spreadsheet once a week, month, or quarter (depending on how fast your receipts build up), there wouldn't be any of that last-minute scurrying before April 15th.

Coming Attractions

Save your file. Take a break. We're done for the moment. In the next chapter, we'll fiddle with formulas to get totals for each row and column, and then get a grand total for the whole spreadsheet.

Still later, we'll edit the information, pretty it up, print it out, and even create charts from it. But let's burn those bridges when we come to them. In the meantime…

The Least You Need to Know

➤ Plan your spreadsheets ahead of time; it will simplify the process.

➤ You can start a new spreadsheet by using the Task Launcher; just click on the **Spreadsheet** button on the **Works Tools** page of the Launcher.

➤ Labels make it easy for folks to figure out what your spreadsheet is all about.

➤ To enter information in a cell, click on the cell to select it, and type in your information.

➤ Pressing **Enter** will place your information in the cell, but leave the same cell selected (say *that* three times fast).

➤ Pressing **Tab** after an entry will also place your information in the cell, but it moves you to the next cell in the row or column you're working in.

➤ Save early; save often.

Chapter 14

Secret Formula Secrets

In This Chapter

➤ What's a formula, anyhow?

➤ AutoSum: We're having SUM fun now

➤ Do it yourself formulas

➤ Functions and Easy Calc

Previously on "Spreadsheet Math…"

In the previous chapter, we created a little spreadsheet to dabble in deductibles for our taxes. We entered some column labels to identify the deduction categories and entered a few receipts, one to a row.

Then we took a break. Well, *you* took a break. I was working. I entered a few more receipts in my copy of the spreadsheet, poured another cup of coffee, and did some chair dancing to the Spin Doctors' "Two Princes." (God, I love my job.)

In this chapter, we're going to crack the whip and get Works to do some math with our receipts: add the contents of cells, and a range of cells, to make tax time a whole lot easier. If you're playing along, make sure your PC is turned on, Works is up and running, and that your saved spreadsheet is open.

To cope with the math concepts, it helps if you're up to speed on basic addition, subtraction, multiplication, and division. For later work, it couldn't hurt if you've had (and remember) some basic algebra—if you don't, don't panic. I'll be gentle with you.

Formulas Defined

In general, a spreadsheet formula is a set of instructions, such as a recipe. When they think of the word "formula," most people either think of baby formula, or of mad scientists: "With this formula, I can *rule the world! Mwah-hah-hah!"*

(Suddenly I'm channeling Pinky and the Brain.)

In terms of Works' spreadsheet, a formula is a shorthand way to express a mathematical operation. Like a grammatical sentence, a formula usually includes a command (a subject) and then something on which to perform the command (an object). All formulas begin with an equal sign (=).

A common formula would look something like this:

=SUM(C2:C7)

These are the individual pieces of that formula:

= tells Works that this is, indeed, a formula (not numbers or text), so listen up and be prepared to do math.

SUM is the command. SUM means add.

(C2:C7) is the object of the SUM command. The parentheses ( ) indicate that it's a range of cells.

In real human-type language, the formula would read something like this: "Hey Works! Add the numbers in all of the cells from C2 through C7." Since this formula also happens to be one we'd use in our spreadsheet anyway, let's use it.

Entering a Formula

In the following figure, you can see where I've added some new things to my spreadsheet (you may add them to your own spreadsheet if you're following along at your PC).

I've added three more receipts and a **Totals** label in cell A8. That's because we're going to enter some SUM formulas at the bottom of each column of our spreadsheet. We're going to enter them three ways: manually, using AutoSum, and by a sneaky copy-and-paste method.

| C8 | =SUM(C1:C6) |

95Expenses.wks

	A	B	C	D	E	F
1	DATE	DESCRIPTION	OFFICE	SUPPLY	POSTAGE	PHONE
2	05/12/95	Software/supplies	$129.00	$110.00		
3	03/21/95	Postage			$15.95	
4	04/01/95	diskettes		$15.99		
5	06/02/95	Lamp/ink refill	$29.95	$24.99		
6	04/02/95	desk chair	$59.95			
7						
8	TOTALS		$216.90	$150.98	$15.95	

Zoom 100%

Having SUM fun with our office deductions.

Prepare for Manual Entry!

You enter a formula the same way you enter any information into a spreadsheet. Click on a cell to select it; then type in the formula.

The **=SUM(C2:C7)** formula will total the column of expenses we labeled **Office** in the last chapter. To enter the formula, do the following:

1. Click on cell **C8** to select it.

2. Carefully type the formula **=SUM(C2:C7)**. There are *no spaces* between any of the characters.

3. Press **Enter**.

Techno Talk

blah blah blah blah bl b

Check Yourself

If you aren't sure you've entered this (or any) formula correctly, click on the check mark to the left of the text entry box in the Formula Bar. Works will make sure that the formula makes sense (*not* that it's the right formula, only that it will work as a formula). Works then, instantly does the math and inserts the result in the cell, just as if you'd pressed Enter.

When you press **Enter**, the formula will stay in the entry box in the Formula Bar, but the result of the formula (the total) will appear in cell C8 (as shown in the figure at the top of the section). Your first formula—you must be so proud!

Using Auto(Sum)Pilot

Since adding a range of cells is the most common operation a spreadsheet performs, Works gives you a quick and easy way to get it done: *AutoSum*.

AutoSum skips all that manual formula entering *mishegaas* and cuts right to the chase. Here's how to use it:

1. Click on the cell where you want your sum to appear. (For this example, let's use **D8**.)

2. Click on the **AutoSum** button (it's the one with the Greek letter that looks like a wonky "E" on it—what is that, Sigma?).

AutoSum—it's not brilliant, but it tries.

That's all there is to it, but AutoSum is *not* a rocket scientist. If you'll look at the preceding figure, you'll see that AutoSum took a guess at which cells I wanted, but got it wrong. It skipped cells D2 and D3, and included the blank D7. That's okay, Works isn't a mind reader (thank goodness). It's easy enough to fix.

Just click on the formula in the text entry box, and edit the cells so they say **D2:D6**. (Spreadsheet entries edit much the same as text in the word processor. There are more editorial techniques in the next chapter, but I think you can wing this.) Then press **Enter**.

Now, if you repeat the AutoSum on subsequent columns, you'll see that Works learns (if only briefly) from its mistakes and will select the same range of cells in later columns.

Sneaky, Underhanded Formula Copying

Once you enter a formula, and you want to repeat a similar formula (with a different range of cells, say) in other rows or columns, there's a sneaky, underhanded, way to do that. Here's how.

1. Click on the cell that contains the formula you want to copy. The formula will show up in the Formula Bar.

2. Double-click (or click-drag) on the formula to select it.

3. Select **Copy** from the **Edit** menu (or use the keyboard shortcut **Ctrl+C**).

4. Click on the cell where you want to use the formula.

5. Select **Paste** from the **Edit** menu (or use the keyboard shortcut **Ctrl+V**).

6. Edit the range of cells so it represents the new column or row (for example, from (C2:C6) to (D2:D6) or whatever).

7. You may also need to delete a quotation mark (") from in front of the formula, since Works on my PC (for some reason) treats *all* pasted data as text. Don't ask me why.

Between AutoSum, manual formula entry, and this sneaky copy-and-paste method of entering formulas, you'll have no trouble at all adding row after row, column after column of deductions and other numerical data.

If you care to continue practicing, you can use these methods to enter SUM formulas in each of the remaining spreadsheet columns. But only if you *really* want to. I'm not your mother, after all. I won't be upset.

Grow Your Own Formulas

Sometimes, simple addition won't be enough for your spreadsheet figuring needs. You can do a lot more than just add.

You can perform a range of simple mathematical operations on two or more cells by writing your own formulas. Don't make that face; it's easy. You just need to know the symbols.

Any Two Cells Can Play

Let's use two cells from our expenses spreadsheet, and put them through the mathematical wringer. Cells C2 and D2 contain some pretty big numbers ($129 and $110, respectively), so we'll fiddle with them.

The first step is to click on the cell where you want the result to land. Then type the formula in it.

To add these two cells together, the formula would be: =C2+D2. It's just a little backward from how you learned to write a problem in addition, because we put the equal sign *first* in a spreadsheet.

To subtract one cell from the other, the formula would be: =C2-D2 (or =D2-C2, which would result in a negative number).

To multiply these two cells, the formula would be: =C2*D2.

To divide these two cells, the formula would be: =C2/D2 (or =D2/C2).

Three or More Can Play

To perform addition on three or more cells, just add them to your formula. For example, to add cell E2 to our addition formula in the last section, we'd literally just add it. The new formula would be: =D2+C2+E2.

That's simple, but awfully tedious with more than two or three cells; that's why there's AutoSum and the ability to use a range of cells.

You can do the same thing with subtraction. The formula =D2-C2-E2 will subtract the contents of cell C2 from cell D2 and then subtract the contents of cell E2 from the remainder of the first subtraction.

Similarly, the formula =D2*C2*E2 will multiply cell C2 by cell D2 and then multiply that result by the contents of cell E2.

Other math operations aren't as simple, though. For example, you can't have a division formula like this: =C2/D2/E2. Works will get cranky. This, and other formulas, take a little special handling.

Multiple Math

If you want to perform two or more simple math operations in one formula, you can. It's just a question of separating the math operations with parentheses ( ).

For example, to make that bogus division formula (=C2/D2/E2) actually work, you'd need to make it look like this: =(C2/D2)/E2. That tells Works to divide C2 by D2 and then to divide the result of that by the contents of cell E2.

Using parentheses to separate mathematical operations allows you to build some fairly complicated formulas (if you care to). For instance, to get an average of our three victim cells, first, we have to add them together. The formula that adds them would be =C2+D2+E2. To average that result, we need to divide it by the number of things we're averaging, in this case three (3). To divide by three, we need to add /3 to the end of the formula. Now it reads =C2+D2+E2/3 but that still won't work. We need to separate the math functions by putting parentheses around the first portion, and that will give us a workable formula that looks like this: =(C2+D2+E2)/3.

Getting Complicated

That average from the last section could, conceivably, include a much larger range of numbers. Instead of typing each cell ID with a plus sign in between, we can work with a range of cells and an additional formula instead.

As you may recall, you indicate a range of numbers by enclosing them in parentheses () and by putting a colon (not *that* kind of colon, this kind (:)—*geesh*) between them.

So, instead of the long and cranky formula we previously used, we can replace the (C2+D2+E2) with a simpler formula (SUM (C2:E2))—well, it *would* be simpler if we were adding together a larger range of cells. Our final, simplified formula to average a range of cells would look like this: =(SUM (C2:E2))/3.

The ability to include multiple math operations, even multiple cell ranges, into a formula can let you do some pretty heavy-duty math in a spreadsheet—math so complex that I don't even remember what it's for or how to build a formula for it. Fortunately, I don't have to remember. Works remembers a lot of it for me.

Functions: Predefined Formulas

The formula we worked out to average a range of cells is also known as a *function*. A function is a generic mathematical formula that's already built-in to Works' spreadsheet. You access formulas with the Easy Calc button on the toolbar (it's the one with the calculator on it).

Works includes functions for basic mathematical operations (sums, multiplication, subtraction, division, and averages) and even some for more esoteric operations (such as finding the SYD function, which calculates the depreciation and salvage (resale value) of a capital investment over a defined period of time).

I don't pretend to understand what half of the over 70 built-in functions are, do, or how they do them. What's more, I don't have to. Easy Calc explains them and holds your hand through the process of using Works' functions.

Additionally, Works' extensive online Help explains each function in detail (how do you think I knew what SYD was—I thought Syd was the guy who does my dry cleaning).

Easy Calc: Uniting Form(ula) and Function

Using Easy Calc is a fairly simple affair. Let's use it to automate that average formula we were fooling with earlier. Easy Calc considers averaging to be a common calculation.

Common Calculations

To begin, click on the cell where you want to insert the Average function. Next, click on the **Easy Calc** button. That will bring up the Easy Calc dialog box shown in the following figure.

Easy Calc makes calculations easy— even confounding Calculus calculations.

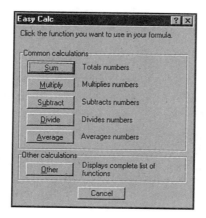

Click on the **Average** button. That will bring up the dialog box shown below. This dialog box explains what the AVG (average) function is, and what you should do next.

Easy Calc holds your hand all the way through the process— just follow the simple instructions on the dialog box.

Explains this function

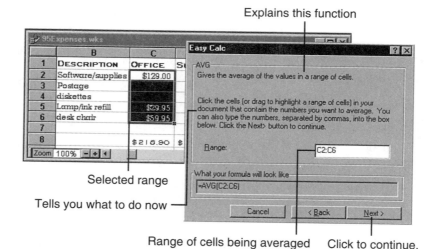

Selected range

Tells you what to do now

Range of cells being averaged   Click to continue.

In this case, you should select the cells you want averaged by clicking on them (you can move the dialog box out of your way by click-dragging on its title bar), or click-dragging to select a range of cells. Then click **Next**. That will bring up the Final result dialog box.

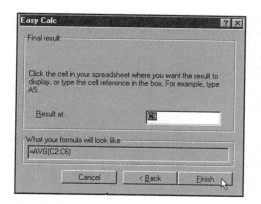

Where would you like that average placed?

All this dialog box wants to know is where you want the final result (the average) placed in your spreadsheet. The Result at text box will show the cell you selected before you started. If it's correct, just click **Finish**.

If you want to change the cell, you can type the cell ID or simply click on the cell and Works will place the result there. Then click **Finish**. Works will insert your newly created formula into the selected cell. Press **Enter** and it will do the math and show you the result, too. It's pretty easy, compared to the Byzantine steps you need to go through to create a complex formula all on your own.

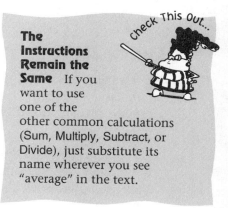

The Instructions Remain the Same If you want to use one of the other common calculations (Sum, Multiply, Subtract, or Divide), just substitute its name wherever you see "average" in the text.

Other Functions

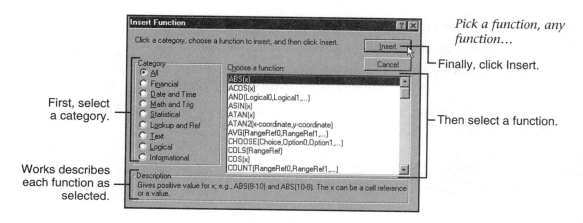

First, select a category.

Works describes each function as selected.

Pick a function, any function...

Finally, click Insert.

Then select a function.

If you want to use one of the other 70+ functions built into Works, it only takes one additional step.

When you first call up Easy Calc, click the **Other** button at the bottom of the dialog box. That will bring up the Insert Function dialog box. You can select a category from the Category box to eliminate unnecessary functions from the list box.

Next, click on a function in the list box. If you aren't sure what each is, Works displays a description of the selected function at the bottom of the dialog box.

When you find the function you want, click **Insert** and Easy Calc will walk you through the process of using that function as simply as it did with averages in the last section.

If you're like me, you'll have done some fabulous math with absolutely no clue about what it means, or how it's done manually. Ah, well, such is life.

A Quick Recap, Then Onward

In this chapter, we used the simple spreadsheet we created in Chapter 13 to fiddle with formulas and functions. You should now have a pretty good understanding of what formulas are, and how to use them—even if you don't understand the math itself.

In the next chapter, we'll do some fancy editing: adding rows and columns; making rows and columns wider and/or narrower, and other funky stuff. For now, take a break. Math, or just talking about math, can bring on an Excedrin headache for many (me included). While you get yourself a refreshing beverage, snack, or take a nap, ponder the following.

The Least You Need To Know

➤ You enter formulas in a spreadsheet the same way you enter any information: click on a cell to select it and type in the formula.

➤ All formulas must begin with an equal sign (=).

➤ The AutoSum button will take care of basic addition.

➤ Complex mathematical operations may need to be separated by parentheses (as in =SUM(C2:E2))/3).

➤ But why create your own complex formulas when Easy Calc can automate the process?

➤ Works' predefined formulas are called *functions*, and Easy Calc will gently walk you through the process of using them.

➤ Math gives me a headache.

Chapter 15

Editing: The Art of Fiddling With Spreadsheets

In This Chapter

➤ Add a row; add a column

➤ Row and column juggling

➤ Changing the height and width of rows and columns

➤ Sorting it all out

It's official, kids: I have no life. The jury was out on the subject for a while, but now that the votes have been tabulated, it's a unanimous decision.

I was able, on a Sunday evening, to just drop everything and go be an extra in a movie filming here in Philadelphia. I spent the night pretending to be a bar patron for ten and fifteen minutes at a time. The rest of the time we spent wisecracking on a street corner until 5:30 a.m., while pretending to not be exhausted.

Look for it: it's a little independent film called "Lies, The Radio Told Me." I'll be the big bearded guy at the end of the bar, smoking and not drinking his fake beer (it was nasty).

Thanks for letting me share, but that's really neither here nor there. What *is* here is a spreadsheet in rough shape. In this chapter we're going to work some editing magic on it, the kind you won't find in a movie. A lot of the editing stuff you'll see here will be old hat to you (if you're reading this straight through, anyhow), but some of it applies only to spreadsheets, so it will be new and fresh (unlike my tired, stale self).

Back to Editing Basics

You've already mastered a great big chunk of basic spreadsheet editorial skills—and you didn't know it. That's because editing information in individual spreadsheet cells is very much like editing words and phrases in a word processing document.

Since we're building on previously learned skills, I'll only summarize here. If you need major refreshing, skip back to Chapter 8 for the details.

Ye Olde Delete and Backspace Keys

You can use your Backspace and Delete keys to delete individual letters, characters, and spaces from a cell entry. Simply click on the cell you want to edit. Click again to place the cursor in the word or number in the formula bar. Then, move the cursor with your arrow keys to exactly the right spot. Finally, delete/backspace to your heart and cell's delight. Enter the correct information, press **Enter**, and you're done.

Cutting, Copying, Pasting, & Other Words That End In -ING

After selecting a cell, you can also cut, copy, or clear the information in it by selecting the appropriate command from the Edit menu.

You can also use drag-and-drop editing (also covered in Chapter 8). Click on a cell to select it, and then click-drag it to its new location. Release the mouse button, and Works will plunk the information down in its new cell location.

Once you've copied or cut some information, you can paste it into another cell by clicking on a new cell and selecting **Paste**, also from the **Edit** menu.

You can copy and paste a *range* of cells in a spreadsheet, just be certain that you select the same number of cells to paste *into* or Works will give you a cranky "number mismatch" message and make you try again. You can also select only one destination cell, and Works will figure out the rest.

Techno Talk

If The Math Doesn't Seem to Work...

If you edit a formula in your spreadsheet, but the result (answer) doesn't seem to change, you can goose Works into doing the math *right now*. Just select **Recalculate Now** from the **Tools** menu.

If the result changes to display a set of number signs (#####), then the cell isn't large enough to accommodate the answer. I'll show you how to fix that a little later. If there's something wrong with the formula, and Works will let you know what *it* thinks is wrong, take a deep breath and try it again.

When You Do That Undo That You Do So Well...

While you experiment with editing individual cells in our expenses spreadsheet, keep in mind that this is practice, so who cares if you mess something up? You can always undo the very last thing you did by using the **Undo** command in the **Edit** menu.

Inserting Rows and Columns

	A	B	C	D	E	F
1	DATE		DESCRIPTION	OFFICE	SUPPLY	POSTAGE
2	03/21/95		Postage and lots of other stuff			$15.95
3						
4	04/01/95		diskettes		$15.99	
5	04/02/95		desk chair	$59.95		
6	05/12/95		Software/supplies	$129.00	$110.00	
7	06/02/95		Lamp/ink refill	$29.99	$24.99	
8						
9	TOTALS			$218.94	$150.98	$15.95

95Expenses.wks — Zoom 100%

At the crossroads of a new row and a new column...

In the figure above, the selected cell (the one with the box around it) was the starting point for adding both a new blank row (number 4) and a new blank column (column B). Thank goodness it's a simple enough chore because I *always* end up doing one, the other, or both.

Always, without fail, I remember that I need to add a category, or that I forgot an important row of information somewhere in the middle of a spreadsheet.

Inserting an extra row, column, or a few of each is a simple matter. Here's how to do it:

First, click on a cell to select it.

For a *column*, the cell should be to the *right* of where you want the new, blank column placed, because Works will place the column to the *left* of the selected cell.

For a new *row*, the cell should be in the row *below* where you want the new, blank row placed, because Works will place the new row *above* the selected cell.

Select **Insert Row** or **Insert Column** from the **Insert** menu.

Works will insert a row or column (whichever you selected) into your spreadsheet. It will also, very kindly, move the existing columns and renumber/reletter them. And, very, very kindly, it will adjust all of the formulas in your spreadsheet to work with the new set of cell names. Isn't that nice?

Deleting Rows and Columns

I don't need to do this as often, but it happens. You hear on C-SPAN that the Capitol Hill gang has just eliminated an entire class of tax deductions. Poop. Now you need to remove them from your deductibles spreadsheet. The way I designed my example, that would mean deleting an entire column (and would probably put me into a new tax bracket).

Similarly, you may find out that a receipt you entered as a deductible business expense actually turned out to be for fifty pounds of cat litter and cat nip. Not deductible. Now you need to delete a row, too.

To delete a *column*, click on the column's header (the gray box above it labeled A, B, C, and so on). Then select **Delete Column** from the **Insert** menu.

To delete a *row*, click on the row's header (the gray box to the left, numbered 1, 2, 3, and so on). Then select **Delete Row** from the **Insert** menu.

Poof, those deductions go the way of all good things.

Drag-and-Drop a Row or Column

If, by some quirk of nature, you accidentally insert a row or column in (*gasp!*) the wrong place, you can drag-and-drop it in the right spot.

To move either a whole row, or a whole column, click on the appropriate column or row header to select it; then click-drag on the box that surrounds the row or column and drag it to its new position.

A thick line will appear when the move cursor touches an appropriate "seam" between columns or rows (you can see what I mean in the before and after figures here).

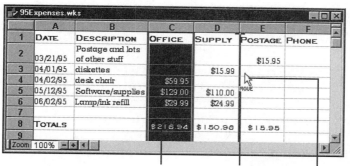

Moving a whole column to a new spot on the spreadsheet.

The row being moved Indicates where column will land The move cursor

After the move (moving is so draining—don't you find?).

When the cursor touches the spot where you want to reposition the column or row, release the mouse button. Works will think about it for a second, and the column or row will jump to its new home (as shown in the bottom figure).

Taller Rows and Wider Columns

Check This Out...

It's Not Just for Wider/Taller...

You may want to make your columns narrower, or your rows shorter. The instructions below work for that, too.

If you're entering width or height figures manually, just type in smaller numbers. The buttons at the bottoms of both dialog boxes will automatically decide whether to make your rows and columns shorter or narrower, depending on their contents. They're a no-brainer.

Sometimes, as in the case of the **Descriptions** label we put on column B of our spreadsheet, we need to enter a word or number that's longer than a 10 character-wide column will hold.

More often (for me, at least) I get too verbose (have you noticed?) and enter more information than will fit comfortably in a cell. Instead of making the whole column wider, I'll just make that row taller to accommodate my extra babbling. It's a simple matter to adjust the width of columns and the height of rows.

Changing Column Width

To change the width of a column, click on the column header to select the whole column (or just click on a cell in the column—either works). If you want to adjust a bunch of columns, you can click-drag on a range of headers.

From the **Format** menu, select **Column Width**. That will bring up the following tiny dialog box.

The Column Width dialog box.

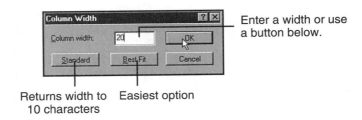

Enter a width or use a button below.

Returns width to 10 characters   Easiest option

You can manually enter a column width by double-clicking on the number in the Column width text box, and entering the new number—but that's too much like work.

It's easier to simply click on the **Best Fit** button at the bottom of the dialog box. That automatically changes the width of the column so it's a little bit wider than the column's widest entry. No guesswork, no counting characters, just a simple click.

If you select a single cell before clicking Best Fit, the column width will be adjusted for *only the selected cell*.

The Standard button will change the setting back to Works' default setting of 10, if you decide later that your changes were unnecessary.

Changing Row Height

The ever-popular Format Row Height dialog box.

The process for changing the height of a row in a spreadsheet is remarkably similar (as you can see in the preceding figure) to changing column width.

To begin, select the row (or a cell in that row) that you want to adjust. If you care to, you can tinker with a range of rows, by click-dragging the row headers. Select **Row Height** from the **Format** menu. The Format Row Height dialog box appears; it works exactly the same as the Column Width dialog box except it alters row height.

The Sneaky Way To Adjust Height And Width

With the previously discussed dialog boxes, you can precisely control the width and height of your columns and rows. Sometimes, that precision just isn't necessary. There's a way to alter the width and height of your columns and rows without getting all obsessive about it.

The lazy way to adjust heights and widths.

The adjust cursor

Simply move your cursor to the seam/line dividing two column or row headers (they're column headers in the preceding figure). The cursor will change to the Adjust cursor shown in the figure. Click-drag the cursor, and Works will resize the row or column in question.

For rows, Works will adjust the row *above* the cursor. For columns, Works adjusts the column to the *left* of the cursor. The other rows or columns are automatically moved to accommodate your chances. Try it; it's cool.

Laziness 101

Personally, I tend to adjust the height and width of rows and columns by this sneaky method while I'm filling in a spreadsheet. Later, when I finish (or nearly finish) the spreadsheet, I'll go through and adjust all the rows and columns to *Best Fit*.

For me, it just seems to save time and thought while doing the important (and tedious) work of typing in spreadsheet information. That way, I don't break my train of thought with a dialog box, but I can still see all of the information I'm entering in my spreadsheet. Just a tip.

Sorting All Sorts of Stuff

An untidy spread-sheet—those dates are a mess!

	A	B	C	D	E	F
	DATE	DESCRIPTION	SUPPLY	OFFICE	POSTAGE	PHONE
1						
2	06/02/95	Lamp/ink refill	$24.99	$29.99		
3	04/02/95	desk chair		$59.95		
4	03/21/95	Postage and lots of other stuff			$15.95	
5	05/12/95	Software/supplies	$110.00	$129.00		
6	04/01/95	diskettes	$15.99			
7						
8	TOTALS		$24.99	$29.99	$0.00	
9						

95Expenses.wks — Zoom 100%

In this figure, the spreadsheet is nice, but a little messy. For the purpose of, say, quarterly taxes, you might want to get all of those receipts into chronological order so you can summarize quarterly expenses. Well, you *might*.

To sort information in a spreadsheet, follow these simple steps:

1. Select the cells you want to sort by. For example, in the spreadsheet in the preceding figure, I want to sort by the date, so I would select cells A2:A6.

2. Select **Sort** from the **Tools** menu. The first sort dialog box will appear.

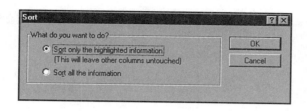

The first Sort dialog box.

3. Click on the sorting option you want to use, then click **OK**. For this example, I want to **Sort all the information** in the spreadsheet, because the receipt information is associated with the dates.

   In other cases (where the information to be sorted isn't associated with the rest of the information in the spreadsheet), you might want to select **Sort only the highlighted information**, which will leave the rest of your columns/rows unchanged.

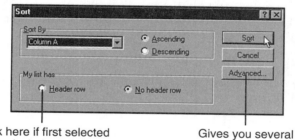

The second Sort dialog box. How do you want that sorted?

Click here if first selected row includes labels.

Gives you several sorting criteria

4. When the second Sort dialog box appears, select a **Sort By** strategy. The column will be the one you selected in the spreadsheet. If it's incorrect, choose the correct one from the pop-up list. You also need to choose **Ascending** (low to high) or **Descending** (high to low) order for the sort.

5. If the information you selected in your spreadsheet includes a row of labels (like those used in this example (Date, Description, and so on), be sure to select **Header row** in the My list has box. Otherwise, Works will sort the header information in with the rest of the data, and that's not good. It might get you all out of sorts.

6. Apologize for tacky pun in the previous step. (I'm so very sorry.)

7. Click **Sort**.

Works will think about it for a moment or two, then rearrange the information in your spreadsheet by the method you selected. The finished sort of our expenses spreadsheet is shown below. Isn't it lovely?

After sorting...

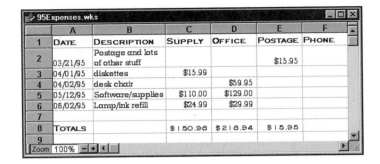

The Least You Need to Know

Editing a spreadsheet isn't tough, mainly because we've used these tools before in the section on word processing (and many of them re-appear in the section on the database, too). The only completely new thing we looked at was sorting information in a spreadsheet. Some important things to remember when sorting are:

➤ Select the information you want to sort, first.

➤ If you only want the selected information sorted, remember to select **Sort only the highlighted information**, which will leave the rest of your columns/rows unchanged.

➤ Remember to tell Works that you have a header row in the selected information; otherwise your labels could wind up in the middle of your spreadsheet, where they won't do you any good.

Chapter 16

Lovely to Look At: Spreadsheet Beautification

In This Chapter

➤ Automatic formatting options

➤ How fonts help readers understand your spreadsheets

➤ Making money *look* like money

➤ Alignment tactics and formatting antics

Getting a spreadsheet created, labeled, and edited so everything is shipshape is just the beginning. Once you enter all that data, it helps if you present it in such a way that your reader can make sense of all that information.

Formatting helps. All along, I've done some basic formatting to our sample expenses spreadsheet (see the next figure). The labels (Date, Description, and so on) are all in larger font (12-point) than the actual entries (10-point). The labels are also in a bold, sans serif font for easy scanning. The actual entries are in a nice, simple serif font that's easy to read even at its relatively small size.

Some basic formatting. Not really pretty, but practical.

Bold labels ⌐

Nice, easy-to-read font ⌐

	A	B	C	D	E	F
1	DATE	DESCRIPTION	SUPPLY	OFFICE	POSTAGE	PHONE
2	03/21/95	Postage			$15.95	
3	04/01/95	diskettes	$15.99			
4	04/02/95	desk chair		$59.95		
5	05/12/95	Software/supplies	$110.00	$129.00		
6	06/02/95	Lamp/ink refill	$24.99	$29.99		
7						
8	TOTALS		$150.98	$218.94	$15.95	
9						
10						

95Expenses.wks — Zoom 100%

Bold labels

There are two basic rules of formatting a spreadsheet: point out helpful information (like headings); and make the data as easy to follow and read as possible.

You already know more than you think about formatting spreadsheets. All of the formatting tools in this chapter you've seen before in Chapter 10, when you formatted a word processing document. Things need to be handled a little differently with spreadsheets, and there's a few spreadsheet-specific options, but there are no big surprises in here—so wipe that slick of panic-sweat off your forehead.

Do It Yourself? Or AutoFormat?

As in most complicated Works functions (that's complicated as in "more than one or two steps," not as in "I'll never be able to do that!"), you can have Works do the work for you by using an AutoFormat.

For spreadsheets, AutoFormat is a set of 16 predefined spreadsheet designs (and some of them are quite nice, really). To access them, select **AutoFormat** from the **Format** menu. That calls up the dialog box shown here.

AutoFormat: able to format tall spreadsheets in a single bound...

1. Choose a format here.

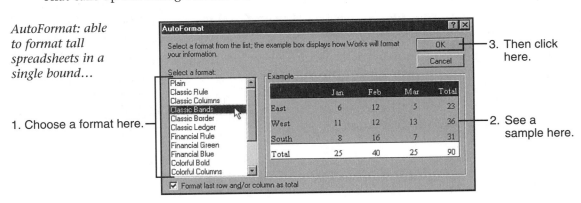

3. Then click here.

2. See a sample here.

In the **Select a format** list box, click on a format. The Example box shows you what the selection looks like. When you find an AutoFormat that you want to use, click **OK** and Works will gussy up your spreadsheet as promised.

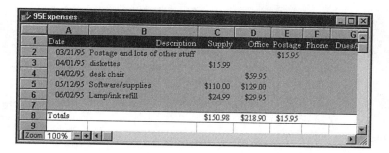

Old faithful, formatted with the Classic Bands AutoFormat.

If AutoFormat Doesn't...

AutoFormat automatically selects all of the information in your spreadsheet for formatting—at least it tries. Sometimes, AutoFormat guesses wrong. It picks the wrong cells, or not enough cells; in short, it screws up.

If it screws up, do this: immediately select **Undo** from the **Edit** menu. That will undo the AutoFormat. Next, click-drag over all of the cells with information in them (don't use Select All; it selects all the blank rows and columns, too, which is a waste of time and formatting). AutoFormat again. That should take care of it.

In case you're wondering, the Format last row and/or column as total check box at the bottom of the screen does just what it says: formats the last row and/or column of your spreadsheet to draw attention to the fact that there's important information there.

If your spreadsheet doesn't contain a total row or column, click on the check box to turn this option off (the check mark will go away). Otherwise, I'd leave it on most of the time.

Since tastes vary, and I'm sure you couldn't care less what I think of all these predefined designs; just try them on for size. Click on each and see what the samples look like. You'll know what you want when you see it.

Techno Talk blah blah blah blah blah bl

Pick Apart a Format to See What Makes It Tick

To learn how each AutoFormat format is put together, apply one you like to a sample document (maybe our friend the expenses spreadsheet).

Click on an interesting portion of the formatting (color, shading, white text on a black background, whatever) to select it. Then call up the Format Cells dialog box (covered later in this section) and flip through each tab to see which options you can use to give you the selected effect.

That way, if you only like a portion of an AutoFormat, you can recreate the good part yourself, whenever you want.

If you don't care to use AutoFormat (or you're just tired of using AutoFormat), be creative and do some funky formatting.

Just Fonting Around

You apply fonts in a spreadsheet the same way you apply fonts to a word processing document: select the cell(s) you want to change, and then select a font, size, and style using the toolbar (or by selecting **Font and Style** from the **Format** menu). The dialog box is exactly the same as the font dialog box we used back in Chapter 10. Nothing to it.

General Spreadsheet Font Tips

In no particular order:

➤ Use bold, eye-catching fonts for labels.

➤ Avoid novelty, script, or other hard-to-read fonts.

➤ The bigger, the better. Larger point sizes make numerical data easier to read. Try to keep your information at between 10–14 points. Labels can be a point or two larger.

Check This Out...

How much space can you spare? Be warned. Large fonts will increase the size of your spreadsheet: more pages, wider columns, taller rows.

Keep in mind as you make your font choices that sans serif fonts (the ones without the little tails and curlicues on the letters) are more *legible*, that is, easier to recognize individual characters. Select sans serif fonts for labels and other information that should standout from the crowd (totals, maybe?).

Serif fonts (the ones with the little tails and curlicues) are more *readable*, meaning they don't strain a reader's eyes after a page or two. Select serif fonts for your data in longer spreadsheets.

If you've completely blanked on the whole serif/sans serif thing, it's covered back in Chapter 10.

Formatting, Body and Cell

Certain kinds of information require special handling. Percentages, for one, need that % sign after them. Dates, on the other hand, are more flexible. You can use one of several formats: 12/1/60; Dec. 1, 1960; and 1 Dec. 1960. They're all the same date in different formats.

This section is about telling Works what special formatting you want applied to cells in your spreadsheet, so you don't have to do it one cell at a time. Yuck.

Generally speaking, formatting involves two steps: selecting the cell(s) you want to format, and then applying the formatting with the Format Cells dialog box. Since numbers will take up most of the space in a spreadsheet, let's look at those first.

Playing the Numbers

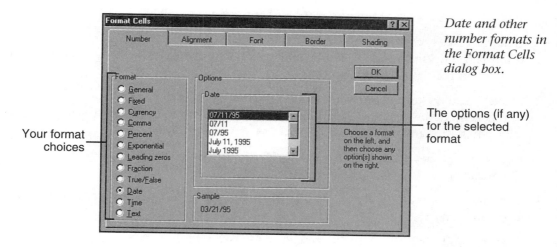

Date and other number formats in the Format Cells dialog box.

Your format choices

The options (if any) for the selected format

Works gives you a wide range of number formats to choose from (as you can see in the figure). Select **Number** from the **Format** menu and the Format Cells dialog box appears. (We're just looking, right now. If we were actually going to apply a number format, of course, I'd have told you to select some cell(s) to format first—but you knew that, didn't you?)

There are three main parts to the Number section of the Format Cells dialog box: your format choices, a selection of options for each format, and a sample that shows what your choice will look like in your spreadsheet.

I'm in the Red

Several of the number formats (currency and fixed, to name two) give you the option of having negative numbers automatically appear in red. That's especially good for accounting spreadsheets, so you know… well… when you're in the red.

If you only look at your spreadsheets on-screen, why not use it? It's an easy way to draw attention to a financial deficit (an attention deficit?).

If you print out your spreadsheets and don't have a color printer, you may want to think twice about using it. Your printer will convert the red numbers to a gray-looking dot pattern that may be hard to read. Try it and see how legible the result is.

These are your number formats (in order of appearance):

General   Like everyday dishes, the general format is good for nonspecific alphanumeric information (it isn't good for money or dates). It automatically aligns numbers to the left and text to the right. That's about it.

Fixed   Lets you keep your figures to a set number of decimal places. Works will round the numbers up or down to the closest decimal place. Many other options also give you the ability to set the number of decimal places as part of the format.

Currency   Money stuff. Adds the dollar sign ($) to selected cells and fixes the decimal places to two.

Comma   Automatically places commas in longer numbers (for example: 1,000,000) so you don't have to.

Percent   Automatically adds the percent sign (%) after numbers.

Exponential   You'll only use this if you do some very complicated mathematics in your spreadsheets. It's a shorthand notation for long numbers that are too long to fit into a spreadsheet cell.

Leading zeros If you want all of the numbers in a particular row to contain, say, five digits, formatting the row as Leading zeros will automatically add zeros to the front of the number so it contains five digits. 123 would appear as **00123** in our 5-digit example.

Fraction Say you're using Works' spreadsheet to figure out how much lumber you'll need to build a picnic table. You can set the number options to Fraction, and then tell Works to round any fractions up to the nearest, oh, ¼-inch. You can also tell Works not to round fractions *down* (just click in the Do not reduce box, when it's active). That way, if anything, you'll wind up with a little extra lumber, instead of not enough (which is always a pain in the buzz saw).

True/False With this option, results that equal 1 appear in the spreadsheet as "true." Results that equal 0 appear as "false." I can't think of a reason in the world to use this, but it's there if you need it.

Date Lets you choose how dates will appear in the spreadsheet, no matter what format you use to enter them. Works will convert them to the chosen format.

Time Works the same as the Date options but with the various time formats.

Text Lets you format numbers (and alphanumerics) as text so Works can sort them, rather than perform math operations on them. For example, you might want to sort a spreadsheet that contains catalog, serial, or Social Security numbers, by those numbers. Format them as text, first.

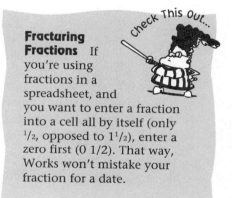

Fracturing Fractions If you're using fractions in a spreadsheet, and you want to enter a fraction into a cell all by itself (only ¹/₂, opposed to 1¹/₂), enter a zero first (0 1/2). That way, Works won't mistake your fraction for a date.

As you can see, Works' Number formatting choices cover just about every imaginable kind of number.

Proper Alignment Makes for Easy Reading

Alignment, as we discussed in Chapter 10, is whether things fall flush against the right or left margin or are centered on the page.

In the case of spreadsheet alignment, think *cell* instead of margin or page. The Alignment portion of the Format Cells dialog box gives you these options plus a few more.

Works' Alignment options for spreadsheets.

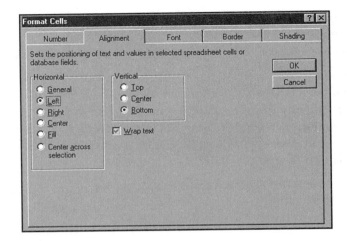

To call up the Alignment options, you can select **Alignment** from the **Format** menu. If the Format Cells dialog box is still open, you can just click on the **Alignment** tab. As you can see in the preceding figure, you can align information in a cell horizontally (from side to side) or vertically (from top to bottom).

Horizontally speaking, the Left, Right, and Center options are the same as we saw with the word processor. Each option places the content of the cell to the left, right, or center of the cell.

The Fill option is similar to the Justify option in the word processor, where the cells contents are forced to fill the cell from side to side.

The options that differ from those we've seen are General and Center across selection.

General horizontal alignment is the same as the General number format we saw in the last section. Text automatically aligns to the left side of the cell, while numbers automatically align to the right.

The Center across selection option lets you take the contents of one cell, and center it across two or more blank, adjoining cells. It's handy for labels, commentary about a set of figures, or other important, can't-miss information.

The Vertical options align text at the Top, Center, or Bottom of the selected cell(s). If, for example, you were going to separate your rows of information by drawing a line between them (with the border options coming up in a little bit), vertically centering the contents of the cells would keep them up, away from that dividing line, making it easier to read them.

The Wrap text option lets you fit more words into a narrow cell, by making the row tall enough to accommodate two or more lines of text (see the next figures).

Why Align Numbers to the Right?

Aligning numbers to the right is a good rule of thumb to follow. Here's why.

If you align numbers of different length to the left, then their decimal places (if any) won't line up on the page, making it hard for the reader to quickly spot large numbers. You really have to think about it.

$1000.00

$100.00

$10.00

At a glance, it's hard to tell the difference between these numbers. However, a little alignment jump to the right, and it's easy to differentiate between these three, similar-looking figures:

$1000.00

$100.00

$10.00

See what I mean?

	A	B	C
1	DATE	DESCRIPTION	SUPPLY
2	03/21/95	Postage and lots of other stuff	

Without Word wrap. Very unattractive.

	A	B	C
1	DATE	DESCRIPTION	SUPPLY
2	03/21/95	Postage and lots of other stuff	

With Word wrap— much prettier.

Borders and Shading Suggestions

The two remaining parts of the Format Cells dialog box are Border and Shading. These, like the Font dialog box, are exactly the same as the ones we used back in Chapter 10 to add borders and shading to a word processing document (except you don't have the option of adding a drop shadow—that's okay, because drop shadows will make your spreadsheet look murky).

Instead of covering this ground again, let me just make some suggestions about the uses of borders and shading in spreadsheets. Actually, it's just one big suggestion with some examples. Here's the suggestion: **keep it simple.**

The point of being able to add borders and other formatting to a spreadsheet is not to make it pretty, it's to make it easy to read. If, in the process, you can make it pretty, too, well—more power to you.

Again, I will recommend (as I did in the AutoFormat section) that you take the time to pick apart how your favorite AutoFormats work. It will give you an excellent grasp of how all the formatting options come together to create an attractive, readable spreadsheet.

Some things to think about:

➤ If your important information is broken down into rows, think about separating each row with a simple line. It will help the reader's eye track across the row without accidentally wandering. You do that with the Bottom border option.

➤ If your important information falls into columns, maybe divide those with a thin line. Use the Left and/or Right border options to draw those.

➤ Don't use both column and row dividing lines, though. That turns your spreadsheet into graph paper.

➤ If you have a column or row that contains nothing but totals, consider a very light shading to draw attention to it. Select the column or row; then select **Shading** from the **Format** menu. Make sure you can read the text through the shading (check the sample before you apply it). You can also box the entire row, or column, and it would be just as effective.

➤ If you must use dark shading, consider making the text white, or another light color, so you can easily read it. Change the color of text with the Font portion of the Format Cells dialog box.

Special Spreadsheet Printing Concerns

On the whole, printing a spreadsheet is a simple proposition. However, because of the nature of spreadsheets, there are some things you need to think about, and account for (no pun intended), before you print.

Specify a Print Area

When you create a new, blank spreadsheet, it's 256 cells wide by 1,600+ cells tall. You'll probably only use a small portion of all that.

Once you finish your spreadsheet, before you print, you should specify what part of that 256 x 1,660+ cells you actually want to appear on paper. It will save you time, energy, and probably lots of paper.

To select the print area, click on cell **A1** and drag the cursor to the last cell (at the bottom right corner) with information in it. Then select **Set print area** from the **Format** menu.

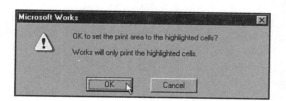

Works asks your permission before it sets the print area.

Works will ask you to confirm your choice with the alert box shown above. If you've selected all of the used cells in your spreadsheet, **click OK**, and only the highlighted portion of your spreadsheet will go to your printer.

If you think your selection is incomplete (or too complete), click **Cancel** and try it again.

Landscape or Portrait?

Since many spreadsheets tend to be wider than they are tall, it's often a good idea to print them in *landscape orientation*. Landscape orientation, you may recall from Chapter 11, turns a standard 8.5-by-11-inch piece of paper on its side, so it is wider than it is tall.

To see if your spreadsheet will benefit from landscape orientation, click on the **Print Preview** button in the toolbar (the piece of paper with the magnifying glass over it), or select **Print Preview** from the **File** menu.

You'll get a glimpse of what your printout will look like, without wasting paper. Our sample expenses spreadsheet is wasteful of paper in either orientation, however we can fit more of the columns across on one page (which makes it easier to read) in landscape orientation, so that's what I'd use.

You change page orientation by using the Page Setup dialog box's Source, Size, & Orientation page, as discussed in Chapter 11.

You can also save *more* paper by making the spreadsheet's margins as small as your printer can handle. That's covered in Chapter 11, too.

But Is It Legal (Sized)?

For very large/wide spreadsheets, you may want to consider laying in a supply of legal-sized paper (8.5-by-14-inches). That will cut down on the number of pages printed, and fit more information on each page—again, making the spreadsheet easier to read and follow.

If your printer can't handle legal-sized paper (many can, but you never know, so check your printer manual for details), you can always tape your printed letter-sized pages together to show the full width of your spreadsheet.

Freeze, Mister!

If you have a spreadsheet that uses column or row labels (as our expenses spreadsheet does), and the whole thing will print out on three or more pages, you can make sure that those labels will print out on every page by *freezing* them.

Freezing titles makes your spreadsheet easier to read, because you don't have to flip back to see which label goes with what column. Freezing titles also affects the display on your computer, too, so you won't have to scroll back to the beginning of your spreadsheet to see your labels, either. Very convenient.

To freeze your labels, click on the row or column header to select the whole row or column. Then select **Freeze Titles** from the **Format** menu. (A check mark will appear in front of the menu item when you select it.)

Use a column *and* a row of labels? Click in the first cell you *don't* want to freeze. Then select **Freeze Titles** from the **Format** menu. All of the rows above, and all of the columns to the left of the selected cell, will be frozen.

To unfreeze titles, repeat the process. Select the frozen rows or columns (or the first unfrozen cell) and select **Freeze Titles** from the **Format** menu again. That unfreezes them. Cool.

Other Printing Options

The last printing options that you need to consider are two spreadsheet-only options, shown in the preceding figure. They're on the Other Options tab of the Page Setup dialog box.

The Print gridlines option will print all of the gray lines that divide rows and columns in a spreadsheet while you're working on it. The gridlines can (if you don't do any other special formatting) help readers decipher your spreadsheet.

Techno Talk

Starting Page Number Option

There is a third option on the Other Options dialog box: the Starting page number option.

All document pages in Works are numbered from one, up. If you want the first page number to be something else (you may want two separate spreadsheets to have continuous page numbers, maybe), enter the new starting page number here. Works will handle the rest.

This option is also available in the word processor; if you want to break a large writing project down into smaller files (chapters for a book, for instance) but still want to keep an accurate page count.

However, printing the gridlines adds a lot of time to the printing process (depending on the kind of printer you have). If you want to have the gridlines printed, click in the Print gridlines box. To turn the option off, just click in the box again.

The second option is Print row and column headers. Selecting this option will print the A, B, C, and so on, headings at the top of each column, and the numbered headings in front of each row.

Having Works print the row and column headings is helpful if you use no other labels in a spreadsheet, but actual meaningful labels are more useful.

To print the row and column headings click in the Print row and column headers check box. To turn the option off, just click in the box again.

Printing (Finally!)

Once you have everything formatted, the page set up, and your print area selected, printing is just a matter of clicking on the Print button (the one with the printer on it) in the toolbar, or selecting **Print** from the **File** menu.

Works will ask if you really want to print the file, and give you the chance to set some printing options (which will vary depending on the printer you own). Click **OK** and Works will get to work.

The Least You Need to Know

The goal of formatting a spreadsheet is to make all those numbers and other information as easy as possible to read. No matter what formatting you do, always ask yourself: "Will this make my figures easier to follow?" If the answer is yes, go ahead and format. If not, try, try again.

Sometimes, we get so caught up in formatting and numbers that we can't really judge what's effective—we already know what we're trying to say, and that makes us biased. If you don't feel you can honestly answer the question, ask an innocent bystander for an unbiased opinion.

Chapter 17

What Chart Is This, I Think I Know...

In This Chapter

➤ Chart creation

➤ Chart varieties

➤ Tips and tricks

➤ Printing charts

Charts are an easy way to convert a pile of numerical data into easy-to-interpret graphical information. You *have* seen them before. Ross Perot, in the '92 Presidential election, couldn't go to the bathroom without flapping a chart around. Don't get the idea, just because that's where you see them most, that charts are just for news programs, politicians, and business people. They aren't.

You can use them to prove to your spouse why buying a new car is a good (or bad) idea. A student can use one to show how the popularity of MTV has risen over its 20-year history (compared to how attention spans have declined). An amateur pollster can show the results of an unscientific survey.

You can turn any sort of numerical data that you enter into a spreadsheet into a chart.

Mommy, Where Do Charts Come From?

(Don't panic. This one's easier to explain without blushing than the "Where did *I* come from?" question.)

Charts are born when two conditions are met: first, information from spreadsheet cells (*cellus digitalus*) must be present, fertile, and selected; second, the cursor must contact and click the charting button (*buttono chartibus*). Then the process of cell replication and graphicalization begins (*are you buying this horse hockey?*).

Actually, that's not too far afield. Charts happen when you select data from a spreadsheet, and click the Chart button on the toolbar (it's the one with the little bar chart on it). Works then takes the selected information and (after asking you to choose a chart type) turns it into the chosen graphical representation—a chart is born.

You can then take the charted information and format it, place it in another document (see Chapter 23 for the how-to on that), and add embellishments to make it easier for folks to interpret.

A Chart Warning

Really, two warnings. The first is that creating a chart is easy. Creating a *meaningful* chart is a little more difficult. For example, in the introductory paragraphs to this chapter, I mentioned making a chart comparing the rise in MTV's popularity to the decline in attention spans. That would be a cool chart, but it might not mean anything. You could be charting nothing more than a coincidence.

Just the appearance of two items in a chart implies some sort of relationship (whether it's really there or not). They also lend your information (bogus or not) a certain level of credibility. Many people believe charts without looking at them too closely (why do you think politicians and infomercial hosts use so many?).

Use the power to chart for good, and not for evil.

The second warning is about me. Creating a good and meaningful chart is an art form. I'm strictly an amateur. I don't need 'em, and I don't use 'em. I can only tell you the basic "start here and do this" stuff, and maybe give you a tip or two on prettying them up.

If you need to create really good charts for work or school, *run* (do not walk) to the business or computer section of your favorite library or bookstore. Find yourself a good book on chart making, presentations, or maybe even statistical (*ack*) analysis.

That said, let's look at the basic chart types.

Chart Varieties

You've probably seen all manner of charts in the course of your life. There's at least one in the newspaper every day, and a few on the news.

Works gives you the opportunity to use one of a dozen chart variations. Each has good and bad points, depending on what kind of information you're presenting. The table below shows you your charting choices.

Types of charts available in Works

Chart Type	Description
Area chart	These are good for comparing/contrasting the change in a set of values over a period of time—sales figures by month, for example.
Stacked line chart	Use this to compare a single value (hardware sales, maybe) to the total of all values (total sales) in the chart.
3-D area chart	Same as the area chart, but with stunning 3-D effects (and you don't need those goofy glasses).
Bar chart	A bar represents each set of values (expense categories, perhaps). The bars make it easy to compare the data at a glance.
Y scatter chart	I've only seen these used in statistical analyses (but I'm no expert). They're good for seeing how two or more X-sets of related data overlap.
3-D bar chart	Same as the bar chart, but with 3-D effects (insert your own favorite 3-D movie joke here). (Who says books aren't inter-active?)
Line chart	Similar to the stacked line chart, just not as well stacked.

continues

Types of charts available in Works   Continued

Chart Type	Description
Radar chart	Shows the change in value or frequency of categories in relationship to a central point (how overall or departmental sales fluctuate in relation to the holiday shopping season, for instance). They're cool looking, too.
3-D line charts	Same as the regular line chart (which is similar to the stacked line chart) except the dotted lines are converted to 3-dimensional looking ribbons.
Pie chart	The politician's friend, used to show the percentage (pro portion) each category represents of the total. In a politician's terms, pie charts can show what percentage each tax earns of the government's total tax income.
Combination	Crosses a bar chart with a line chart, giving you the benefits of each.
3-D pie chart	Same as the pie chart, but you can see whether the pie is deep-dish or not.

The easiest way (I think) to select the appropriate chart-type to match your data, is to simply try each chart on for size. It's very simple, and I'll tell you how in just a few pages (I'm such a chart-tease).

How Charts Work

A chart graphically represents the data from a spreadsheet. The information is usually plotted along two axes (that's pronounced "ack-sees" and is the plural of *axis*—the stuff isn't arranged along two hatchets), typically referred to as the X- and Y-axes (they're labeled in the next figure).

The X- and Y-axes typically represent time and data, respectively. You can measure time in seconds, minutes, hours, days, or (as in the figure) weeks. You can measure the data in dollars, or any other numerical value. A dot on the chart represents the value (number) from each cell of the spreadsheet, and a line connects the dots in each series.

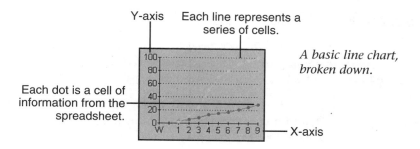

A basic line chart, broken down.

Even without knowing what the chart above represents, you can tell by looking at it that one element (represented by the top line) has changed a lot faster than the other (the bottom line). That's the power of a chart; one glance and you have a pretty good idea of growth or change, even if you don't know what's growing or changing.

Creating a Chart

A chart begins with a spreadsheet.

To create a chart of your very own, you need to start with a spreadsheet. Since you're probably tired of looking at our old friend, Mr. Expenses, I created a new one, shown in the preceding figure. Don't ask where I got the idea for it; it just came to me.

This is a very simple spreadsheet—there aren't even any formulas in it. The first column is the number of the weeks I've been writing this book. The second column is the cumulative number of chapters I've written in those weeks. The third column is how badly I need to get away to Atlantic City for some R & R as the work progresses.

199

Select What You Want Charted

In order to chart this drastic need for a vacation, first select the information from the spreadsheet you want charted. In the preceding figure, I'd select the range of cells A3:C13. (Notice that I selected the column headings.)

I would not select any part of the first row, because that's just a title I slapped on the spreadsheet, and it isn't something that needs charting. If you select it, Works will try and work it into the chart, no matter how pointless the information.

Once the information is selected, click the **Chart** button on the toolbar (or select **Create New Chart** from the **Tools** menu).

Pick a Chart, Any Chart...

*Define your chart
with the New Chart
dialog box.*

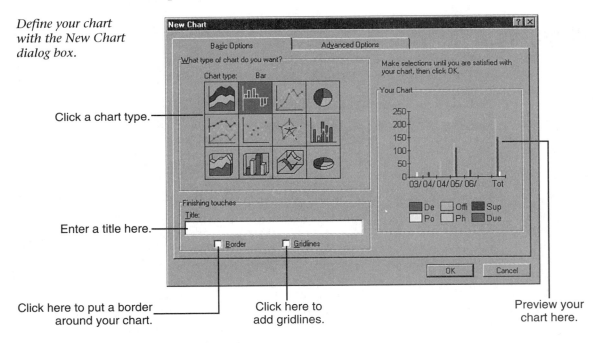

Click a chart type.

Enter a title here.

Click here to put a border
around your chart.

Click here to
add gridlines.

Preview your
chart here.

When you click the Chart button, you'll get the New Chart dialog box. The Basic Options tab (as shown in the preceding figure) will be foremost.

First, click on the type of chart you want in the box labeled **What type of chart do you want?** If you aren't sure which kind you want, click on each and check out the preview in the **Your Chart** box. You'll be able to decide from the preview which chart best meets your needs.

In the box labeled **Finishing touches**, you can type in a name for your chart (just click to place the cursor in the **Title** text box, and type the name).

You can also put a border around your chart by clicking in the **Border** check box. You can add gridlines (which can make some charts easier to interpret), too. Just click in the **Gridlines** check box. Any changes you make will appear in the preview, so you can try them on for size before you commit to them.

If none of these options give you a chart you can use, you may need to tinker with the Advanced Options. To do that, first select the chart type that's closest to what you want, then click on the **Advanced Options** tab at the top of the dialog box.

Oh, Those Advanced Options

The Advanced Options let you tell Works a little more about your spreadsheet, so it can build you a better chart.

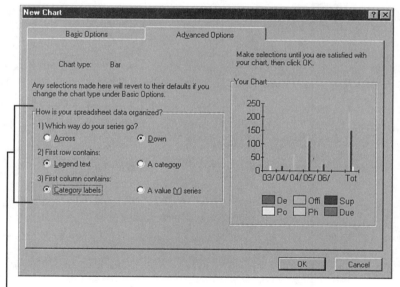

Works may need more information to do your spreadsheet justice.

Provide more info about your spread- sheet here.

There are three specific bits of information Works needs. You'll find the questions in the box labeled **How is your spreadsheet data organized?**

The first question (Which way do your series go?) wants to know if you have arranged the data in your spreadsheet across, in rows, or down in columns.

In the sample, the information is grouped in columns, so I'd click the **Down** option. If your information is grouped by rows, you would click **Across**.

The second question, First row contains (which isn't actually phrased in the form of a question), wants to know the kind of information contained in the first row of your spreadsheet. Is it column names or other labels? If it is, click **Legend text**. Is it numerical data? If it is, click **A category**. In mine, it's column labels, so I selected **Legend text**.

Finally, Works wants to know what's in the first column (First column contains—which is also not in the form of a question, so these last two wouldn't count on *Jeopardy!*).

If the first column is another set of labels, click **Category labels**. If it contains data that you want charted, click **A value (Y) series**. In the sample, the first column (Week #), though numerical, is actually just a label. It doesn't need to be charted, so I selected **Category labels**.

As always, any changes you make to these options will appear in the sample chart at the right of the dialog box. When your chart looks good, click **OK**.

If the Advanced Options don't help the chart type you selected, you can repeat the process. Go back to the Basic Options tab and select a new chart type; then try the Advanced Options on the new kind of chart.

Don't go feeling all stupid and inadequate if it takes you a few tries to get the chart looking the way you want it. It took me three tries to get one close to what I wanted, and I'm still not happy with it (you can see it here—the "Need for Slot Machines" label is too long to fit). To fix that, I need to shorten the label in the spreadsheet, and that's the sort of thing the next section is about.

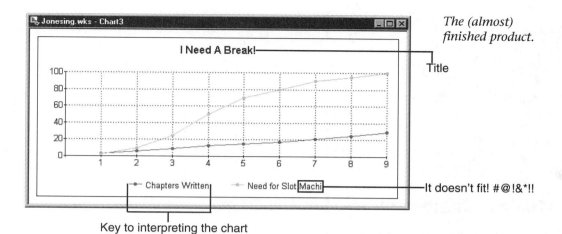

The (almost) finished product.

Title

It doesn't fit! #@!&*!!

Key to interpreting the chart

Who Do You Think's the Idiot, Here? It's Me!

I let that "Need for Slot Machi" mistake go because, judging by the mail I get, a lot of readers think people who write these books never make mistakes.

Everybody makes mistakes. Everybody faces that learning curve when they tackle new software and hardware. In fact, I think the *more* you know about computers, the more qualified you are to make bigger, more horrifying mistakes. You should see the PC I took *completely* apart, chip by chip, thinking I could put it back together again. It's over there, in a box. 'Nuff said?

Change That Chart!

You'd think that, in order to change a *faux pas* like the too long label in the last figure, that I'd have to scrap this chart and start again. No way. Works is much more forgiving than that.

Your spreadsheet and chart are not two separate documents; they're linked. If you discover, in the course of creating a chart, that a label is too long, or the information would chart better if listed another way, you can fix it in the spreadsheet, and the chart will follow suit.

You Can't Fix Everything; However...

This correction process will make changes to the appearance, but it won't change the selected data. If you want to use a different set of rows and columns from your spreadsheet, you need to start over from scratch.

Close the chart you've created, by clicking on its **Close** box. You'll return to the spreadsheet. Select the new range of data, and click the **Chart** button. Repeat the charting process as previously described. It's the only way, sorry.

Making Changes on the Spreadsheet

To fix an atrocity like the too-long label, here's what you'd do.

1. Select the spreadsheet's name from the **Window** menu. The spreadsheet will jump to the front, so you can work with it.

2. Select the cell(s) you want to change.

3. Make your changes. (In the sample, I changed the label **Need for Slot Machines (1–100)** to simply **Need for Slot Play**.)

4. Select the chart's name from the **Window** menu. The chart will jump to the front. Wonder of wonders, the changes you made to the spreadsheet will show up in the chart.

This process will work with cell entries, labels, anything you've included in the spreadsheet that's also included in the chart.

If You Exit Works and Come Back Later...

You'll open your spreadsheet file and (gasp!) your chart's gone! Don't panic. It's still around (plus every chart variation you tried on). Select **Chart** from the **View** menu. Works will ask you to select the chart you want to open (if you created more than one). Select the chart you want from the list, and click **OK**. It will open right up.

Refining the Chart (or Changing It Completely)

Once all the information is to your liking, you may decide to fine-tune the chart you have, or turn it into another sort of chart entirely. You can. Here's how.

When there's a chart on your screen, Works' toolbar changes to show a new assortment of buttons (shown in the next figure), each one representing one of the basic chart types.

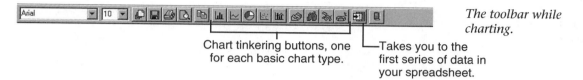

The toolbar while charting.

Chart tinkering buttons, one for each basic chart type.

└─Takes you to the first series of data in your spreadsheet.

To refine your chart further, click on the button that represents the type of chart you're creating. Our sample is a line chart, so I'd click the second button in the preceding figure, the one with a little line chart on it. That will call up the Chart Type dialog box shown here.

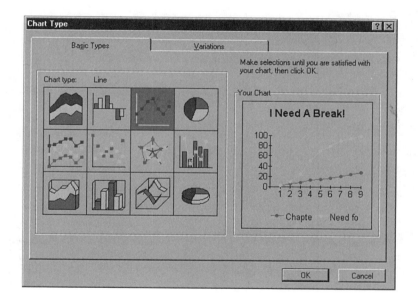

The Chart Type dialog box—what chart's your type?

Next, click on the **Variations** tab; that will give you variations on your chart type. You can select one of six variations and apply them to your existing chart. Just click a variation and click **OK**, and your chart will reflect the change.

Variations on a charting theme.

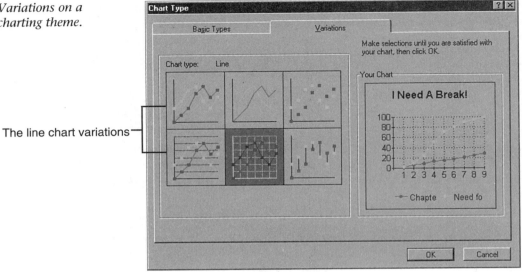

The line chart variations

If you want to change the type of chart you're using completely, click on the **Basic Types** tab. Click on the new type you want to use. (You can also click on the **Variations** tab again, to see what variations there are for your new chart type.)

When you've made all the changes you want, click **OK**. Your chart will reconfigure itself to the new chart variety.

What I Did...

The finished product.

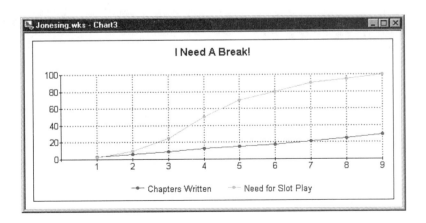

I didn't want a whole new type of chart—I like the line chart just fine. However, I did want to add horizontal and vertical gridlines to make it easier to figure out where each point falls on the chart. I also fixed the label, as mentioned earlier, and you can see that the new one fits beautifully.

This chart is so persuasive now, I simply have to go to Atlantic City for a couple of hours and throw quarters away. I'll see you later.

If You Have an Axis to Grind...

Works tries, based on the information you selected in your spreadsheet, to create the appropriate X- and Y-axes in your chart. Usually it gets it right, but if there's too much information displayed, you may need to thin it out.

For example, in one of my first chart attempts for this chapter, Works guessed that the **Week #** information was actually a variable to be charted (you can see it in the next figure), instead of just a plain ol' count of weeks slipping past. It took a perfectly good X-axis and turned it into meaningless dots on a chart.

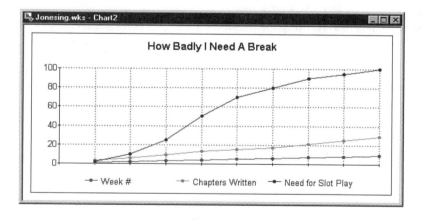

Works made a bad guess here—there's no X-axis.

If you want to fine-tune your chart's axes, you can use commands in the Format menu.

X Marks the Axis

To tinker with the horizontal (X) axis, select **Horizontal (X) Axis** from the **Format** menu. That will give you the Format Horizontal Axis dialog box. There are three categories of options you can tinker with.

Set your X (horizontal) axis options here.

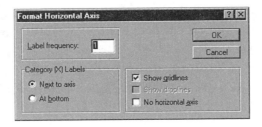

Label frequency sets how many labels Works will display from your spreadsheet. A setting of 1, as in the figure, displays all the labels. A setting of 2 displays every other label. Set it to 3 and you'll get every third label, and so on. It's handy for crowded spreadsheets, where labels overlap and are hard to read.

The Category (X) Labels options let you position your labels either Next to axis (as in my sample chart) or At bottom (which puts your labels at the bottom of the chart). I prefer my labels right next to the axis, where it's easy to tell what they refer to, but that's a personal preference.

The last three options are:

Show gridlines   Draws dotted lines across the chart from each of the labels, making it easy for the reader's eye to follow across the chart from the label to the data.

Show droplines(grayed out in the figure)   Only an option for 3-D and area charts that shows where one marker ends and the next begins, which can be hard to see in these chart varieties.

No horizontal axis   Tells Works that your chart has no X-axis.

Y Axis Y?

(What is this, a beer commercial?)

To change the settings for your Y, or vertical axis, select **Vertical (Y) Axis** from the **Format** menu. That calls up the Format Vertical Axis dialog box.

If you look at the figure, you'll see that it gives you four sets of options (or it would, if one set wasn't grayed-out), Range, Type, Y-Axis Tick Labels, and the three options at the lower right.

The Range options let you specify the range of values you want displayed along the Y-axis. Minimum lets you specify the lowest value you want displayed, Maximum the highest. If your spreadsheet has values from 0 to 1,000, but you're only interested in the data in the 50 to 500 range, you can set the Minimum to 50 and the Maximum to 500, and Works will not chart the rest of the unwanted parts of the range.

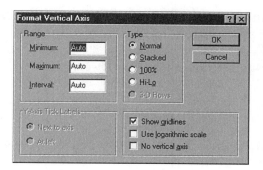

Your Y-axis options—talk about your axis powers!

The Interval sets how the minimum and maximum values are broken down—for example, a setting of 10 will display your Y-axis values in steps of ten (10, 20, 30, and so on). In my chart, earlier, they're stepped by 20 (0, 20, 40).

To change any of these settings, double-click in the text box after the option, and enter the setting of your choice.

The Type options tell Works what kind of values to display along the Y-axis.

Tick Not the comic book and cartoon character who shouts "Spoon!" as he leaps into action. A tick is one of the little hash marks that appear in the X-and Y-axes of a spreadsheet that show what increments the chart is measuring.

Normal   Means your average, run-of-the-mill numerical values.

Stacked   Means you're using a stacked line chart, where the values represent a cumulative effect of the series shown.

100%   Tells Works the Y-axis represents a 100% scale.

Hi-Lo   Adjusts the vertical axis to show values from high to low, between your minimum and maximum values (discussed earlier) for each category. A Hi-Lo chart is a line chart variety.

3-D Rows (grayed out in the figure)   Only for 3-D type charts. It adjusts the Y-axis to show the values as charted in 3-D chart.

The Y-Axis Tick Label options (grayed out in the figure) are similar to the label options we saw in the Format Horizontal Axis dialog box (but these affect the Y-axis). You can place your labels next to the Y-axis (click **Next to axis**), or at the left side of the chart (click **At left**).

Finally, there are three straggler options that don't fit nicely in any of the other catego-ries. The Show gridlines option is the same as we saw in the last section, except the gridlines run across the vertical axis. Use logarithmic scale tells Works that you're using logarithms (something I would never do). No vertical axis tells Works not to bother, there is no Y-axis.

Other Options

There are a handful of other chart formatting options. They vary depending on what kind of chart you're creating.

If you're creating a new chart, explore the Format menu for your options before you finalize it. Play with the various settings to see what they do. It's a lot more fun and interesting than reading about them here.

Chart Tips and Tricks

This section includes some very basic advice on chart creation and beautification. Let's begin, shall we?

Pretty but Simple

No, that's not a comment on myself (no one's ever called me "pretty"), but on how little you should tinker with your charts. Basically, you only have a few options you can change, but even those few can make it difficult to skim the information quickly from a chart.

You can change fonts, and you can change the color and/or pattern of your series indica-tors (the lines in a line chart or the bars in a bar chart).

Changing fonts is a two part process. First, to change the font used for tick (the graduated measures along the X- and Y-axes) and data labels, just select **Font and Style** from the **Format** menu. It will give you the Format Font and Style dialog box you've used a few times already, so I won't bore you with it again.

You know the drill: select the font from the Font scroll box, a size from the Size scroll box. Select a color from that drop-down menu, and, if you care to, a style from the box o' Style check boxes. Click **OK** when you're done.

The second part is changing the title's font (if you use one, like "I Need A Break!" in the sample). To change the title's font, you need to click on the title to select it. Then select **Font and Style** from the **Format** menu. You get the same kind of dialog box, and it works just the same. Easy as pie (charts).

Stylize Those Indicators!

You can stylize the series indicators (the bars in a bar chart and wedges in a pie chart, and so on), though, personally, I like Works' default colors. To fiddle with them select **Shading and Color** from the **Format** menu. That will call up the Format Shading and Color dialog box.

First, click on the **Series** number you want to change (you can tell which is which by a glance at the key at the bottom of your chart).

Next, select a color from the **Colors** list. If you're printing to a black-and-white printer, you might want to select a pattern from the **Pattern** list instead—but there's no reason why you can't do both (unless it makes your chart hard to read, which it can).

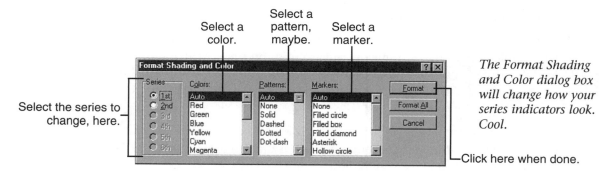

Select a color.

Select a pattern, maybe.

Select a marker.

Select the series to change, here.

The Format Shading and Color dialog box will change how your series indicators look. Cool.

Click here when done.

From the Markers list box, you can select a marker. A marker is how your line chart shows where your actual figures fall on the line. In my chart, they're filled-in circles, but you have some other lovely/lively choices here. Hollow diamonds are nice.

The point of changing the color, pattern, and markers for your series is to make it easier to tell the lines apart in your chart. They should be as different as possible, so there's no guessing which series is which.

You can format one series, and click **Format**, and then do the next series. Or you can format all your series (by repeating the process after clicking each series number in the dialog box) and click **Format All**. Whichever works better for you.

> **Check This Out...**
>
> **Little Miss(ing) Markers** If you're creating a chart other than a line chart (a bar chart, for example), the Markers list will be blank. Bar charts don't use markers, so you can't select one. Go figure.

KISS Me Again

I try to keep the KISS principle in mind when creating charts, too: Keep It Simple, Stupid. Charts can be fairly complex beasties to begin with. If you clutter them up with a lot of fancy fonts and formatting, they can get extremely difficult to read.

I try to limit myself to one simple font (maybe with bold and italic variations). For the series indicators, I keep them simple, letting color or pattern variations make them easy to identify. The more series that are represented in the chart, the simpler I keep things. You don't want formatting to overshadow your data.

Printing a Chart

It's nice to print out your charts when you're done. People are always impressed when you pass out charts and graphs in a meeting or use them as overhead transparencies.

I don't have a clue about what kind of printer you have. It may be color or black-and-white, a laser or an inkjet; it may be able to print on transparency film, or it may not. Fancier printers (like some laser printers) can reduce the size of a printed image so it fits on one page, where it would take two or more pages to print it full-sized. Only you know what your printer can do for you. Check your printer's manual for help.

I can, however, tell you that charts are often wider than they are tall, and may benefit from being printed in landscape orientation (as discussed in Chapters 11 and 16). The best printing tip I can give you for your charts is to use that Print Preview button on the toolbar to see if you need to change your page setup to accommodate your chart. Just click on the **Print Preview** button (the one with the page and a magnifying glass on it) before you waste paper and ink printing a test run of your chart.

If you create a color chart but are printing it on a black-and-white printer, you can get an idea of what it will look like by also selecting the **Display View as Printed** option from the **View** menu. It will give you an idea of what your colors will look like when you print it out.

The Least You Need to Know

As I said early in this chapter, creating an effective and meaningful chart is an art form, and I am no artist. To make truly excellent charts, you may want to consult a book on business presentations, statistics, or (if there is such a book) chart making.

To create a chart with Works, you need to:

➤ Create a spreadsheet

➤ Select the data in that spreadsheet that you want charted

➤ Click on the **New Chart** button in the toolbar (or select **Create New Chart** from the **Tools** menu).

Part 4
Your Basic Database

In many ways, a database is a lot like a spreadsheet: both involve lots of information presented in an organized manner. Spreadsheets crunch numbers in a fairly standard format. Databases, on the other hand, are very flexible. You control the horizontal; you control the vertical. Wait, that's the "Outer Limits."

Use databases for any sort of information you care to enter—names, words, numbers, or anything. The real power is searching and sorting through all that information and generating reports (which sounds dull, but can be fun in a twisted way). In this section, we'll create a database from scratch, enter data, sort it, search it, and print that sucker out in a very spiffy-looking report.

Chapter 18

Database, First Base

In This Chapter

➤ Database basics

➤ Before you start

➤ Creating a database

➤ Working with your new database

In many ways, a database is a kissing-cousin to a spreadsheet. Where a spreadsheet can make the presentation of numerical information easier (with a little text thrown in for giggles), a database can simplify the presentation of text-based information (with some numbers thrown in for laughs).

The ideal use for a database is for a big, fat catalog of related information that you need to sort (names and addresses, libraries of books or audio CDs, inventories) or pull snippets of information out of a little bit at a time (a few names and addresses; the information on a book; the name of the drummer on Carly Simon's "Boys in the Trees" CD).

Forms and Fields: Database Building Blocks

Spreadsheets, you may recall, have cells as their basic components. Those cells appear into rows and columns, and all the rows and columns make up a spreadsheet.

With a database, the basic element is the *field*, which is similar to a cell in a spreadsheet. A field is the place where you put *one* kind of information: a first name, a last name, or a street address.

An address database, such as the Works Address Book, might contain these fields plus more (phone numbers, maybe, birthdays, and anniversary dates) for each person.

One complete set of those fields is a *record*. For an address database, one record would include all of the information you have on one person; for a CD catalog, it would be one CD per record. You may have hundreds or even *thousands* of records in a database (depending on how many people you know or CDs you own). All together, all those records make up your database, literally a base, a foundation of raw information that you can manipulate to suit your needs.

You can do many things with information in a database. You can pull up a list of everyone you know who has a birthday in August. You can sort all of your CDs first by their release dates and then alphabetically by the artist. You can arrange your home library by the Library of Congress's cataloging system (or the Dewey Decimal System, if you prefer).

However, in order to have a database that will let you do all that keen sorting and selecting, you need to think about all the things you're going to want to do with your database *before* you even create it.

Before You Start

You need to think and plan before you start a new database. You need to think about all the information you want in each record and how you want to break down that information. Here's why.

If you create a database of all your friends and neighbors (so you can easily see who has a birthday or other special event coming up) and have the address handy to send a card, you've already defined three fields: Name, Address, and Birthday/Anniversary.

But wait. *Everybody* has a birthday. If somebody has an anniversary too, you'll only have space for one date. Better make that *four* fields: Name, Address, Birthday, *and* Anniversary/Other.

But wait. What if you want to find all of your out-of-town friends and family members with birthdays, a month or two in advance? You need time to shop for, and ship, a gift or card. You'll need to break the address field into component parts: street address; City,

State, ZIP code. That way, you can search for the out-of-towners by City or State. That takes you up to seven fields.

Better make it eight, since some of those folks live in apartments, or have other special address information (such as 2nd floor front). But wait, if you throw a bachelor or bachelorette party, you'll want to be able to sort folks out by gender. That's *another* field (so we're up to nine).

You could create a gender field, or include a title (Mr., Mrs., Miss, Ms.). However you do it, you want some way to tell that your seldom-seen second cousin, Chris, is a Christine, not Christopher, and she gets invited to the right prewedding bash.

Get the idea? The more delicately you break up the information you include in your database, the more power you'll have when you sort and sift through that big, fat, hairy pile of information later.

Before You Start, Part II

Naturally, before you begin the process of creating a database on your own, you should check out the Works TaskWizards already built-in to Works to see if there isn't one that will meet your needs. Why put in the time and energy if Works will create one for you automatically?

These are the database TaskWizards:

Accounts For accounts receivable or payable, or even your checking account.

Address Book It has its own chapter: Chapter 25.

Business Inventory Keep track of your capital investments and office supplies.

Customers or Clients Mail your customers your latest brochure or flyer, easily.

Employee Profile Keep track of who's doing what, where, and when you hired them.

Home Inventory Keep a record of all your worldly possessions for insurance purposes.

Phone List Be able to hand the baby sitter a printed list of names to contact in case of emergency.

Sales Contacts Who's in charge of acquiring the goods or services you offer?

Student & Membership Information Keep track of the students in your class or the members of your club.

Suppliers & Vendors Who sold you that gross of widgets two months ago?

You start a TaskWizard by selecting it from the list of TaskWizards on the Task Launcher, and clicking **OK**. Then follow the step-by-step instructions on-screen.

But you knew that, already.

Starting a Database

Instead of firing up Works and creating a database right away, sit down with a good, old-fashioned pencil and paper. Consider all of the information you want to include in your database. Write it down. Then think about it again. Is some of that information too big? Too vague? Can it be broken down into smaller chunks? Write the list over and include the finer divisions.

You may want to repeat the process once or twice (beyond that, you may just be splitting hairs). A good rule of thumb is to ask yourself if the new division provides a useful chunk of information. If it does, use it. If not, skip it. I mean, are you *really* going to search your database for folks who live on avenues, rather than streets or boulevards? Probably not.

It's best to do this first and think it through. There comes a point in the life of any database where it's a real pain in the hindquarters to go through it to add a new field to each and every record—especially once you get past 20–30 records. *Oi!* The tedium. If you overindulge at first, you can always delete unused fields—and that's *much* easier than typing in twenty or more *new* bits of information.

For a sample database, I'm going to create a catalog of my pathetically skimpy CD collection (I don't have a CD player except for the CD-ROM drive in my computer—isn't that sad?). That way, there won't be too much work, and nobody gets hurt, see? You can play along or create one of your own.

Creating a New Database

With your list of potential fields (not to be confused with Tootie or Strawberry Fields) ready, you can fire up your PC and Works.

When the Task Launcher appears, click on the **Works Tools** tab. Then click on the **Database** button. Works will create a new, blank, untitled database just for you.

The first thing you'll see is the Create Database dialog box, and it will ask you to define the fields you want in your database—that's a fancy way of saying "tell me what information you're going to store in this thing."

In the Field name box, type the name of the field you want to create first (for my CD database, I'm entering **Artist/Group**).

Enter a field name.

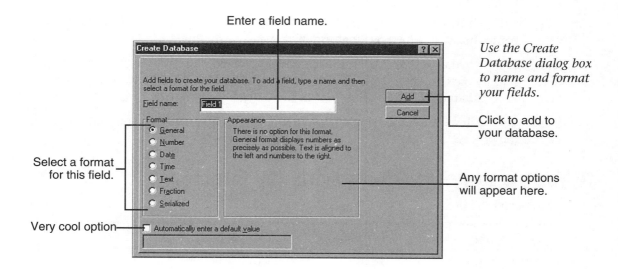

Use the Create Database dialog box to name and format your fields.

Click to add to your database.

Any format options will appear here.

Select a format for this field.

Very cool option

Next, select a format from the Format box. These options should look familiar to you; they're very similar to the ones used in the section on spreadsheets.

General Generic format that aligns text to the left and numbers to the right.

Number Gives you a variety of number formats to choose from (they appear in the Appearance box when you have options).

Date Gives you a variety of date-related format options.

Time Gives you a number of time-related format options.

Text Specifies that this field will contain nothing but text information (even numbers will be treated as text).

Fraction Tells Works that this field will contain fractions, nothing but fractions.

Serialized Numbers the chosen field from one to whatever in each record. The assigned number sticks to the field no matter how it gets moved around. That's handy if you need to keep a running count of clients, students, or whatevers, as you get them.

Once you select a format, you can select an Appearance option (if there are any).

If you're creating a database where a field will usually contain the same information (such as your local area code, city and state name, or ZIP code), you can make Works enter it automatically in the selected field.

While you're defining the field, click **Automatically enter a default value**. Then type the value (word, phrase, or whatever) that usually appears in that field in the text box.

Now, whenever you see that field in the database, it will contain whatever you entered here. You only have to enter different information for the few exceptions. What a time-saver! (Unfortunately, there's no use for it in my CD catalog. Oh, well.)

When you finish defining the field, click **Add** and that field is added to your database. Repeat the process until all your fields have been defined and entered.

If You're Playing Along with My Sample...

... these are the fields and their formats that I entered.

Field Name	Format	Appearance
Artist/Group	Text	(A blank here means no choice available)
Title	Text	
Label	Text	
ID #	Number	1234.56
Track 1	Text	

(I entered 13 more Track labels 2–14, all formatted as text—who needs to see all *that*?)

Producer	Text	
Year Released	General (because there's no date format that's *only* the year)	
Drummer	Text	
Bass	Text	
Lead Guitar	Text	
Rhythm Guitar	Text	
Piano	Text	
Horns	Text	

It's a very simple database. Others might want more information (for example, I only have one producer slot while most albums have two or more producers; there's no slot for the songwriters after each track; no track or total playing time; there's no space for guest musicians). My brother, the musician, would be *very* unhappy with this database design. For me, however, it should do nicely.

When Your Fields Have All Been Entered...

(That kinda sounds like the beginning of a country/western song—Garth Brooks, you sing it, I'll write it.)

When you've entered all the fields you need, click **Done**. Works will think about it for a moment and then present you with the blank database, all of your fields present and accounted for, ready for you to enter data. It looks a little something like the next figure.

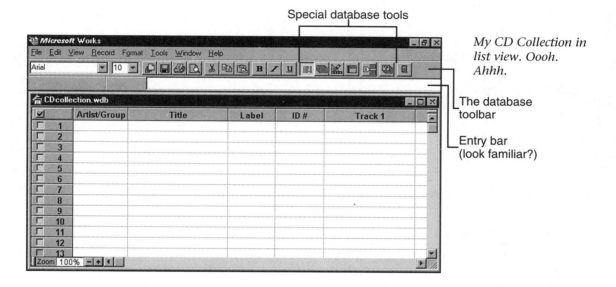

Special database tools

My CD Collection in list view. Oooh. Ahhh.

The database toolbar

Entry bar (look familiar?)

The first time you see your new database, Works presents it to you in *list view* (as shown here), which even looks a little like a spreadsheet. List view shows you all of your records at once, in a list, which can speed up the entering and editing of data.

Check This Out...

A Point of Personal Preference

Even though list view can speed up data entry, I prefer to work in *form view*. Form view shows your database one record at a time, which keeps me from getting lost and confused in the sheer number of records being displayed.

You can use form view to enter and edit information in any record in your database. We'll look at form, list, and two other views you can use in the next chapter.

The Database Tools

As long as we have this nice, blank, nonthreatening database form, let's take a look at the special database tools Works offers.

Déjà Vu: The Entry Bar

As you saw in the previous figure, there's an entry bar that looks remarkably like the one we used to enter and edit data and formulas in a spreadsheet. It *looks* the same because it *is* the same—and, in case you didn't know it, you can enter formulas in a database, too.

Since you've seen it and used it (skip to Chapter 12 for the scoop if you've been skipping around), I won't belabor the point.

The Toolbar Tools

You probably noticed in that previous figure that you have the usual assortment of buttons on the toolbar to work with. The first few are from our cast of regular buttons: Task Launcher, Save, Print, Print Preview, Cut, Copy, Paste, Bold, Italic, and Underline. Seen 'em, used 'em, know 'em, movin's on.

The table below shows you the new database tools, in order of appearance.

Database Toolbar Icons

Icon	What it does
List View	Displays your database contents (all records) in a big, fat list (covered in the next chapter).
Form View	Displays your database so you see only *one* record at a time. You can use this view to enter and edit data in your fields.
Form Design View	Lets you format all of your records with fonts, graphic elements, and other pretty stuff. You can also format individual fields and arrange them on the form (more about this in Chapters 19 and 20).
Report View	Where you can search, sort, and otherwise juggle the information in your database to look at only the information you need. You can also print out a spiffy report based on that information. (Chapter 21 has the details.)

Icon	What it does
Insert Record	For the inevitable moment when you realize you forgot to enter a very important record in your database, you can slip one in (read the next chapter).
Filters	Calls up powerful searching tools to let you filter out unwanted records, leaving you with the database records that meet your search criteria. (Confused? See Chapter 21 for clarification.)

The last button on the toolbar is the ubiquitous Address Book button; you'll click that one 'til it hurts in Chapter 25.

Save It or Lose It

So, we've created a blank database and entered some formatted fields to hold our information. Now we should save the blank form.

You remember how to save, right? Select **Save** from the **File** menu. Enter a name to the file (I'm calling mine **CDCOLLECTION** so there will be no mistaking this for a mailing list). Navigate to where you want Works to store the file (to a particular folder on your hard drive or to a floppy disk). Click **Save** and Works writes a copy of the file to the selected location. Now you can't lose this file unless something really oogy happens to your disk or hard drive.

The Least You Need to Know

In the next chapter, you'll enter some data into your database and then play around with it. For now, hang onto a few kernels of truth (and advice masquerading as truth).

➤ Before you go through all this thinking and entering, check to see if Works has a TaskWizard that will create a database that meets your needs. If it does, use it.

➤ You need to plan your database in advance to cut down on adding a new bit of information to hundreds of records later.

➤ To create a new database, click on the **Database** button on the Works Tools tab of the Task Launcher.

➤ Define your database's fields before you even enter any information.

➤ When you first see your database in the flesh, so to speak, it's in list view, where you get to see your whole database, with each record filling one row. (It looks kind of like a spreadsheet in this view.) You can enter and edit information in fields.

➤ As always: save early, save often. These words (followed regularly) soothe the soul and prevent data-related heartburn.

Chapter 19

Getting to Second Base: Entering Data and Printing

In This Chapter

➤ Entering database data

➤ Using form view

➤ Editing saved data

➤ Adding and deleting fields and records

So, now we have this empty database just crying to be filled up with my small, yet terribly bizarre—I mean eclectic, yeah, that's the ticket, *eclectic*—audio CD collection. This chapter shows you how to enter data into your database.

Entering Data

Entering data into a database is surprisingly simple, and awfully familiar: it's just like entering data into a spreadsheet. It's as easy as 1-2-3:

1. Click on the field in which you want to enter data. That selects it.

2. Type the data.

3. Press enter, or hit the **Tab** key.

Pressing **Enter** enters the data into the field but keeps that same field selected. Pressing the **Tab** key also enters the data into the field, but moves the selection to the next field. Tabbing can save you a little time. (You can change how Works moves the selection, if you care to. There are details in Chapter 28.)

This works for entering any sort of data into a field; however (as with the spreadsheet), Works guesses about the kind of data you're entering, or goes by the format you applied when creating the field. If you want to cut to the chase, you can tell Works what kind of data you're entering as you enter it.

Telling Works That You're Entering Text

You let Works know you're entering text by typing a double quotation mark (") followed by the text you're entering without any space between them (**Spin Doctors** would be the first entry in my database).

You can also put a double quotation mark before numerical information you're entering that won't require Works to perform any special math-type handling.

The **Year Released** field, in the sample database, is a good candidate. I don't plan to do any math with those years, so I could enter them as text ("**1994**, for example) to let Works know not to worry about them as numbers.

What About Entering Numbers?

If there are some numbers you want Works to treat as numbers, just enter them with no special character in front. Works will know it's a number and occasionally check to make sure you don't want any math done with it.

Check This Out...

Why Do Math in a Database?

Oh, for any number of reasons, really. Say you're a baseball card collector, and you want to keep track of how many you actually have, their value, condition, and such. You could have Works count your entries and put the result in a total box somewhere. That way, as you add or delete cards from the list, the number will change. I'll tell you how when we get to Chapter 21.

Entering Formulas

Entering a formula in a database follows the same steps as entering one in a spreadsheet. A formula starts with an equal sign, then there's a command, and then there's a range of fields for it to work the math upon:

=SUM(*Reference1:Reference10*)

In a spreadsheet, you identify a cell by its position in the spreadsheet (the cell in column A, row 5 is **A5**). A range is the first and last cell separated by a colon (A1:A200), or nonsequential cells separated by commas (A1,A5,B10,Z23).

In a database, you identify entries by their field name and record number. The third entry in my Title field would be called **Title3**. The first five entries in the Title field, expressed as a range, appears as **(Title1:Title5)**. A nonsequential range would look like this:

(Title2,Artist/Group5,Track 1515)

Other than the way you identify entries and ranges of entries in database formulas, all of the other formula information (back in Chapter 14) applies, except Works' database doesn't give you access to that handy pair of tools: AutoSum and EasyCalc.

Editing Data

You edit the data in a database much the same way you edit data in a spreadsheet. First, you need to click on the field you want to edit; that selects it. Next, click on the information in the entry bar, to place the cursor there (or click-drag or double-click to select the whole entry). Edit at will.

Works also lets you use the spelling checker in the database (select **Spelling** from the **Tools** menu), and you won't have to edit each typo individually. The details on the spelling checker are spelled out back in Chapter 8, if you missed them.

The Four Faces of Your Database

In the last chapter, we saw the CD database in list view, which looks a bit like a spreadsheet. List view, as you may recall, allows you to enter and edit data in a field, insert and delete a record or field, format a field, resize a field, and perform a few other tasks that are handy when creating a database.

There are other ways to view your data, and each lets you do different things to and with that data. Keep reading.

Form View

The CD database in form view.

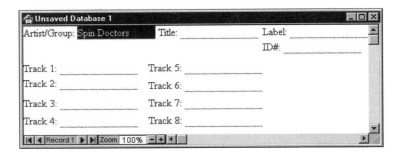

Form view, as you can see in the preceding figure, lets you look at your database one record at a time. Each field is on a line by itself, and the fields all line up flush with the left margin. In form view, you can enter data into fields (as I'm doing in the figure), edit existing data, and insert or delete records (not fields).

I prefer entering data in form view, because I like working with one record at a time. That's a personal preference thing. It can get complicated, though, if I haven't done my preplanning. Having to switch between list and form views to fiddle with fields can be a pain, but that just encourages me to plan better.

Form Design View

The CD database in form design view—it looks like form view, with boxes.

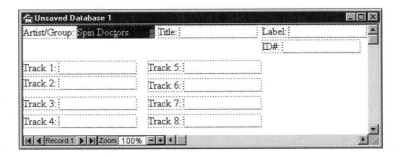

Form design view looks exactly the same as form view, but each field and field name is in a box. In the preceding figure, you can see what I mean.

Design view lets you move stuff around, change fonts, add and delete fields, add graphic elements (pictures, boxes, borders, shading) and otherwise beautify the design of your records. You can see that I've used form design view to move the fields into an arrangement that looks better and conserves space.

We'll work the heck out of design view in Chapter 20. Stay tuned.

Renaming Fields

When I was entering the fields for this database, I must have blinked when I was typing **Track 13** because it turns out I entered **Thrack 13**. *Sheesh.*

There are two ways to fix gaffes like this. First, in list view:

1. Select the offending field.

2. Select **Field** from the **Format** menu. That calls up the Format Field dialog box, which is exactly the same as the Create Database dialog box we used to create all of these fields in the last chapter.

3. Edit the field name (you may also change any format and appearance options, too).

4. Click **OK**.

Thrack becomes **Track** in nothing flack—*flat.*

In form design view, you click on the offending field name. That will put its name up in the entry bar (shown here). Edit as you would any field entry. Press **Enter** when you're done.

Editing a field name in the entry bar.

Resizing Fields and Records

If you haven't noticed, there's no standard length for song titles (nor should there be—how anal do you think I am?).

Some song titles are really long (like Spin Doctors' "How Could You Want Him (When You Know You Could Have Me?"), while others are really short (like Spin Doctors' "Two Princes"). Chances are, you'll wind up with both short and long entries in the same field of different records in your database.

You have two options for getting field entries to fit, without wasting a lot of valuable space (and paper, when printing them out). You can widen the field or make the record taller (to accommodate a second line of type).

Check This Out...

Patience Is a Virtue

When I'm working with a database (or a spreadsheet for that matter), I tend not to worry about information fitting in a field or cell until after I've entered it all.

If you change field width or record height on an as-needed basis, while entering data, you could wind up changing the same thing several times. Bummer. Instead, save resizing for last. Then you can adjust everything at once and be done with it. Just a thought.

Wider Fields

Depending on the data you're working with, most of the time you're going to need more room than the skimpy 10-character width Works starts you off with anyhow. To make a field wider, and show a complete, long entry, click on the field to select it (this should be in list view, by the way).

Caution: widening the load.

Enter a size here.

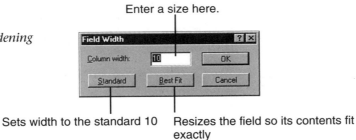

Sets width to the standard 10   Resizes the field so its contents fit exactly

Then select **Field Width** from the **Format** menu. That will call up the Field Width dialog box. You can type a specific size in the text box, if you know what it should be (I never know). You can also just click **Best Fit,** which resizes the field to accommodate the data (this is what I do most).

All of your records will have the selected field resized to the new width.

I wouldn't resize a field in 50+ records to accommodate one or two longer entries. Widen your fields to accommodate *most* of the records. The remaining, cranky records might look better if you make the field taller, so the extra information can wrap to a second line.

Taller Records

If the field is the only one with a longish entry, you may do better to only increase the height of the odd-sized record, and leave the field width alone.

By making the one record taller, you can fit in a longer bit of data, without adding unneeded space to the rest of your records. Here's how to do it (this should also be in list view):

1. Select the record by clicking on the record number at the beginning of the row. That will highlight the whole row.

2. Select **Record Height** from the **Format** menu. The Format Record Height dialog box appears. It looks exactly the same as the Field Width dialog box and works the same, too.

Going for a record height.

3. Enter the new height number (I usually just double whatever's already there—in the preceding figure, I'd enter 24).

4. Click **OK**.

    That makes the record taller, but in order to get the entry to wrap around and use the extra height, you have to turn on the text wrap option, and that's a couple more steps.

5. With the row still highlighted, select **Alignment** from the **Format** menu. It brings up Works' Format dialog box with the Alignment tab in front. (That you've seen, what? Three times now? Four? You'll also see it again in Chapter 20.)

6. Click the **Wrap text** check box.

7. Click **OK**.

The entry in your newly heightened row will wrap around onto a second line. If there still isn't enough room for the entry, repeat steps 1–4.

Two, Two, Two Dialog Boxes in One

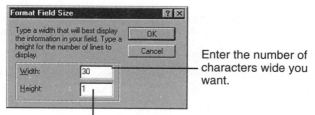

Enter the number of characters wide you want.

Doing double duty with the Format Field Size dialog box in form design view.

Enter the number of lines tall you want.

You can take care of both field width and height in one dialog box if you make these adjustments in form design view. While in form design view, select the troublesome field. Then select **Field Size** from the **Format** menu. That will give you the dialog box in the preceding figure.

Enter the number of characters wide you want the field to be in the text box labeled Width. Then (and this is a little different from the earlier method), enter the number of lines tall you want the record to be, in the text box labeled Height. Click **OK**.

Works will reconfigure the height and width to your specifications.

The Lazy Eyeball Method

We talked about a similar method back in Chapter 15, with spreadsheet rows and columns. You can resize a field, or record, manually by click-dragging on the dividing line between record numbers or field labels.

When your cursor touches the dividing line, it changes into one with two arrows and the word **ADJUST** in between. Click-and-drag the dividing line to resize the field or record to your liking. And there's no messy dialog box to wash up after.

Adding and Deleting Fields

You may have wondered, back in the last chapter, when you were looking at the list of fields for the CD database, where the heck the music category (you know, Pop, Rock, Easy Listening) field was. Truth is, I meant to leave it out. Really. I did. Now I can show you how to insert a field in your database, should you accidentally forget one.

Add A Field Here...

To add a field to all of the records in your database, first you need to be in list view—click on the **List View** button on the toolbar, if you aren't in list view already.

Next, select a field next to where you want to insert the new field (just click on the field label at the top of the field column).

While the field is highlighted, select **Insert Field** from the **Record** menu. A submenu will pop up. If you want the new field inserted to the left of the selected field, select **1 Before**. If you want it to the right of the selected field, select **2 After** from the pop-up menu.

Whichever you select, Works will present you with an Insert Field dialog box that is an exact copy (except for the name) of the Create Database dialog box we used to create our fields in the last chapter.

Where shall I insert this? Hmmm...

You can use it to enter a name for the field, select a format (and Appearance options, if any). When you finish, click **Add**. Works will add the new field to your database. Now all you have to do is backtrack and fill in the appropriate information in all of the existing records.

To be honest, I not only forgot a category field, but I also was lazy when creating Track # fields: I should have created a lot more than 14. The soundtrack of *Gypsy* has 17 tracks, and the one for *The Adventures of Priscilla: Queen of the Desert* has over 20.

Did I mention my music collection is eclectic?

Delete This Field

Sometimes, I get carried away in the planning stages of a database and create fields that really serve no useful purpose. You can delete unwanted fields easily enough, and nobody will be the wiser.

To delete a field, select it by clicking on its label at the top of its column. Then select **Delete Field** from the **Record** menu.

Click here to select field.

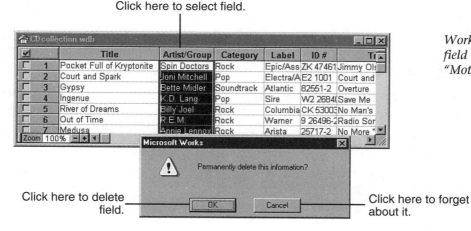

Works won't delete a field without asking "Mother, may I?"

Click here to delete field.

Click here to forget about it.

Adding and Deleting Whole Records

Once you've entered a pile of records into your database, you may discover that you skipped one somewhere in the middle of the pile, you need to add one, or you got tired of a CD and traded it in at your local swap meet. You can delete a record easily, too.

Add One

To add a record, start in list view; then select the record below where you want the new one inserted. Select **Insert Record** from the **Record** menu. *Poof!* There's a new, blank record above the one you selected.

Delete One

To delete a record, you also start in list view. Click on the record number to select the whole record. Then select **Delete Record** from the **Record** menu. *Poof!* The selected record is gone, vanished, no more. It is an ex-record.

Oops Alert! Works doesn't ask your permission when it deletes a record. If you accidentally delete a record, *immediately* select **Undo** from the **Edit** menu, and that should bring the deleted record back.

Moving Stuff Around

In list view, you can juggle the position of your fields and whole records by click-dragging them to their new positions.

If you want to move a field, select it by clicking on its field label at the top of the column. Then click-drag it to its new position (a thick line will appear where Works will place it). Release your mouse button.

It works the same for whole records, except you select the record; just click on the record number at the beginning of the row. Then drag-and-drop as previously described.

Printing Out a Database

The concerns that face you when printing out your database are much the same as those we discussed for spreadsheets, back in Chapter 16.

Printing from List View

Printing from list view, your database can be a lot wider than it is tall, so you may want to change your page orientation to *landscape* and maybe print it on legal-sized paper. (Chapter 11 tells you how to use the Page Setup item on the File menu to do both.)

Additionally, you may want to have Works print your record numbers and field labels, so it's easier to figure out which record is which. You can also have Works print the gridlines that divide fields and records, so it's easier for your eye to follow across rows and down columns. You do both with the Other Options tab of the Page Setup dialog box.

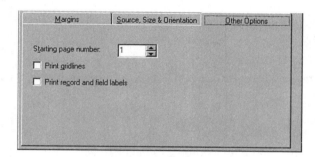

Pick an option, either option—or both.

To use either option (or both), click in the check box in front of the option you want to use. When you've made whatever Page Setup adjustments you want, select **Print** from the **File** menu to send your list view to your printer.

Printing my CD database (even with only nine records entered) in list view, took four pieces of paper—that's how wide it had become.

Printing in Form View

When you print from form view, each record in the database will print on a single page. You probably won't need to make any Page Setup adjustments (unless you changed them in the previous section) because each record usually fits nicely on an 8.5-by-11-inch page in portrait orientation.

If you aren't sure if one record fits on one page, you can use the **Print Preview** button on the toolbar to check (it's the one with the page and a magnifying glass on it). Since, at the moment, my database has nine records, it will take nine pages to print it out from form view.

In case you were wondering, printing from form design view works much the same as printing while in form view, except form design view prints only one page: a blank form with field headings. No actual data from your database prints. This is a paper-saving tip if all you want to do is test-print your form's design to see how it looks.

Other Printing Stuff

Printing a report involves some different concerns, but you don't know what a report is yet, so don't sweat it. It's all coming up in Chapter 21.

The Least You Need to Know

We looked at a lot of database tinkering in this section: entering and editing your data; adding, deleting, resizing, and moving both fields and records; printing. That's a lot.

You probably noticed that many tasks were the same as the related operations in spreadsheets. You may want to read the relevant chapters in the spreadsheet section (indicated in this chapter), if you haven't read them. The big difference is how the different database views affect what you can and cannot do to your data.

➤ **List view** gives you the most entering, editing, moving, and field formatting options.

➤ **Form view** gives you fewer editing options but lets you focus your attention on one record at a time.

➤ **Form design view** lets you arrange and beautify your fields and will be covered in detail in the next chapter.

➤ **Report view** is where you sort and sift through your database looking for the one or two records you need from the pile. It's covered in Chapter 21.

Chapter 20

Prettying Up a Database

In This Chapter

➤ Labeling data

➤ Fooling with fonts

➤ Gridlock

➤ Sorting for sense

All together now, *"I feel pretty, oh, so pretty..."*

I'm sorry. As I write this, we're having our 15th straight day of temperatures in the 90s (with a heat index of 105 degrees, and more). Every fan I own is pointed at me. I think my brains have fried, or melted. I'm *almost* beginning to wish for the second ice age Thornton Wilder wrote about in *The Skin of Our Teeth*: "Here it is the middle of July and the coldest day of the year—the dogs are sticking to the sidewalks!" That's starting to sound pleasant. I must be insane, so you'll excuse me if I babble.

At this stage of the game, you see an almost well-developed database of audio CDs, but it isn't quite finished. I've entered the data, yes, but haven't prettied it up. Let's do it.

(And, in case you're wondering, you already know how to do most of this. The procedures remain pretty much the same as they have for gussying up word processing documents and spreadsheets. There are very few surprises here.)

Design That Form!

Nearly everything in this chapter is in *form design view*. On the one occasion where you need to switch, I'll point it out.

If you've forgotten, form design view is the database display that lets you do everything from adding new fields and labels, to changing fonts, and even adding clip art. Click on the **Form Design View** button (the button with the drafting tools) on the toolbar to get into form design view.

When we last saw Works' form design view, it looked something like the following figure. I was using it to click-drag the various fields into a more efficient arrangement than just having them all flush with the left margin.

Yoo-hoo! Remember me? Form design view?

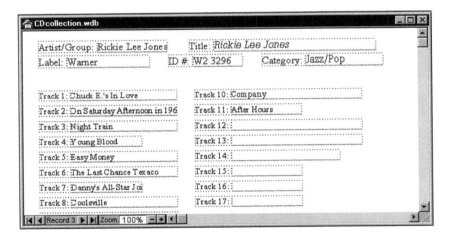

The dotted lines around each field show its width and height. To move a field, drag it to its new position on the page. In the figure, you can see I've grouped all of the production credits together in a nice little tableau.

I also grouped all the song titles (Tracks 1–17) into two columns in the center of the form, and the Artist/Group, Title, Label, ID #, and Category fields together at the top of the page. You, as always, place your fields wherever you like. I won't tell.

To Grid, or Not to Grid, That Is the Question

Having trouble with fields sticking to your form? I hate it when that happens—that, and peanut butter on the roof of my mouth. What's going on is Works' Snap To Grid feature (on the Format menu) is at work—there's a check mark in front of it on the menu.

When turned on, Snap To Grid activates an invisible grid, like graph paper, behind the form. When you drag something around, it automatically jumps to the nearest grid position when you release the mouse button.

Snap To Grid makes it easier to line fields up evenly, that is, unless you don't want them even. Then it's a pain in the tuchas. To turn **Snap To Grid** off, select it from the **Format** menu. The check mark will go away, and your fields won't jump around uncontrollably. (I wonder if it works on cats? Hmm.)

If you want to move several fields around at once, you have two selecting options.

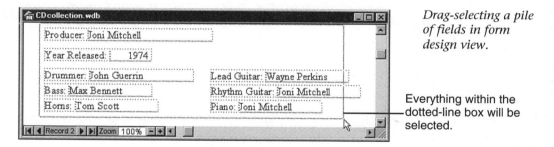

Drag-selecting a pile of fields in form design view.

Everything within the dotted-line box will be selected.

For fields that are together in one place, you can drag over them to select them all. Start at the top left corner, and drag down to the bottom right. A dotted-line box will trail out from the cursor as you drag it, and everything enclosed in the box will be selected when you release the mouse button. You can see it happening in the preceding figure.

If you want to select a few fields here-and-there from a group, press and hold the **CTRL** key while you click fields. That will let you select a field here, a field there, and none of the surrounding fields will come along for the ride.

Once you've arranged your fields to your liking (you can see my arrangement in the next figure), you might want to add some labels to your form (other than the field labels, I mean), and tinker with fonts. Both are coming right up.

How I've arranged things.

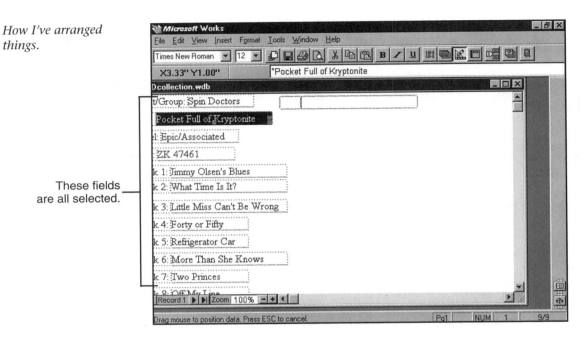

These fields are all selected.

Labeling Your Data

If, like me, you've decided to group relevant bits of information together in chunks on your database form, it might be handy to label those chunks for easy identification.

I've lumped stuff into three groups: information about the CD in general, a list of the songs, and a rundown of the production team. It might help a stranger reading the database if you slap an appropriate label near each chunk of information. There's two ways to do it.

Using the Insert Label Command

To insert a label, you can select **Label** from the **Insert** menu, which will give you this handy, little dialog box.

Inserting a label with a dialog box.

Type your new label here.

Click here to insert it.

You type the label you want in the text box (as indicated in the figure); then click **Insert**. Works then places the label in your form, already selected for you, and you drag-and-drop it to where you want it.

Just Type It—Entering the Label Manually

If a dialog box is too much to handle (even a teeny-tiny one), there is another way to create a label: simply click the form where you want the label to go. That places the insertion point cursor (just like you used to edit database, spreadsheet, and word processor files) on the form.

Type your label (but don't include a colon—I'll explain why in a second). Press **Enter** and your label appears.

You can also insert a whole new field in your database this same way. Follow the preceding directions, but end the label with a colon (:) and Works will turn the label into a new database field. That's why you don't want to include a colon in your labels with this method.

If you want to use a colon in your label, use the **Label** command in the **Insert** menu instead.

My Label Choices

At the top of the form, I added the label **The Compact Disc**. Above the listing of tracks, I used **The Songs** as my label. Finally, above the producer and musician listings, I added **The Team**.

Maybe not the most inventive labels I could have come up with, but they're meaningful, if a little dull.

After adding the labels, you can fiddle with their fonts and sizes to make them stand out from the rest of the information on the form. Here's how…

Stylize Your Fonts

The process of changing fonts in your database is exactly the same as all the other times we've done it. First, I'll refresh your memory with a little list. Then it's "Show and Tell" time; I'll show you what I did, and tell you why I did it.

Font Changing Recap (It Has Been a While)

1. Select the item(s) you want to change.

2. Choose a new font from the font drop-down list on the toolbar, or use the **Font and Style** command on the **Format** menu.

3. Choose a new font size from the font size drop-down list on the toolbar (or continue with the Font and Style dialog box).

4. Click one or more font style buttons (bold, italic, or underline) on the toolbar (or carry on using the Font and Style dialog box; and remember to click **OK** when you're done with it).

5. Repeat the process as needed to change all the fonts you care to change.

The main thing to keep in mind while changing fonts in form design view is that you can use the selection tricks, mentioned earlier, to select several fields or labels at once. That will help cut down on the amount of time it takes to deck out your database in new fonts.

My Font Choices

Now, don't go getting all jealous. I'm an admitted font junkie, so I probably have *wayyyy* more fonts than you. Besides, bitterness ages the face. Ask Leona Helmsley.

For my font choices (you can see them in the figure at the end of the section on moving fields around), I picked a bold font for the field headings (Artist/Group and such). I used a font called Tekton because it's stylish, but simple (much like me). It looks like the printing architects use to write on blue prints and drawings.

I used the same font, in a larger size, for the labels used in the "Labeling Your Data" section. For the field entries, I chose a nice, simple serif font: Boton. I italicized it for CD titles. The combination of bold headings and labels, with simpler entries, I think, makes it easier to scan the database for information.

The results look good (judge for yourself, in the next figure), but I think a little more tinkering may be in order.

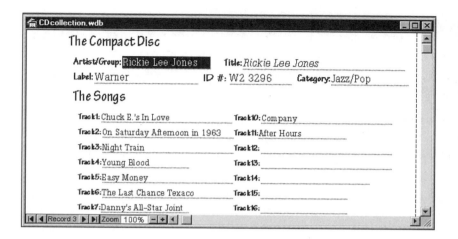

The not-quite-finished product.

Alignment Options

Sometimes, information in a database can pile up and become difficult to read, especially when you group it into columns as I've done with the fields in my CD database. One way to make things a little easier to read is to fool around with the alignment options.

First, select the field(s) you want to realign. Next, select **Alignment** from the **Format** menu. The Format dialog box appears. (You used a similar dialog box while aligning cells in a spreadsheet, back in Chapter 16.)

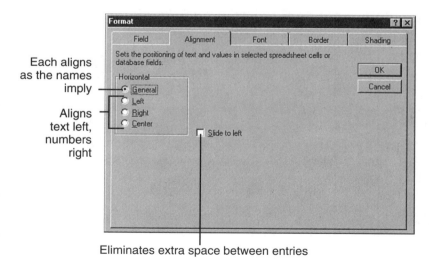

Each aligns as the names imply

Aligns text left, numbers right

Eliminates extra space between entries

Changing your alignment—you can even slide left.

The horizontal alignment options are the same as we saw when aligning cells in a spread-sheet. General is a multipurpose alignment that sends text to the left side of the field, and numbers to the right. Left, Right, and Center do pretty much what you'd expect them to.

The coolest option on the page is the Slide to left check box. (It won't help my CD data-base, but it's still very cool.)

When you check **Slide to left**, Works eliminates any extra spaces between the selected fields. For example, if you're creating an address database for cranking out personalized junk mail (as we will in Chapter 24), you would use Slide to left for your City and State fields.

Normally, a City will take up the full width of a field, whether the state name fills it or not. Entries wind up looking like this, when printed:

> Philadelphia PA
>
> Fresno   CA

However, if you select the **Slide to left** option, Works will eliminate the unused space, so the same entries will look like this (regardless of the assigned size of the field):

> Philadelphia PA
>
> Fresno CA

The Slide to left option only works when you're printing from form view; it has no effect on either list or form design view.

You can experiment with different alignments for different fields in your database form and see if they make it easier to pick out the information. If not, the **Undo** command in the **Edit** menu will reset the alignment to what it was just before you changed it.

Boxes, Color, and Shading

Still caught up in the endless quest to draw attention to the important information in my database, I decided to add some boxes, color, and shading to certain elements.

Insert Rectangle

I thought a box around all of the **Track #** fields would make them stand out a little more. To insert a rectangle:

1. Select **Rectangle** from the **Insert** menu. Works drops a small rectangle into your form.

2. Click-drag the rectangle's handles (little boxes in the center of each side, and in each corner; they're labeled in the next figure) to grow or shrink it to the proper size.

3. Drag the rectangle and place it where you want it on the form (in this example, place it so it surrounds the **Track #** fields).

    With the rectangle selected, you can use the Color and Shading options, coming up, to change the rectangle's color and fill it with a pattern. (I chose not too; it made the song titles too hard to read.)

4. When the rectangle is positioned where you want it, click somewhere else on the form (not on the rectangle) and Works will fix its position there.

Inserting a rectangle—watch out for sharp corners

Now the focus of the form is the song titles. The eye gets drawn by the box, and you pay attention to what it contains. That may or may not be a good thing, depending on what you put a rectangle around.

I think to offset the effect of the rectangle, we need to punch up the labels.

Bordering and Shading Labels

One of the more eye-catching treatments you can give to important information is to put it on a colored background with white (or light) lettering. It really stands out on the printed page. (Actually, this will work for field entries and file names, too.)

First, select an important something. I'm going to use the labels added in the "Labeling Your Data" section. Next, select **Border** from the **Format** menu. That will call up the Format dialog box. (Notice that your border options are limited in the database. You only have one choice, an outline-style box.)

The database version of the Border Format dialog box.

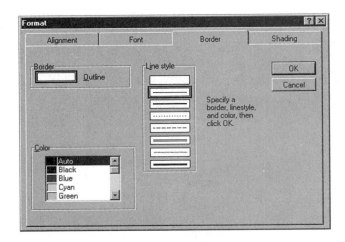

Because I intend to fill the border with black, I selected a plain, thin, solid line style for the border (as shown in the figure). You could also select no border and let the shading define the edges. For other uses, you may want to select a different line style.

Next, click on the **Shading** tab to call up the shading options. These are the same options you've been seeing and using all along, so there are no new things here.

If you look at the figure closely, you'll see that I chose solid shading and made both the foreground and background colors black (which actually makes all of the shading options, except None, solid black).

246

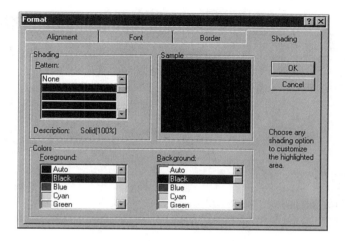

Our box is being made in the shading... .

Finally, click on the **Font** tab to see the Font options. Here, I left the font, size, and style options as I had them, and selected **White** from the drop-down Color list for the font color.

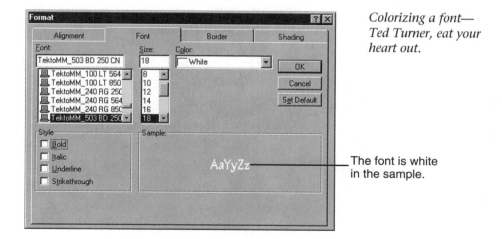

Colorizing a font—Ted Turner, eat your heart out.

The font is white in the sample.

After all that, simply click **OK**. Works will take and apply the box, shading, and font color options to the three selected labels. Here's the finished product—very eye-catching, I think.

The finished label.

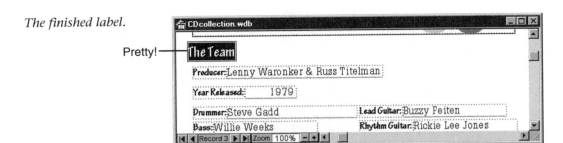

Pretty!

Adding Some Art

At a glance, the database form looked a little too serious to me. Too work-like. I decided to add a little whimsy, by adding ClipArt from Works' built-in collection.

To add ClipArt, select **ClipArt** from the **Insert** menu. The ClipArt Gallery appears. It's the same one we saw back in Chapter 11 (and we'll see again in Chapter 22).

The ClipArt Gallery—where's the wine and cheese?

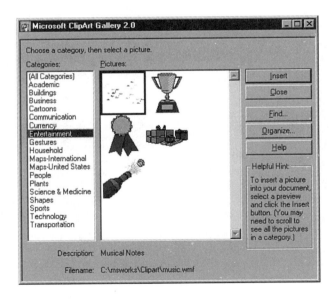

Select the ClipArt you want to use from the Gallery, by clicking on it (I chose the Musical Notes clip). Then click **Insert**. Works places a copy of the selected art in your form.

From here on out, it's much like placing the rectangle earlier:

➤ Drag its handles to resize the ClipArt to the size you need. (I made mine the same size as the rectangle around the song list.) Be careful when making the clip much wider, or taller; you may distort the picture.

➤ Drag the clip to where you want it (I put mine inside the rectangle around the song list).

➤ If you're placing the ClipArt in an area that has text, or something else that shouldn't be hidden behind the artwork, select **Send To Back** from the **Format** menu. That places the ClipArt behind everything else on the page, so everything can still be seen.

➤ Finally, click somewhere else on the form (not on the ClipArt) to place it.

Voilà! You not only have an informative database, it's artistically inclined, too.

The Last (Re)Sort

The final touch I added to the CD database was to have Works put it in some kind of order. When I grabbed the CDs off my desk to enter them, I grabbed them randomly and entered them higgeldy-piggledy, too.

To have the database make a little more sense, I sorted it in two steps. First, I had Works sort it so all the CDs were listed from oldest to newest (by Release Year), and then alphabetically (by Artist/Group).

First, you need to switch to list or form view. Next, select **Sort Records** from the **Record** menu. You see the Sort Records dialog box.

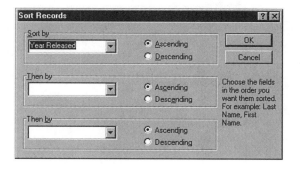

Sorting your records—and you don't need to know the alphabet.

You can do up to a three-level sort, if you care to. First select a field to sort by from the Sort by drop-down list (it already has all of your field names on it). I chose **Year Released**. Then click on a sort order, either Ascending (low to high) or Descending (high to low).

Next, select a second field to sort by from the Then by drop-down list, and another sort order. I chose **Artist/Group** here. Finally, you can repeat the process a third time in the other Then by drop-down list. I didn't, but you certainly can.

When you've made your choices, click **OK**. Works will sort your database by the first sorting method (in this example, from oldest to newest by release date). Then it will take the new arrangement (where two or more records meet the first sorting criteria—have the same release date) and sort those duplicates according to the second criteria (Artist/Group). Finally, it will sort them by the third.

In my CD database, records were arranged by year first. Then, any CDs that came out in the same year were put in alphabetical order by the Artist/Group field.

If I had chosen a third sorting option, it would have been title. Then Works would have taken any records of the same Artist/Group, released in the same year, and sorted them alphabetically by Title.

And it would have done it all in a fraction of a second. Pretty amazing.

Drumroll, Please! The Finished Product

The final product, seen in Page Preview from form view.

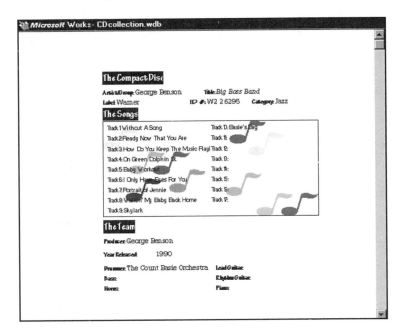

So, to summarize:

You started with a bland database. Using form design view, you juggled fields around to make them more organized and take up less space on the page.

You added labels to help readers identify the new arrangement of information on the page.

Then you changed the fonts; added a rectangle; played with the labels' border, shading, and font color options; and added ClipArt.

Finally, you sorted the database (in form or list view) into an order that makes sense (by year, and then by Artist/Group). All in all, a good day's work.

You now have an attractive database. But what if you just want to find, say, all the CDs that feature Steve Gadd as drummer? For that, you need to generate a *report*. You'll do that in the next chapter. In the meantime... .

The Least You Need to Know

You performed most of the beautification to your database in *form design view* (except for sorting—that was in *form view*). Since most of the tools we used to change fonts, and add boxes, shading, and color have been consistently the same throughout Works, here's a summary of the new things:

➤ You can drag-select consecutive fields in form design view, and select a bunch at once.

➤ You can also select nonconsecutive fields: press and hold the **CTRL** key while you click, and everything you click will be selected (or deselected, if it was selected already).

➤ You can insert a label in a database form by either using the **Label** command in the **Insert** menu or just by clicking on the form to place the insertion point and type the label.

➤ You don't have as many border options in the database as you do in Works' spreadsheet.

➤ You can sort a database by as many as three different fields, using the **Sort Records** command on the **Record** menu.

Now, go take five. You must be exhausted. Me, I'm just crazy with the heat.

Chapter 21

Reports: Data, Reporting for Duty

In This Chapter

➤ Why bother with reports?

➤ Filtering data

➤ Using the ReportCreator

In the last chapter, you put the finishing touches on a database, making it as pretty as possible and sorting it into a logical order. That should be enough for any intelligent being, right?

Well, no. Not necessarily.

It depends on a couple of things: the intelligent being in question, the kind of information he wants to pull out of a database, and (most important) the database itself.

Pulling particular information out of a database can be accomplished with a *filter* (explained in a bit), and then the information you've retrieved can be prettied up and presented as a *report*.

So, Why Create a Report?

Here's the scenario: you're a music maven. If it's been recorded, you own a copy. You've worked long and hard putting together a database catalog of your music collection.

Now and then, to celebrate important musical events (Mahler's birthday, the anniversary of the first performance of Gershwin's *Rhapsody in Blue*, Snoop Doggy Dog's graduation from obedience school—stuff like that), you like to throw shindigs featuring the music being celebrated.

With a couple of hours to kill, you could go through the *thousands* of records you have in your database by hand, looking for just the right background music.

On the other hand, even with only ten minutes 'til party time, you can do the same research by filtering your database or generating a report—and have your CD player stocked before the first guests arrived.

Which would *you* rather do?

I thought so.

Filtering Data

A database *filter*, like a pool filter, is a tool used to remove extraneous floaty things (information in a database), so you're left with a clear pool of information.

With a database filter, you tell Works to look for any and all information that meets certain criteria. These criteria are expressed in logical expressions, like the IF/THEN statements you probably learned in high school Geometry class. Essentially, you tell Works IF a record contains a certain kind of information, THEN do this (show it to me, don't show it to me).

You can strain the information in your database through as many as five filters at once, so you can be pretty picky about the records you cull from your database.

Easy Filter

To start filtering your data (I'm going to be sifting through my skimpy CD database, but you can use whatever database you have handy), click the **Filters button** on the toolbar (it's the one with three pages, and a question mark on it).

The first thing Works does is ask you to *Name That Filter*—the rollicking game show where contestants compete for cash and fabulous prizes... sorry. Too much daytime television.

You see the teeny-tiny Filter Name dialog box. Just enter an appropriate name (I'm calling all these filters CDFilter1, 2, and so on) and click **OK**.

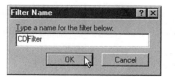

What are you gonna call this filter, sunshine?

Works then presents you with the Filter dialog box (shown here) with the Easy Filter options displayed. Easy Filter allows you to construct a filter from built-in arguments (those logic statements) and data you supply. Check out the figure.

Select a field to filter.

Choose a comparison statement (argument).

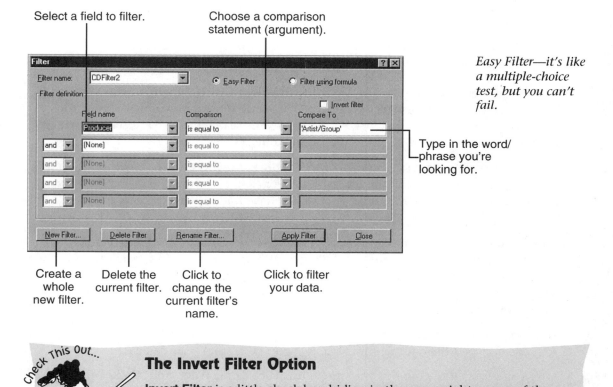

Easy Filter—it's like a multiple-choice test, but you can't fail.

Type in the word/ phrase you're looking for.

Create a whole new filter.

Delete the current filter.

Click to change the current filter's name.

Click to filter your data.

The Invert Filter Option

Invert Filter is a little check box hiding in the upper right corner of the Filter definition box. If you click on it, it inverts, or reverses, your search results.

For example, if you set the filter to find every record that lists John Guerrin as Bass player and then click **Invert Filter**, the filter will select every record that *doesn't* list John Guerrin as Bass player. It turns Works into a three-year-old that does the exact *opposite* of what he's told.

To create a filter:

1. Select a field to filter from the Field name drop-down menu. It contains all the fields in your database. If you're looking, say, for a particular bass player, you'd select the Bass field.

2. Select an argument from the Comparison drop-down list. It includes logical statements like **is equal to**, **contains**, **does not contain**, and more (see the "What Those Comparison Options Mean" sidebar a little later in this chapter).

   If you're still looking for that bass player, you'd select **is equal to** or **contains**. If you want anyone *but* a particular bass player, you'd select **does not contain** or **is not equal to**.

3. Type the word or phrase you're looking for in the Compare To text box. To find or eliminate records that contain bassist John Guerrin, you'd enter his name here.

You can further refine the filter by repeating the process with the subsequent filter levels. The process is the same, except you need to tell Works whether to apply the next filter to the records turned up with the first (that narrows the search more) by selecting from the little drop-down list in front of the later Field name choices.

"And" narrows the search because Works will only choose records that meet both (or all, if you use more than two) of the filter criteria. For example, with Works you can find records that list John Guerrin as bass player *and* have Joni Mitchell playing piano.

If you want to widen the search, you would choose **or** from the little drop-down list in front of subsequent Field name choices. Filtering with secondary "or" statements will return more information because you're giving Works more ways to select. You're saying "Show me records that have John Guerrin on bass *or* Joni Mitchell on piano." You can find records that have John Guerrin on bass, records with Joni Mitchell on piano, and records that have them both.

You can have up to four additional and/or arguments in an Easy Filter, which will let you get very, very picky about the information Works pulls from your database.

After you select all the options you care to use, click **Apply Filter**, and Works will show you any and all records that meet the filter criteria. Once you have them, you can print them out, or you can start over and try another filter combination.

Before you click that filter button again, make sure you click the **Record** menu, and select **1 All Records** from the **Show** submenu. That will return all of your database records to the screen. The following table explains what the different comparision options mean.

What Those Comparison Options Mean

is equal to	The entry in the selected field is *exactly the same* as the entry in the Compare To box.
is not equal to	The entry in the selected field is *not the same* as the entry in the Compare To box.
is less than	The number in the selected field is *lower than* the entry in the Compare To box.
is greater than	The number in the selected field is *higher than* the entry in the Compare To box.
is less than or equal to	The number in the selected field is *the same or lower than* the entry in the Compare To box.
is greater than or equal to	The number in the selected field is *the same or higher than* the entry in the Compare To box.
contains	The entry in the selected field includes the entry in the Compare To box as part of its contents.
does not contain	The entry in the selected field doesn't include the entry in the Compare To box.
is blank	The selected field contains no information.
is not blank	The selected field contains *any* information.
begins with	The entry in the selected field starts with the entry in the Compare To box.
does not begin with	The entry in the selected field doesn't start with the entry in the Compare To box.
ends with	The entry in the selected field ends with the entry in the Compare To box.
does not end with	The entry in the selected field doesn't end with the entry in the Compare To box.

Filter Using Formula

Easy Filter *is* easy, and it will probably fulfill the needs of most users, most of the time. However, it is limited.

You can only use Easy Filter to compare the entries in a selected field with your filter. If you want to do something a little more challenging, say, compare two different fields, you need to click on the **Filter using formula** option at the upper right corner of the Filter dialog box. That will change the filter dialog box so it looks like this figure.

Click here to enter your own formula.

"Filter using formula" lets you get very fancy with your filtering.

Type your formula here.

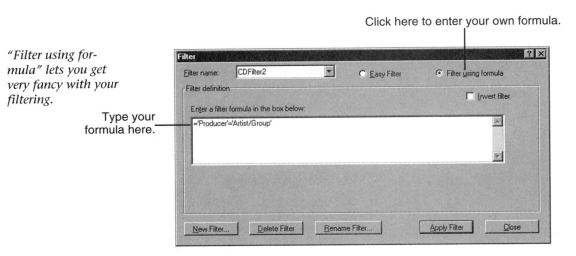

To use it, click in the box labeled Enter a filter formula in the box below. That will place the cursor there. Type your formula. And then, click **Apply Filter**.

(The details on database formulas are back in Chapter 19, if you need a refresher).

In the preceding figure, I entered the following formula:

='Producer'='Artist/Group'

This is what it's telling Works to do:

=	Tells Works that this is a formula.
'Producer'	Tells Works that it will be comparing the contents of the field labeled **Producer**.
=	Here, the equal sign is the same as selecting the **is equal to** comparison back in Easy Filter.
'Artist/Group'	Tells Works to compare the contents of the field labeled **Producer** (above) with the contents of the field labeled **Artist/Group**.

In short, it says "show me all the records where the entry in the Producer field is the same as the entry in the Artist/Group field."

In my database, this formula turned up two records—CDs by Joni Mitchell and George Benson. Again, you can print out the results or click the **Record** menu, and select **1 All Records** from the **Show** submenu to try another filter.

Odds are, you won't ever, or at least rarely ever, need to use the Filter using formula option. If you do, keep the following in mind. Creating a formula to filter your database is not horribly difficult, but it is a challenge. The best advice I can give you is to study how Works builds its own formulas.

To see how Works writes a formula, use Easy Filter as described in the last section to put together a filter similar to one you want create. Then click **Filter using formula**.

The text box will display the Works formula, which you can dissect and adapt to your own needs. With a little patience, you can figure out (as I did) that you need to enclose field names in single quotation marks ('), and to enclose text in double quotes (") when entering them in a formula.

Using ReportCreator

Using a filter, by itself, is very convenient for just pulling the information you need out of a large database. However, sometimes, you want more than just a simple set of records. You want a count of how many records meet your filter criteria, plus you want the information you retrieved broken down into categories so you can scan it quickly for pertinent details. *ReportCreator* lets you do all that, and more.

ReportCreator Is...

ReportCreator is similar to a TaskWizard, in that it walks you step-by-step through the process of creating a report.

You can use ReportCreator while in any of the view modes we've looked at (list, form, or form design). It asks you the relevant questions, lets you select the report options you want, and then hands you your report on a silver platter. Well, practically.

To start the ReportCreator, click the **Report View** button on the toolbar (the one with the bound report on it), or select **ReportCreator** from the **Tools** menu.

First thing you'll be asked (just as you were with filters, earlier) is to name your report with the Report Name dialog box. Just type in the name you want to use (I called mine **CD Report**), and click **OK**.

That will call up the ReportCreator dialog box.

ReportCreator: Title

The choices begin: the ReportCreator Title tab.

Type in a new title if you want.

Select a page orientation.

Choose a font and font size here.

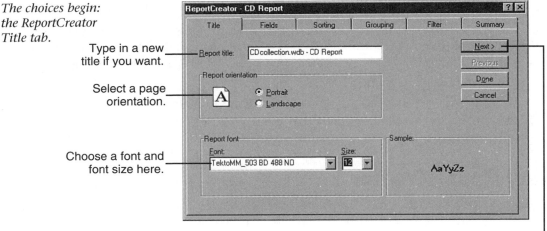

Click to move on.

The ReportCreator automatically assigns a title to your report (the name of the database file, plus the report name you just entered). You can edit it (in the Report title box), type in a whole new one, or just leave it as is.

Next, select a page orientation (Portrait or Landscape) in the Report orientation box. Portrait is the default option. If you're not sure which you need, leave it alone. You can always change it later with the **Page Setup** command in the **File** menu.

Finally, select a font and font size from the Report font box. Whichever font you select will be the only font used in the report: pick a nice, easy-to-read one.

When you're happy with your choices, click **Next.** The Fields tab comes to the front.

Database Fields Forever

The Fields tab lets you select which fields (from all of the fields in your database) you want to include in your report. To add fields to your report, click the first field you want to add and click **Add.** Click the next field and click **Add** again.

The chosen fields will appear in your report in the same order you select them, so you don't have to choose them in alphabetical (or any) order if you don't want to.

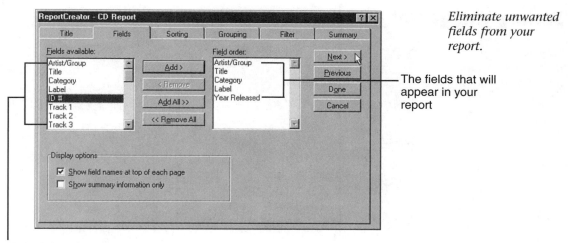

Eliminate unwanted fields from your report.

The fields that will appear in your report

All the fields from your database

If you want to add all of the fields from your database to the report, click **Add All**. Add a field by accident? Click on it in the Field order box; then click **Remove**. It's gone. Hate all of your field choices? Click **Remove All** to remove all the entries in the Field order box, and you can start over.

Once you've selected the fields you want to appear in your report, you can select their options from the Display options box at the bottom of the dialog box.

Clicking **Show field names at top of each page** will print the selected field names on each page of the report. That's a good idea for multipage reports, since it saves the reader from flipping back to see what information is in each column.

Show summary information only eliminates field names, and even field entries from the report. It only shows a summary of the information in the database. It's good if you want a report specifying how many CDs you own that are Jazz, Pop, Rock, and so on, without actually printing out all of the CD artists and titles. (These summary options are explained shortly.)

When you're ready, click **Next** to continue. If you click **Previous**, you'll return to the last tab displayed (Title).

Sorting Things Out

Your sorting op-
tions—you've seen
these before.

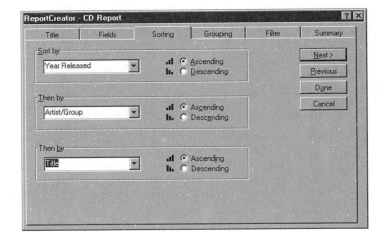

The Sorting tab gives you the chance to sort the records, by up to three different fields, that land in your report.

This page works exactly the same as the sorting options we used in the last chapter to sort the whole database. You can check Chapter 20 for the sorted details. (A horrible pun. I apologize.) When you've picked your sorting options, click **Next** to continue.

Grouping Groupies and Groupers

Records of a feather
can be grouped
together.

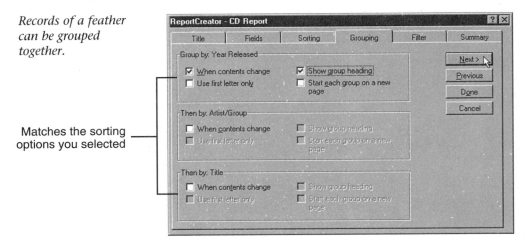

Matches the sorting
options you selected

The Grouping tab is set up to complement the Sorting tab. It gives you the chance to group the sorted data together.

For example, in the preceding figure, I sorted information by the Year Released field. In the Group by: Year Released box in the figure, I've selected **When contents change** (it's checked in the figure). That means that Works will group all of the CDs that had original pressing in 1967 together, the CDs released in 1994 together, and so on.

Because I selected **Show group heading**, too, Works will label each group with the appropriate year.

The remaining two options aren't selected. I didn't select Use first letter only because that would make the group headings all "1" (since all of the CDs were released in 1900-something), and that won't be useful. If this were an alphabetical list of names, for instance, the Use first letter only option would make the headings A, B, C, and so on and would be very useful.

The Start each group on a new page option isn't selected because I didn't want all the 1967 CDs on a page by themselves—there aren't enough CDs in my collection to make that practical. In another kind of database (for example, of regional sales managers sorted by region), that might be a useful option.

Additionally, you can group information together by any of the secondary Then by sorting options you've chosen. Each has the same set of four options as discussed.

If you select any of the grouping options in a Then by category, Works will add the appropriate subheading to each grouping. For example, the 1967 CDs will then be broken down and labeled by the Artist/Group name, if I select the same options in the Then by: Artist/Group box as I did in the preceding figure.

Click **Next** to continue on to the Filter tab.

Filters Revisited

The Filter tab lets you select from any filters you may have already saved for this database (they'll appear in the Select a filter box). But, I haven't saved any, so we need to create a new one. To do that, click the **Create New Filter** button and type a name; click **OK**. That will give you the Easy Filter dialog box we used earlier in the chapter. It's shown again, here, with my new filter. I'm looking for all records that contain Steve Gadd as drummer.

Filters for days.

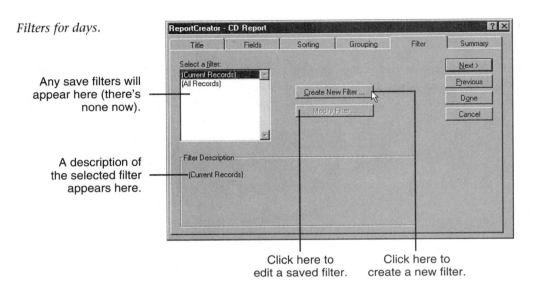

Any save filters will
appear here (there's
none now).

A description of
the selected filter
appears here.

Click here to
edit a saved filter.

Click here to
create a new filter.

*The Easy Filter
dialog box: same
as it ever was.*

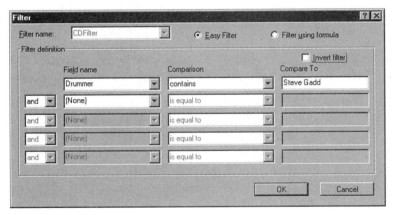

You can use Easy Filter or create a filter using a formula, as described in the "Filtering Data" section at the top of this chapter.

When you're done, click **OK** on the Filter dialog box. Then click **Next** on the ReportCreator dialog box. That will take you to the last and final tab: Summary.

Summarizing Your Summary Options

Adds a summary label to report.

Select a report field here.

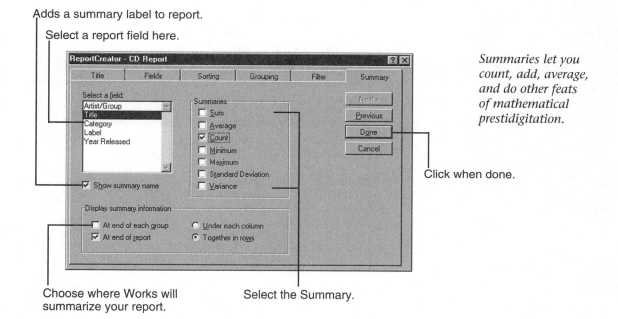

Summaries let you count, add, average, and do other feats of mathematical prestidigitation.

Click when done.

Choose where Works will summarize your report.

Select the Summary.

The Summary tab lets you collect and create summary information from the records chosen for your report.

Select a field from the list box, one you want to summarize. Choose a summary from the Summaries list.

Sum	Adds all the records in the selected field together and gives you a total—numbers only, please.
Average	Adds all the records in the selected field together and then divides the sum by the number of records. Again, numbers only need apply.
Count	Counts the number of entries in the selected field.
Minimum	Gives you lowest number from all the entries in the selected field.
Maximum	Gives you highest number from all the entries in the selected field.

Standard Deviation	Calculates the standard deviation among all of the figures in the selected field. It's a statistical thing.
Variance	Calculates the variance between all of the figures in the selected field. It's another statistical thing.

You can select more than one summary for a field. For example, if you're calculating a student's grades, you might want Minimum, Maximum, and Average to show the highs and lows, plus the final grade, for a semester's work.

Click in the check box labeled **Show summary name** to add a summary label to each summary in your report. Finally, select where and how you want the summary information displayed by clicking one or more Display summary information options.

At end of each group places summaries at the end of each of the groupings specified on the Grouping tab.

At end of report places the summary information on the last page(s) of the report.

You can also decide to have the summaries placed **Under each column**, or **Together in rows**.

After making your choices, click **Done**. Works will put an alert on the screen that says: **The report definition has been created. Do you wish to preview or modify the report definition?**

Preview It

If you click **Preview**, Works will generate the report and show you what it looks like in Print Preview mode.

Techno Talk

Report View Oddity You don't actually get to see any of the data in your report in report view. To see the database information and actual summaries, you need to print the report, or check it out in print preview. Isn't that odd?

If you like the preview, you can click **Print** to print your report out. If not, click **Cancel** and you'll automatically go to *report view* (shown next).

In report view, you can adjust field width, height, and formatting the way we did in the last chapter. After you make your format changes, click the **Print Preview** button on the toolbar to see how you like the changes.

If you decide, while reformatting the report, that you'd like to make changes to your Sorting, Grouping, or Filter options in the report definition, select **Report Sorting**, **Report Grouping**, or **Report Filter** from the **Tools** menu, and make your changes. If you want to change other parts of the report definition (the selected fields or summaries), you need to create a new report from scratch, with a different name.

The selected fields   Report name

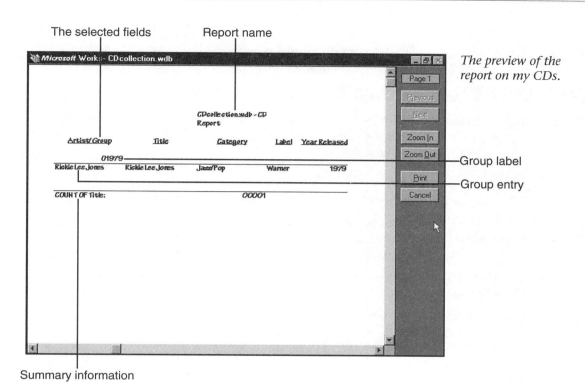

The preview of the report on my CDs.

Summary information

The report in report view—there's no data, just formulas and formatting.

Modify It

If, when Works asks "**The report definition has been created. Do you wish to preview or modify the report definition?**" you click **Modify**, you'll go to report view, directly to report

267

view, do not pass "Go," do not collect $200. Your options are the same as those previously discussed, except you won't even get a peek at the print preview of your report first.

The Least You Need to Know

To milk your database files for every useful bit of information you want, and *only* the information you want, you'll use filters to eliminate unnecessary records, and then create a report to present the necessary ones.

➤ Easy Filter will meet most of your needs.

➤ Filter using formula allows for more complicated filtering, but it isn't for everyone.

➤ Filters will pull only the records that meet your filter criteria from the database. Filters won't count records or do any other math on the contents of your database. To do that fancy-schmancy stuff, you need to generate a report.

➤ ReportCreator will help you create exactly the report you need—and hold your hand along the way.

➤ You don't actually get to see the information that makes it to your report unless you print it out, or use Works' Print Preview option.

Part 5
Works Working Together

Now that you've seen the major *components of Works for Windows 95, it's time to look at (I don't want to use the word minor) some of the smaller parts of this integrated suite of applications. In this section, we'll look at things such as Draw and WordArt (Chapter 22), the communications module (Chapters 26 and 27), and the Address Book (Chapter 25). We'll also look at all the ways in which Works is integrated, and why it always gets a plus in "plays well with others."*

It's no secret that Works can share its own documents, but it can also merge an Address Book into a letter and create personalized form letters (Chapter 24). Works can also share information with other applications on your PC (Chapter 23). Check it out.

Chapter 22

Picture Perfect: Art Accessories

In This Chapter

➤ Using Microsoft Draw

➤ ClipArt revisited

➤ Turn a word into WordArt

As my friend Teresa is fond of noting: life is cheap, it's the accessories that will break you. Not so with Works. You get a number of art accessories to help you deck out your documents with glorious works of art—and you don't have to be a Rembrandt or Picasso to use them (I'm certainly not).

In this chapter, you'll look at Microsoft Draw, recap ClipArt, and play around with WordArt. These are really *accessories*, not stand-alone components. In order to use them, you need to be working with a word processing document, spreadsheet, or database (in form design view).

Since we used ClipArt in Chapters 11 and 21, and since we at least *saw* WordArt in Chapter 11, let's look at Microsoft Draw first.

Draw!

To start off on the right foot, make sure your PC is running and Works is going. Open a new, blank Word Processing document (Chapter 5 explains how, if you're roaming).

With the word processing document open (you may want to save it before we begin—that's in Chapter 5, too), select **Drawing** from the **Insert** menu. Works will churn and burn for a moment or two; then it will open Draw (shown here). It looks like a miniature version of a complete application (it even has its own menus and tools), because that's what it is.

Draw gives you a blank slate to work with.

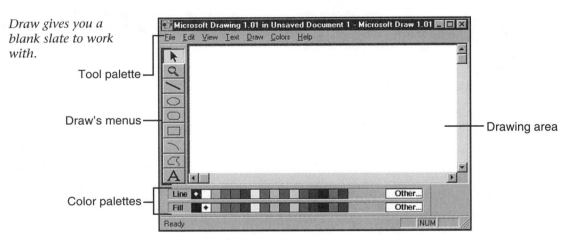

Tool palette —

Draw's menus —

Color palettes —

Drawing area

A drawing program, such as Draw, is designed to let you create simple graphics from discrete pieces (a circle, a box, a chunk of text) that you can move and compose into a pleasing arrangement.

The Drawing Tools

The tools available to you in Draw appear down the left side of the application window. Check them out, from top to bottom.

Pointer

For the usual clicking, dragging, and selecting.

Zoom

Zoom in on your drawing so you can see the finer details. To Zoom out again, press the **Shift** key while you click. The View menu performs the same functions.

Line

For drawing straight lines. Click where you want the line to begin, drag the cursor to where you want it to end, and click again. You can change the thickness and pattern of the line with the Line Style submenu on the Draw menu.

Oval drawing

Draws ovals and circles automatically—just click-drag.

Rounded rectangle

The same as the Oval tool, but this one draws rectangles with rounded corners.

Rectangle

The same as the Oval tool, but this one draws plain rectangles and squares.

Arc

Works the same as the Oval tool, but draws arcs—not Noah's boat, not a welding tool, but arc as in a portion of a circle. An arc is shaped like a funky triangle that's flat on two sides, and rounded on the third.

Freeform

This one does double duty: click once and drag, and it works like the Line tool but lets you click then drag several times, creating a nongeometrical shape, until you double-click.

If you click-drag (holding down the mouse button), it behaves like a pencil, so you can draw freehand.

Text

Lets you insert text into your drawings. You can choose font, size, and styles for this text with the Text menu.

When you use a tool to create something (a circle, rectangle, or whatever the tool creates), it is automatically selected. While it's selected, you can use the handles to shrink or stretch your creation (as we did with the ClipArt we added to the database form in Chapter 20).

You can also change the selected object's color (with the color palettes), pattern (with the Patterns submenu on the Draw menu), and line style (with the Line Style submenu on the Draw menu).

The Draw menu also lets you select whether what you're drawing appears Framed (has a visible border) or Filled (colored in). When you check the Framed and Filled options in the Draw menu, your object appears framed and filled. To turn either option on or off, just select it from the Draw menu.

Line And Fill Colors

The color palettes—
how colorful.

The Line and Fill color palettes (see the figure) let you select the color of the Framing line, and Fill (from the last section) for an object, by simply clicking on the color you want to use for each. In the figure, the default selections are indicated by diamond-shapes on the default colors. Lines are black, and the fill is white.

To change either, just click on the color you want, from the appropriate palette, while the object you're changing is selected. The color you click will pick up a check mark (to show it's the color being used), and the object's line or fill will pick up the selected color.

If you don't care for the colors in either palette, you can customize each set. First, click on the color you want to replace; then click the **Other** button. (You can also do a lot of the following with the options on the Colors menu.)

When you click the **Other** button, it calls up the Color dialog box shown below (in the figure, it's fully expanded—you may have to **click** the **Define Custom Colors** button to see it all).

Customizing your
Line and Fill colors.

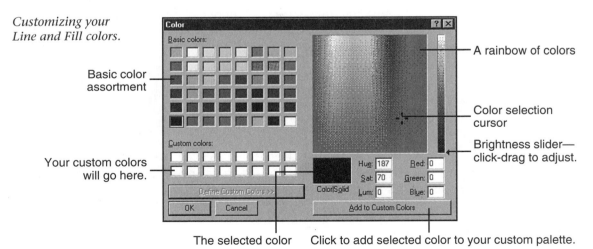

Click on one of the color squares in the Basic colors display, and it replaces your selection in the palette. Or you can select a completely new color by clicking one in the rainbow of colors displayed on the right side of the dialog box. You can adjust the brightness with the brightness slider.

When you like the color, click **Add to Custom Colors** and the color will appear in the **Custom colors** palette on the left side of the screen.

If clicking around in a rainbow isn't your speed, you can manually create a custom color by entering values in the boxes labeled Hue, Sat(uration), Lum(inosity), Red, Green, and Blue, above the Add to Custom Colors button. You can manually create a color, though I've never figured out how to get a decent color this way.

Once you've added custom colors to the Custom colors palette, you can add them to your Line and Fill palettes as previously described.

Learn by Playing

Draw is one of those things that it takes so much longer to explain what to do than it actually takes to do something. Rather than bore you to death with page after page of picayune details, I suggest you set aside 20 minutes or so, and just play with Draw. You'll get a much better grasp of what things are, and what they do, than I could ever put into words.

The following are some fun menu items to play with, once you've created two or more shapes (make sure one is selected before you try these).

On the File Menu

Update   Sends whatever changes you've made to the drawing to your word processing (or other) document.

Import Picture   If you have absolutely no artistic talent, you can use the Import command to open prepared graphics (from commercial clip art packages or Works' built-in ClipArt collection) and place them in your documents.

On the Edit Menu

Send to Back   Places the selected item behind all the other objects, so you can control how things overlap.

Bring to Front   Pulls an item that you've sent to the back (or that's buried behind other things) front and center.

On the Draw Menu

Group   Select two or more objects in your drawing, then select **Group**. Draw fuses the two objects into one.

Ungroup   Breaks apart a grouped object into its component parts.

Pattern and **Line Style**   These two give you a little more variety, with several patterns and line thicknesses to choose from.

Snap to Grid   Works the same as the Snap to Grid business we talked about in Chapter 20. It makes it easy to arrange things symmetrically in a drawing.

Show Guides   Reveals the grid that things are snapping to.

Rotate/Flip   You can turn the selected object to the right or left. Or you can flip it horizontally (side to side) or vertically (top to bottom).

Creating a Logo

This is a practical demonstration of the kinds of things you can create with Draw, even with limited artistic ability.

The Logo, and How to Swing It

Parts is parts, and the tools used to create them.

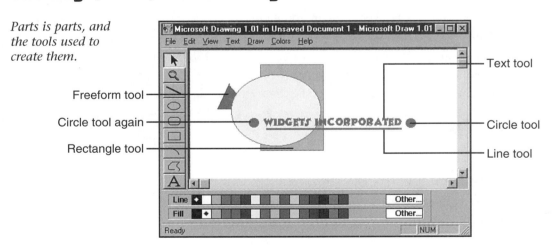

The logo you see in the figure I created with Draw's basic set of tools. The foreground part is made up of a line of text, a 2-point line drawn under the words, and small circles at either end. (Actually, I only drew *one* circle and copied and pasted it to create an exact copy.)

Behind the name are three geometric shapes, a circle, rectangle, and triangle. They were created in that order, and each was sent behind the others with the **Send to Back** command in the **Edit** menu.

Using That Logo

When you finish creating your masterpiece, you can either click the **Close** (X) box or select **Exit and Return** from the **File** menu. Works will ask if you want to save the changes you've made to your drawing. If you want them, click **Yes**. If not, click **No**. Clicking **Cancel** will return you to Draw.

When you close Draw and save your changes, Works returns you to your original document. Your logo (or other creation) is there, too, and selected so you can resize it or move it, if you care to.

With mine, I decided to make it into a letterhead for the fictional Widgets Incorporated. I left the logo in the upper left corner of the document and built a letter around its default placement in a blank document.

Here are the results.

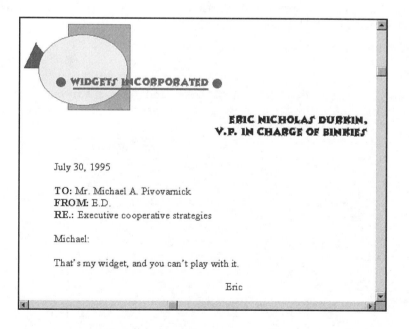

My logo at work. (Logos at work tend to stay at work.)

Once you place your drawing in your document, you can position it on the page by dragging it where you want it in relation to text on the page. You can center it, or left/right align it by clicking the alignment buttons on the toolbar. You can also change how your text flows around the drawing by selecting **Text Wrap** from the **Format** menu.

If you need a refresher on placing graphics and what Text Wrap is and does, you'll find them back in Chapter 11, along with other tips on creating fancy-shmancy word processing documents.

ClipArt Revisited

ClipArt, you may recall from Chapters 11 and 20, is the collection of prepared art that comes with Works. In those chapters, you saw how to select and insert ClipArt into your documents, so I won't repeat that here. However, you should know that you can open Works' ClipArt with Draw and change it to suit your mood, or meet your needs.

Here's how. Start in your word processing program or other Works document. Then:

1. To open draw, select **Drawing** from the **Insert** menu.

2. Select **Import Picture** from Draw's **File** menu. Works will give you a standard Open file dialog box.

3. Use the Open dialog box to navigate to Works' ClipArt collection. It's usually at the path: **C:\MSWORKS\CLIPART**.

4. Click on the ClipArt file you want to use.

5. Click **Open**.

6. Works will open a copy of the ClipArt file in Draw, and you can edit and accessorize it however you like, following the description in the previous Draw section.

A bit of ClipArt with visual sound effects added in Draw.

That's my "Splat!" ——

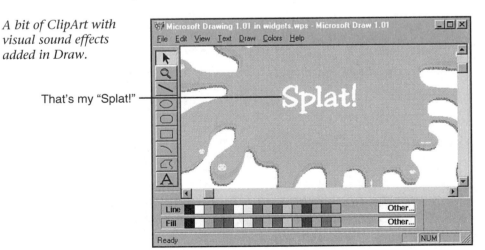

Check This Out...

If You've Already Placed the ClipArt...

If you've already placed a piece of ClipArt in your document and then decide you want to tinker with it in Draw, first, click on the ClipArt to select it. Next, select **Cut** from the **Edit** menu. Then, select **Drawing** from the **Insert** menu. When Draw opens, select **Paste** from the **Edit** menu. Works will paste the ClipArt into Draw where you can tinker 'til the cows come home. Moo.

If you're artistically challenged, like myself, you can purchase packages of clip art from computer and software stores and mail-order companies. If you want them easily accessible to Works, copy the files into the CLIPART folder inside your MSWORKS folder, and they will be available when you select **ClipArt** from the **Insert** menu. Check your Windows 95 documentation for details on copying files.

A Word Can Be Worth a Thousand Pictures

WordArt is the Works feature that lets you turn a simple word or phrase into an impressive graphic element. You saw it at work in Chapter 11 with the title on the *Much Ado About Bubkes* flyer.

This is another tool that's much more fun to play with than to have described and dissected. In this section, I'll show you the various tools at your disposal, and then turn you loose to play and discover on your own.

Starting with WordArt

In order to use WordArt, you need to have a word processing document, spreadsheet, or database (in form design view) open. Click to place the cursor where you want the WordArt; then select **WordArt** from the **Insert** menu. Your document window will change to resemble the one shown here.

Type the word or phrase you want to art-ify in the box labeled **Enter Your Text Here**. Use the Insert Symbol button to add symbols like Π, $\leftrightarrow$, and other funky stuff. After entering your text, click **Update Display**. That inserts your words into the WordArt frame in your document.

With that done, you can play with your WordArt options from the toolbar to distort, color, and otherwise stylize the text you entered.

Creating a work of WordArt.

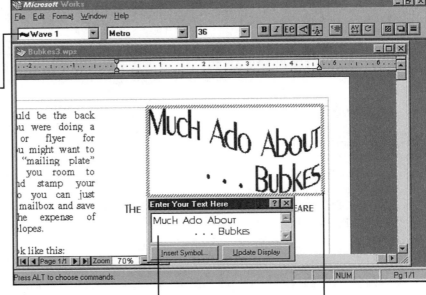

The WordArt toolbar ⌐

Type your word(s) here.   WordArt frame

The WordArt Tools

This is the fun stuff. I'm just going to generally describe what each tool does. You play and explore—trust me, it's too much fun to just *read* about.

A click here shows you a list of ways you can distort/shape your words. There's a little shape in front of the name to give you an idea of the effect.

Metro ▼
Select the font you want to use here. Simple fonts seem to produce the best results. They're easier to read in the finished product.

36 ▼
Select a font size here. Since you're creating a graphic with odd shapes and colors, larger sizes tend to work better. They're also easier to read in the final product.

Puts your font in **Boldface**.

Makes your font *italic*.

Makes upper- and lowercase letters the same size.

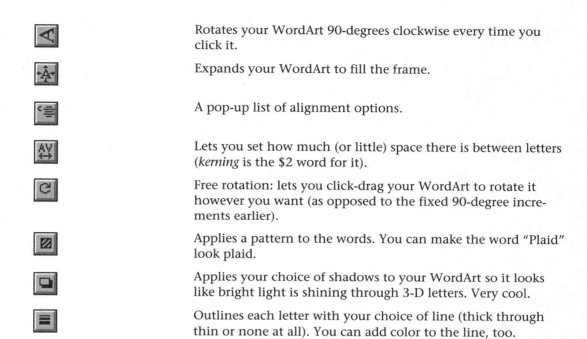

Rotates your WordArt 90-degrees clockwise every time you click it.

Expands your WordArt to fill the frame.

A pop-up list of alignment options.

Lets you set how much (or little) space there is between letters (*kerning* is the $2 word for it).

Free rotation: lets you click-drag your WordArt to rotate it however you want (as opposed to the fixed 90-degree increments earlier).

Applies a pattern to the words. You can make the word "Plaid" look plaid.

Applies your choice of shadows to your WordArt so it looks like bright light is shining through 3-D letters. Very cool.

Outlines each letter with your choice of line (thick through thin or none at all). You can add color to the line, too.

You can apply any or all of these effects to your WordArt (and you can get as tacky as you want while you're experimenting—I won't tell anyone).

When you're done, click in your original document somewhere outside the WordArt frame (you may have to click twice if the Enter Your Text Here dialog box is active), and you'll return to the regular document window.

Later on, if you want to change your WordArt, double-click in the WordArt frame and all the WordArt tools will return.

I'm such a toy-brain, I lost *hours* playing with different words (some of which you can't say on television) in different WordArt variations. Even a non-toy-brain should get at least 40 minutes of fun out of exploring everything you can do with WordArt.

WordArt creations are nice to use for title pages, instead of clip art on sale flyers (20% Off! Today Only!), or for anything you really want to draw attention to in a document.

The Least You Need to Know

A nice assortment of Works' art accessories are at your beck and call. In order to use them, you need to be working with a word processing document, spreadsheet, or database (in form design view).

➤ Draw lets you create your own works of art from scratch. Use the **Drawing** command in the **Insert** menu to start.

➤ ClipArt gives you an assortment of prepared drawings you can use when you don't have the time or talent to create your own.

➤ You can, however, use Draw to alter Work's assortment of ClipArt.

➤ WordArt lets you turn words into fancy works of art, even if you'd be embarrassed to show those words to your Mom.

Chapter 23

Spreading Information Around

In This Chapter

➤ Sharing Works files with your friends

➤ Embedding and linking objects isn't painful—not in Works, anyhow

➤ OLE! It's not just for bullfights, anymore.

Sharing is a good thing. You've probably been hearing that since your second grade teacher asked if you brought enough chewing gum "for everybody." You can continue the tradition of sharing with Works in three ways: sharing your Works files with other computer users; sharing Works files with other Works files; and sharing files between applications on your own computer.

Of course, if you're sharing your files with other computer users, you can reasonably expect that they'll want to share their files with *you* (isn't that what sharing is all about?). No matter how, or with whom, you share your files, Works makes it a simple proposition.

Thanks for Sharing: Works 4.0 to Works 4.0

The simplest way to trade files with another computer user, is if you both use Works 4.0. All you need to do is save the file(s) you want to share onto a floppy disk and hand them to your friend.

She can pop the disk in her PC, and open the files using her copy of Works. Everything in the file will be exactly the same as it was on your PC (unless your friend doesn't have one of the fonts you've used in your document—and if you stick to Windows' basic font set, that won't be a problem).

Share and Share Alike: Works 4.0 to Other Applications

If your friend doesn't have Works for Windows 95, or even an IBM-compatible computer, you can still share files back and forth. Preparing files to give to a friend means saving them in another file format. You do that with the **Save As** command on the **File** menu.

Works' Save As dialog box, with the Save as type menu showing.

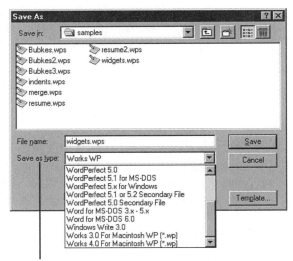

Select an application your friend does have, here.

Whether you know it or not, you've used the Save As command before. Every time you save a new, untitled file, you save it with the Save As dialog box shown here.

To prepare a file for sharing with your friend, find out what applications she has. Then, open the file you want to share, and select **Save As** from the **File** menu.

When the Save As dialog box appears, use it to navigate to the floppy disk you want to save the file on (that's covered back in Chapter 5 if you're reading ahead). Then click on the **Save as type** menu. A list of applications will drop down. Select the name of an application your friend owns from the list. (There are even two Macintosh computer formats, so you can share files with a friend who owns a Mac—see the "Works' Save As Formats" box later in this chapter).

Finally, click **Save**. Works will, in the process of saving the file, *translate* it into the selected application's file format.

Most applications, these days, are capable of doing file translations for many popular applications. If your friend wants to share a file with you, see if her favorite application can save a file in Works 4.0 (or an earlier Works version) format. If not, you can probably still use one of your friend's files.

File Format Different applications store their files differently when they write them to a disk. How the file is stored is called its file format. You don't need to know the details, really.

Translator Works uses a file translator (like a language translator) to change a Works format file into the file format used by another application.

Works' Save As Formats

In addition to the regular Works 4.0 file formats (spreadsheet (SS), database (DB), word processor (WP), and such), Works can also save files in the following file formats:

Works for Windows 3.0 WP
Works for Windows 2.0/Works for DOS
Text
Text (DOS)
RTF (Rich Text Format)
Word 2.0 for Windows
WordPerfect 5.0
WordPerfect 5.1 for MS-DOS
WordPerfect 5.x for Windows
WordPerfect 5.1 or 5.2 Secondary File
WordPerfect 5.0 Secondary File
Word for MS-DOS 3.x-5.x
Word for MS-DOS 6.0
Windows Write 3.0
Works 3.0 for Macintosh
Works 4.0 for Macintosh

Opening a Foreign File Format

If your friend doesn't have an application that can save in Works 4.0 format, don't sweat it. Works may be able to read the format of her file just as it is.

Check This Out...

If Your Friend Has a Macintosh Computer

If your friend has a Mac, make sure she formats the disk she's giving you as a PC disk, not a Mac disk. All Macs running System 7.1 and later can read and format PC disks. Most PCs, on the other hand, can't format or read Macintosh disks.

Just as Works is able to translate a file while saving it, it can perform the same magic on a file while opening it.

To open an alien file format, do this:

1. Launch **Works**.

2. Pop the disk with the file in your floppy drive.

3. Select **Open** from Works' **File** menu.

4. Navigate to the floppy drive with the disk in it (probably A:\).

5. Click the **Files of type** drop-down menu (shown in the next figure).

6. Select the appropriate application name from the menu (or select **All Files (*.*)**).

7. Select the file's name from the files list.

8. Click **Open**.

If it can (and it's only a question if you use the All Files option), Works will translate the foreign file into Works format. Make sure you save the translated file in Works format right after you open it—that will save you time when you open it again.

File Formats Works Can Open

In addition to files created with any version of Microsoft Works, Works 4.0 can also open files with the following file formats:

Excel SS
Text
dBase
Sylk
Lotus 1-2-3
RTF
Word for Windows 6.0
Word 2.x for Windows
WordPerfect 5.x
WordPerfect 6.x
Windows Write
Word for MS-DOS 3.x-5.x
Word for MS-DOS 6.0
Works 3.0 for Mac (SS, DB, and WP)
Works 4.0 for Mac (SS, DB, and WP)

Sharing Within Works

If you create an excellent spreadsheet, say, on the rising costs of orange juice due to inclement weather in Florida, and then chart that information, you may want to include that spreadsheet, chart, or both in a report called *Weather and Economics*.

It's easy enough to do. Here's how:

1. Create your spreadsheet (as described in Chapters 13–16), and save the file.

2. Chart your data (explained in Chapter 17).

3. Write your report in the word processor program.

4. When you're ready to place the chart in your report, click to place the cursor where you want the chart to go.

5. Select **Chart** from the **Insert** menu. That will call up the dialog box shown here.

6. Click on the name of the spreadsheet in the Select a spreadsheet list.

Inserting a chart into another Works document.

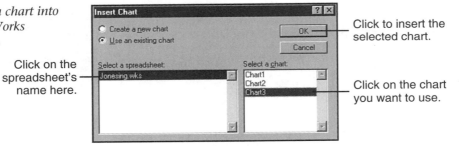

Click to insert the selected chart.

Click on the spreadsheet's name here.

Click on the chart you want to use.

7. Click on the name of the chart you want to use in the Select a chart list.

8. Click **OK**.

Works will open the spreadsheet and chart, and place a copy of the chart in your report. Not just a copy of the chart, but a *dynamic copy*. By that, I mean, that if you add data to the spreadsheet, not only will the original chart change, so will the copy inserted in your word processing document. They're *linked*. More about links in a moment.

You can place a spreadsheet by following the same steps—just swap the word "spreadsheet" for the word "chart" in the previous instructions. Where the Insert dialog box asks you to select a chart, above, it will allow you to select a range of cells when inserting a spreadsheet.

Check This Out...

You Can Work on the Fly

You can, in fact, create a new, never-before-seen chart or spreadsheet to insert in a Works document (click **Create a new chart/spreadsheet** in the appropriate Insert dialog box)—but I find that really complicates the process, especially when you're new to Works.

I *strongly* suggest that you create the chart (or whatever) in advance, at least until you're more comfortable with creating documents in Works. Who needs the extra stress?

Sharing Information with Other Applications on Your PC

A couple of years back, Microsoft added what it calls OLE technology to Windows. OLE stands for Object Linking and Embedding.

What OLE does is allow you to take a file created with one OLE-compatible application and place it in a document created with another OLE-compatible application. The file, when placed in another document, is called an *object* because it's treated like an individual thing (object) that you can move around and fiddle with inside the new document.

Will Your Applications Say "OLE!"?

I don't know. These days most are, but check your application manuals, or online help, to see if they're OLE-compatible.

There are two ways to get information from another file into a Works document. The first is the old, tried-and-true Copy and Paste method. The second is by inserting the object, much the same way we inserted a chart.

The Copy and Paste Special Method

To place an object from another application in a Works document, do the following:

1. Open the other application (for the sake of having a name to use, I'm going to say Microsoft Imager, but this will work with any OLE-compatible application).

2. Create and save the object you want to use (or open the file, if it already exists). For this example, I'm going to use a picture of the new Microsoft Network created with Microsoft Imager.

3. Select all or the part of the file you want to copy.

4. Select **Copy** from the **Edit** menu.

5. Launch Works.

6. Open (or create) the file you want to paste into.

7. Click to place the cursor where you want to put the object.

8. Select **Paste Special** from Works' **Edit** menu. Works will give you the dialog box shown here.

The Paste Special dialog box...it is special, too.

Path to the file you're pasting from

Paste options

Description of what you're doing

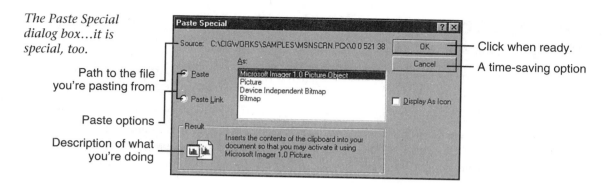

Click when ready.

A time-saving option

9. Select **Paste** or **Paste Link** and an option from the **As** list box.

10. Click **OK** and Works will plop the object into your Works document.

You have two pasting options with this method: Paste and Paste Link. Paste allows you to past the object as something in particular, which will affect how the object will behave later.

In the preceding figure, the object will be pasted as a Microsoft Imager 1.0 Picture Object. That means that later I can edit the object by double-clicking on it. That will open the object in Microsoft Imager; I can edit it but the changes *only* affect the object in my Works file, not the original file. This object is *embedded* not *linked*.

If I select any of the other three options (Picture, Device Independent Bitmap, or plain Bitmap) the best I'll be able to manage is to edit the object with Works' Draw module. These options also just embed, they don't link.

For the most flexibility, click **Paste Link** to place the object in your document but maintain its connection to the original file and application. If I edit the original file with Microsoft Imager, the copy in my Works document will also show the changes. The object is linked to the original, as well as embedded in the Works document.

If I double-click on the object in my Works file, it launches Microsoft Imager. Any changes I make to the object not only appear in the Works file but also in the original file.

The Display as Icon option, when checked, displays a simple icon in your Works document, not the actual object. This can save you time, since objects (especially some graphics) can slow down your system as they gets redrawn over and over when you page up or down.

Even though you only see an icon in the document, the actual object will be there when you print the document.

Inserting an Object

Copying and pasting may be a bit much when you're working quickly. You can also add an object from another application by selecting **Object** from the **Insert** menu. That will call up the Insert Object dialog box.

The Insert Object dialog box gives you two options. You can create a whole new object with the other application, or you can insert an object from an existing file.

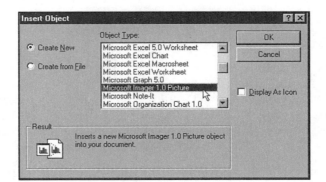

Creating a new object.

Create New

To create a new object, click the button labeled **Create New**. Then select an Object Type from the list box. It contains a list of the OLE-compatible applications on your hard drive. Select the application you want to use to create the object, and click **OK**.

Works will launch the selected application. Use it to create the object you want. Save the object. Exit the application. The newly created object will appear in your Works document.

Create from File

If the object you want to use already exists as a file, click **Create from File** on the Insert Object dialog box. The dialog box changes to look like this.

The application that created the file

Creating an object from an existing file.

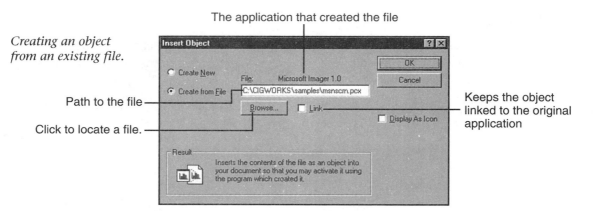

Path to the file

Click to locate a file.

Keeps the object linked to the original application

If you know the location of the file you want to use, you can type the path statement in the File text box (for example C:\CIGWORKS\SAMPLES\MSNSCRN.PCX, as shown in the figure). If not, click **Browse** and use the dialog box to show Works where the file is hiding.

If you want the object to remain linked with the original application that created it, click **Link**. It's a good idea to link information that will probably change (a spreadsheet or chart that's regularly updated, for example). That way, your Works document always has the latest version.

Techno Talk

Update and Save

When you edit an embedded and linked object with the application that created it, saving the changes becomes a two-step process. You save the file the same way, but now you must also select **Update** from the **File** menu. That will send the changes to the linked copy in your Works document.

For pictures and other items that are less likely to change, you may not want to link them. It's up to you. If you want to only display an icon in your Works file, instead of the actual object, click **Display As Icon**. Then click **OK**.

It may take a few moments, but Works will place the selected file in you Works document. It will also open the original file in the original application (so you can make any last minute changes, if you care to).

Working with Objects

Whether you decide to paste the object or insert it, an object looks like this when it first appears in your document.

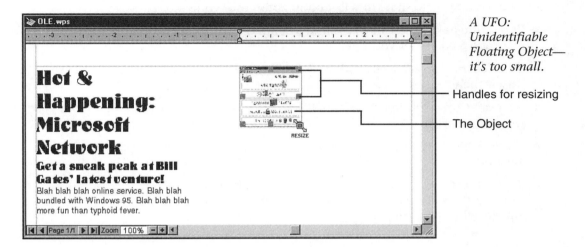

A UFO: Unidentifiable Floating Object— it's too small.

Handles for resizing

The Object

Once placed, you can treat the object like any other inserted item (such as ClipArt). You can click-drag on the object's handles to resize it. You can also click-drag in the center of the object to drag it to a new position in your document. If you double-click on the object, you'll launch the original application and be able to edit the object.

The object from the last figure, after some tinkering.

You can see the object after some moving and resizing.

The Least You Need to Know

Sharing files with your friends and co-workers, or even between applications on your own computer can really simplify your life.

➤ The easiest way to share files is if both parties use Works 4.0.

➤ If not, the next easiest way is to find a common file format that Works can open for you, and **Save As** for your friend.

➤ Place charts, spreadsheets, and other Works objects in your documents using the **Insert** menu.

➤ You can **Copy** stuff in another application and use **Paste Special** to place it in your Works documents.

➤ **Insert Object** lets you embed a file created with another application into a Works document.

➤ If you select the link option, you'll be able to edit an embedded object with the application that created it. Both the original file and the embedded object will update with the changes.

Chapter 24

Grow Your Own Junk Mail: Form Letters

In This Chapter

➤ Putting your Address Book through its paces

➤ The Form Letter TaskWizard

➤ Labels, labels, labels

➤ Do it yourself

Mail merge is the older, technical name for the process of generating form letters. When I was learning computers, *way* back when (we're talking 1980 something), it was such a pain in the behind. I still go all fluttery in the stomach when I think about it—and that was 10 years ago. Still, in terms of computer-time, that's about a million years. Things have changed a little.

Works calls mail merging creating a *form letter* and has automated the process so it's hardly a chore at all, any more. First, there's a TaskWizard to do most of the hard work for you—and there's secondary help to do everything else.

You guys have it *so* easy.

Why Use a Form Letter?

You've probably received form letters from Ed McMahon saying you may have won millions of dollars. You may have received form letters from your bank when a check bounced or interest rates dropped. And how about those form letters from charities asking you for money. (*Geesh, no wonder people hate junk mail so much.*)

Unless you're in business yourself, why on earth would you want to create a form letter? Lots of reasons:

➤ Holiday newsletters (It's Been a Great Year!) or letters to your family and friends with big news (It's a Boy!).

➤ Letters to notify everyone that you're moving and to give them your new address and phone number.

➤ God forbid, but letters to your creditors explaining how you're going out on strike, and not to expect payments until it's resolved.

You can generate a form letter any time you need to let a lot of people know the same handful of information. "A lot" is a relative term—anything over five or six is a lot to me.

Creating a Form Letter: How It Works

Creating a form letter is a two-step process.

First, you need to create an Address Book, using the Address Book TaskWizard, as described in Chapter 25. Or you can create an appropriate database file on your own, as described in Chapters 18–21. Whichever route you take, you must save the file to your hard drive.

The second step is the creation of the form letter itself. You can do it manually (I'll explain how, later) but the *Form Letter* TaskWizard is too simple to resist.

The Urge to Merge

For the sake of this chapter, I'm going to create a form letter using the names and addresses I entered in my Address Book in Chapter 25. You may use whatever Address Book or address database you have on hand.

To begin, fire up your PC and launch Works. When the Task Launcher appears (shown here for, oh, the *billionth* time), click on the **TaskWizard** tab. Then click on the **Correspondence** heading to get at the Form Letter TaskWizard. Click **Form Letter** then click **OK** (or just double-click **Form Letter**).

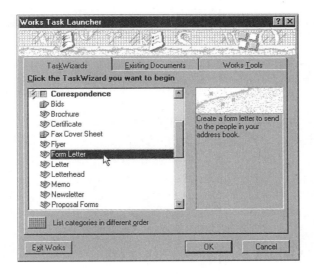

Firing up the Form Letter TaskWizard.

Works may ask if you really, really want to run this TaskWizard. You do, so click the button next to **Yes** and run the TaskWizard.

Take a Letter, Maria...

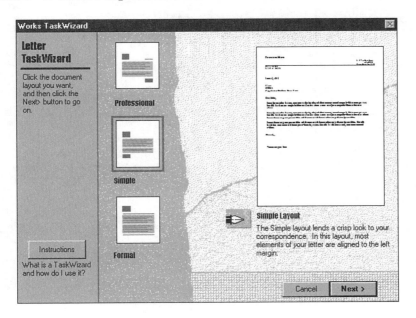

What kind of letter do you want?

Damn, another song stuck in my head. Now I've got to find the oldies station on the radio.

Right off the bat, Works will want to know what kind of letter you're going to write. It shows you three choices in the preceding dialog box. Look them over, then click the button for the style of letter you want.

Your choices are: Professional, Simple (my choice, since I'm a simple guy), and Formal. If you click each button, Works will show you a preview and description of each, on the right side of the screen.

For letters to family and other informal correspondence, I'd choose Simple. For letters to businesses, landlords, or editors, choose Formal. If the form letter you're creating is for *your* business, use Professional. When you've made your selection, click **Next**.

Design That Letter

Your letter options—everything from a cool letterhead to body text.

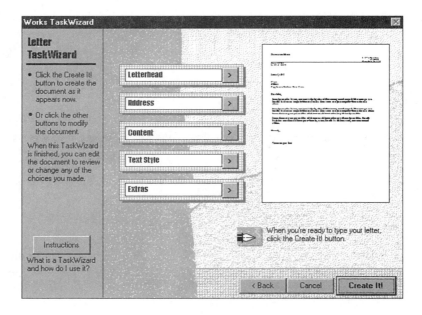

The next screen gives you five sets of options that set the style and content of the whole letter. We'll look at each, in turn.

Letterhead

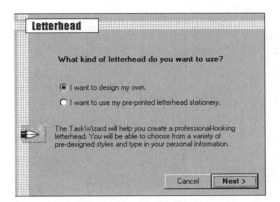

Do you want Works to help you design a new letterhead, or use preprinted stationery?

If you already have preprinted stationery with your name and mailing address on it, click **I want to use my pre-printed letterhead stationery**.

Works will then ask you two questions about your stationery: where is the letterhead on the page, and how much space does it take up? Works needs to know so it can fit the body of your letter on the page. Simply answer the questions. It'll help if you have your stationery handy, and a ruler (to measure it).

No stationery? No problem. Click **I want to design my own** and Works will walk you through five easy steps:

1. Select a letterhead style: you have seven choices, and Works shows you samples of each. Click the style you want; then click **Next**.

2. Pick a name: you can choose to feature a Company name (if you're writing for your business), or your Personal name. Click the appropriate name. If you're using a company name, there's a text box where you can type it. (I used a company name and called my bogus company *PIVovarnick Productions*.) Click **Next** when you're done.

3. Enter your return address on the Letterhead dialog box (there are four text boxes for each part of your address: address 1; address 2; city, state, Postal code; and country). Any line that isn't required for your address (like "country") you can leave blank. Click **Next**.

4. Enter your phone number(s) and e-mail address. There are four check boxes to select which numbers go on your letterhead. Your choices: Work phone number, Fax number, Home phone, E-mail address (for an online service such as America Online or The Microsoft Network). Click **Next** when you're done.

5. Works shows you a preview of your letterhead. Make sure you still like your choices and that you've entered the information correctly. (Nothing takes the bite out of a letter to the editor like misspelling your own name. Trust me.) You can see my letterhead in the next figure.

6. Click **OK** to continue, using the letterhead you've designed. If you're having second thoughts, you can cancel, start over, or go back one screen to make any mendacious emendations.

My finished letter-head, step-by-step (slooowwwly I turned).

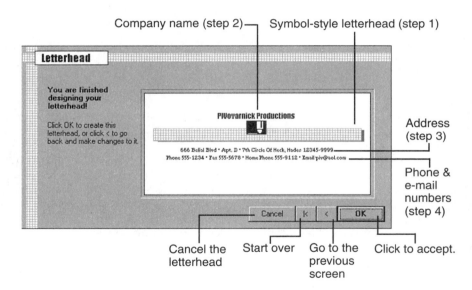

Company name (step 2) — Symbol-style letterhead (step 1)

Address (step 3)

Phone & e-mail numbers (step 4)

Cancel the letterhead   Start over   Go to the previous screen   Click to accept.

Address

When you click **Next**, you'll be back at the Letter options screen we saw earlier. Click **Address**.

Works will ask you: **How do you want to address your letter?** You have two choices: I want to type a single address and I want to use addresses from a Works database. Since the whole point of making a form letter is to use addresses from a database, click **I want to use addresses from a Works database**, then click **Next**.

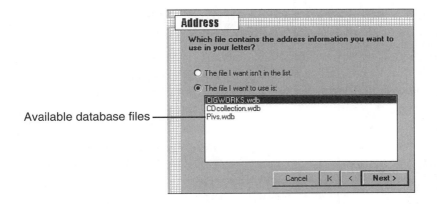

Pick a database file.

Available database files

Works asks which database file you want to use and shows you a list of the all the databases it can find (you can see them in the preceding figure). Click the name of the database you want to use in the list box and click **Next**.

Techno Talk

The Database I Want Isn't in the List!

Hey, calm down. If the file you want isn't in the list, click on **The file I want isn't in the list**, and click **Next**. Works gives you an Open file dialog box. Use it to show Works where the database file you want is located.

Works only keeps track of the files you saved in the Documents folder (C:\MSWORKS\DOCUMENTS). If you save them elsewhere (even just up one level in the MSWORKS folder), Works figures that's *your* problem.

Assemble the Address

When you click **Next**, a dialog box appears (see next figure) that lists all the fields in the selected database. Works is clever, but not clever enough to figure out which fields you need, and where to put them to build an intelligible address. You need to tell it.

To build the address, click on the first field you want to appear (**First name** in the figure) and click **Add**. Repeat the process with the next field and the next. When you add all of the information that belongs on the first line (for example, First name Middle name Last name, as in the figure) click **New Line**, and Works will move down to the next line.

You need to separate some information in an address (such as City, State, Postal code or Last name, Title) by a comma (,). To add a comma, click the **Comma** button between

301

entries. This *sounds* much more complicated than it actually is. If you know how to address an envelope, you know the order and punctuation of all this.

By chance, if you do mess up and need to back track, use the **Remove** button. It will delete the last field, line, or comma you added. Or you can select a field in the list of field names and click **Remove**, and Works removes that field from the address.

After you assemble the address, click **Next**.

┌─ The database fields

It says "Address1" and "Address2" here; you just can't see it for some reason.

Building your "To:" address. It tells Works what information you want and where you want it.

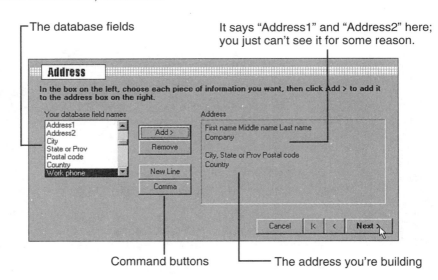

Command buttons

The address you're building

Greetings!

Build your salutation here.

Those database fields again

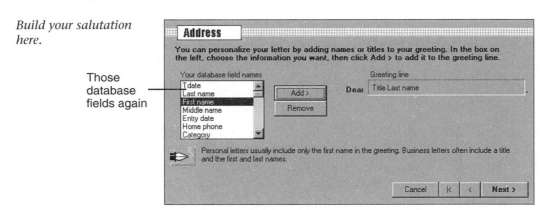

Works next asks how you want the letter's greeting to read. For personal mail between friends, you can use a first name: "Dear Mary." Business correspondence usually says something like "Dear President Clinton," or "Dear Ms. Wempen," using the person's title and last name.

To build the greeting, click the field you want to appear first and click **Add**. Repeat the process for any additional fields you want to use. The Remove button will remove the last field you added to the greeting.

Click **Next** when you finish.

If the Addressee Is Not Actually Dear to You...

Works assumes your salutation will start with the standard "Dear." That isn't always appropriate (I know I don't feel comfortable calling someone I don't know "dear"). Some correspondence should begin with just the addressee's title, last name, and position (**Mr. Davidson**, or **Editor**, for instance). Don't worry about it. You can make it anything you like later, once you create the letter.

When you finish the Greeting, Works will give you the chance to go back and make any address/greeting changes you want to make (just click the < button). If you're happy with your choices, click **OK**. You'll return to the main Letter screen, with the five options on it.

Fresh or Canned Contents?

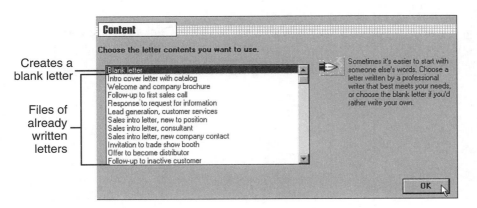

Creates a blank letter

Files of already written letters

You can write your own letter or edit one that has already been written for you.

Your next choice is about the content of the letter, that is, what it will say. Click **Content**. That gives you the dialog box shown above.

Works includes a number of "canned" letters (letters that have been written for you) on a wide variety of topics. You can choose anything from **We've had a baby** to **Your account is over due—pay up, you deadbeat**.

Scroll through the list and see if there's a letter that suits your needs. If so, click its name and click **OK**. Otherwise, you'll have to write one from scratch: click **Blank letter** and click **OK**.

Stylize Your Text

You have four styles to choose from.

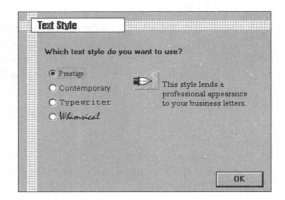

Meanwhile, back at the Letter options page.... Your next choice involves the style of the text in your letter—in plain English: the font.

Click **Text Style** and you'll see the options in the preceding figure. Click the style you want to use and click **OK**. Again, if you don't like any of the choices? (I don't, but I'm a font snob.) Just pick any one. You can choose another font later.

Extras! Extras!

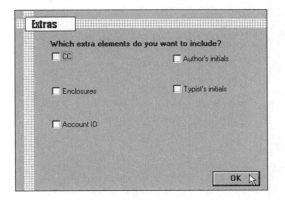

Formal, business-type extras for the end of your letter.

Finally, click the **Extras** button on the Letter options page. You see five options. Any you select will be added to the end of your letter. The options include:

CC	CC stands for "carbon copy." Use this if you're sending a letter, say, to your landlord and a copy to your lawyer.
Enclosures	Click this one if you're including a manuscript, or resume with the letter you're creating. It lets the recipient know there's something else in the envelope.
Account ID	Gives you a space to include your account number (if you're writing to a credit card company, for example) or the addressee's account number.
Author's initials	See next description.
Typist's initials	Use these last two options only if you're typing a letter for someone else. The author's initials are the initials of whoever the letter is from. The typist's initials are (don't freak out, now) the initials of the person who typed the letter. It's an old business practice that says "Hey, I have a secretary. Tremble at my greatness."

(When I first started out as a writer, I used to add a fake set of typists initials to the bottom of my letters to make editors think I was so good, I could afford a secretary. Did it work? No. Did it look impressive? Not really.)

After you've chosen any extras you care to add, and supplied Works with appropriate information for each, click **OK**. You're done!

Check That Checklist!

Do you regret any choices you've made?

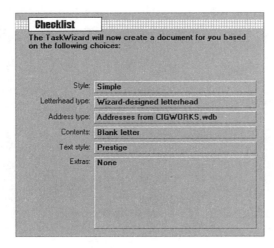

Click **Create It!** and Works will (as with all TaskWizards) present you with a final Checklist, showing you all the choices you've made along the way (mine are shown here).

Give them a good going over. If you're happy with those choices, click **Create Document**. Works will begin to form your form letter. If you want to make changes, click **Return to Wizard**. Fix the things you want to fix, and then click **Create Document**.

Anatomy of a Form Letter

The final product.

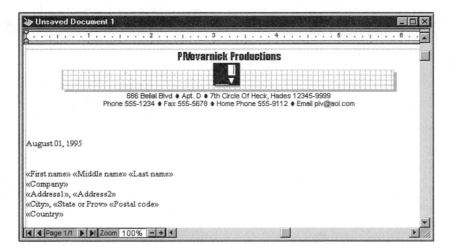

This figure shows you the form letter Works created for me. At the top of the page is the letterhead I created. Next comes today's date—I think the zero in the "01" has *got* to go (we can fix that).

Next, you'll see the addressee's name and address composed of field names put in brackets like this: <<**First name**>>; in the same order you specified in the TaskWizard. The same is true of the greeting, but you can't see it in the figure. Mine looks like this:

Place Holder
The bracketed entries are called *place holders* because they hold the place for the actual data that will be added from your database.

> Dear <<**Title**>> <<**Last name**>>,

If you chose to use a prewritten "canned" letter, the text of it will follow the greeting. Since I picked a blank letter, all mine says is: **Start typing your letter here**; **Sincerely**, and **Your name goes here**.

Editing a Form Letter

Stop. Save your form letter before you start to tinker with it in any way. Go ahead, *shoo*.

You can edit your form letter like any other word processing document. It *is* a word processing document, after all;. there's just some <<goofy-looking stuff>> thrown in.

You can change fonts, enter and edit the body of the letter, change the **Dear** to something appropriate, and get rid of that zero in the date. Change anything you care to change. If you're using a "canned" letter, edit it and add or delete whatever you need to make it fit your particular situation. It wouldn't hurt if it sounded like you wrote it, too.

The only thing to keep in mind when editing a form letter is this: *be careful when editing in and around the <<field name>> entries*. You can move them around, change their order, the font and size, add punctuation between them, and all that jazz. Any formatting you apply to the field entries will also be applied to the information they represent. Make <<Company>> italic, for example, and all the company names in all the letters will be in italic.

The only hard and fast rule to editing a form letter is that you *must keep the field entries surrounded by those brackets* (<<>>). If you accidentally delete a bracket, the field name stops being a field name and becomes part of the text of your letter. You could print out fifty letters that greet everyone as **Dear <Title>>**, and all fifty people will know you screwed up somehow. Check those brackets!

Smooshing the Data into the Letter

This one is a no-brainer. To complete the process and add actual names and addresses to your form letter, print the letter, or use **Print Preview** to peek before you print.

A form letter, with all its address information, in print preview mode.

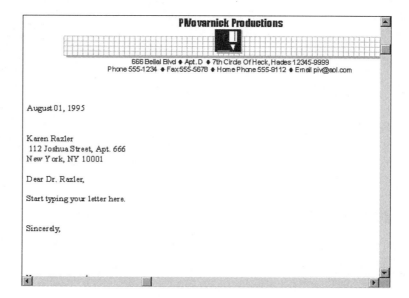

In the process of getting your form letter ready to print, Works replaces the **<<entry>>** place holders with the appropriate field entries from your database.

The information from one record is placed in one letter. That letter is sent to the printer; then the process is repeated with the next record and the next, until your database runs out of records.

Do-It-Yourself Form Letters

You can create a form letter without the help of the Form Letter TaskWizard (although why you'd want to eludes me right now). Here's how:

1. Create your database or Address Book file and save it.

2. Write your letter but leave out the information that's in your database. Don't even try to get all those <<placeholders>> right—it's maddening. Save the letter.

3. With the letter still open, select **Form Letters** from the **Tools** menu. This dialog box will appear.

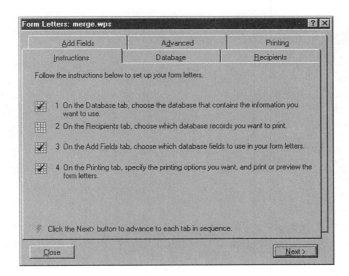

Manually creating a form letter—Look, Ma! No TaskWizard!

The Form Letters dialog box provides you with step-by-step instructions on how to select a database file to use, select field names to add to your letter, and how to print your letters.

The steps are similar to the TaskWizard you've already seen, so you shouldn't have any problem using them. Once you insert the field placeholders in your letter, you can edit, format, and finalize the letter before printing.

All This, and Mailing Labels, Too

Creating a mass mailing is a very professional tool. To make it look even more professional, you can use Works to print address labels.

The first time you try to print labels, I suggest you use the Labels TaskWizard. It's in the group called (oddly enough) **Envelopes and Labels**. It makes the process simple, and will introduce you to the basic concepts I'll be recapping here.

Skip the Labels, Print Envelopes

If your printer can handle printing on envelopes, you can also select **Envelopes** from the **Tools** menu. It will present you with a set of dialog boxes much like those for printing Labels, except (of course) they're for printing envelopes. Check your printer's manual to see if it can handle envelopes (many can, but some can't).

The first time you try, I recommend using the Envelopes TaskWizard. It's in the Envelopes and Labels group on the TaskWizard tab of the Task Launcher. You can go it alone after you've seen it done right at least once.

Later, if you want to tackle labels without the aid of the TaskWizard, here's what you do. While your form letter is open, select **Labels** from the **Tools** menu. Works will ask you if you want to create a set of different labels or a number of labels that all say the same thing. To create mailing labels, click **Labels**. To create return address labels, click **Multiple copies of one label**.

The Labels dialog box appears. Like the Form Letter dialog box we saw in the last section, it gives you step-by-step instructions, and each step is on a separate tab of the dialog box. After you read the instructions, click **Next**.

Creating labels to mail the world a letter.

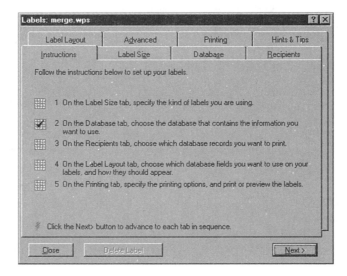

First, Works wants to know what size label you have, click **Label Size**. You can choose a standard size (or Avery number) from the list box labeled **Choose a label size**. You can also click **Custom** and manually enter the label size. Either way, click **Next** when you're done.

On the Database tab, tell Works what database file you want to use. Select it from the list box, or use an Open File dialog box to open a database not in the list. You can even click the **View Database** button to look at the database and see if it's the one you want. After you select the file, click **Next**. That will bring the Instructions tab forward. Click the **Recipients** tab.

On the Recipients tab, select which records you want to use from the database. You can choose All, the Current records (if you've done a report with them), Marked records (if you've marked some), or you can select a Filter and filter them down to the ones you want.

If you don't want all of the records, but haven't done anything to indicate which ones you do want, click **View Database**. Works will open the selected database file, and you can filter the database, or run a report to select the records you want on your labels. Click the **Next** button when you're ready to move on.

The Label Layout tab works just like the TaskWizard's Address. It lists all the fields from the selected database, and you add them to the label in the order you want. The only difference here is that you manually add punctuation to the label: there isn't a Comma button.

Click the **Next** button when you finish.

You can click the **Advanced** tab that will let you use the word processor to change the font and otherwise format the labels (you can even add clip art). The labels, at this point, look like the address portion of your form letter: they're all <<database>><<fields>>.

Finally, there's the Printing tab. It allows you to preview your labels before printing; to print two rows of labels to make sure the text lands correctly on the labels; or Print, to send all of the labels to the printer.

You can also tell Works to print multiple copies of the labels and start printing at a particular row of labels (for example, if you've already used the first two rows on a sheet of labels, enter 3).

The labels you create will be linked to the letter file. If you don't want to keep the labels around, click the **Delete Label** button after they've printed. If you think you're going to use the letter (and labels) again, click **Close** and Works will save the labels with the file until the next time you need them.

The Least You Need to Know

Creating form letters and labels used to be a grueling process (for me at least)—full of trial and error, and tons of wasted paper. Works' Form Letter TaskWizard makes the process so simple, your six-year-old will be creating form letters, hitting relatives up for birthday presents.

The absolute least you need to know is this: you can accomplish everything covered in this chapter with a TaskWizard. At least the first time out, why hurt your brain? Let Works do it. Later on, you can be adventurous and create form letters, labels, and even envelopes on your own.

Chapter 25

Address Book Details

In This Chapter

➤ Step-by-step Address Book creation

➤ Filling in the details

➤ Making the Address Book work for you

It seems like everybody I know has address book troubles. My friend Kevin doesn't really keep one. Tom keeps losing his. Karen, well, I'm not really sure what she does. And my problem? I keep too many of them, and none of them contains the same information—so I'm always left trying to figure out which addresses are the most current.

Works provides you with an Address Book that's neatly integrated into all of Works' various components—and only a mouse-click away.

Works' Address Book is actually a database file, like those discussed in Part 4 of this book, so you can filter, sort, and create reports from it. And you can do all that with any of the Address Books you create—because you can create as many as you need or want.

But, before you can do any of that sorting and filtering, you need to create an Address Book. It's easy; you do it with a TaskWizard.

Start Here...

It all began with a double-click.

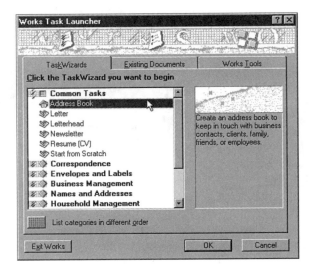

Start with the Task Launcher. Click on the **TaskWizards** tab, and double-click on the **Address Book** entry under the **Common Tasks** heading (see preceding figure).

Works will probably ask if you really want to use the TaskWizard you selected (unless you disabled that prompt with Works' Options, as described in Chapter 28). Click the button by Yes; run the TaskWizard. Works will pull the Address Book Wizard together and then start asking you questions about the Address Book you want to create.

What Flavor Do You Want?

First thing Works asks is, "What kind of Address Book do you want?" You have six to choose from: Personal, Business, Customers or Clients, Suppliers and Vendors, Sales Contacts, and Employees.

For the sake of this chapter, we'll create a Personal Address Book, but the steps are similar for each variety; only the field names and number of fields change. Works is more than happy to spell out your options at every step, when/if you decide to create a different sort of Address Book. For now, click the **Personal** icon and click **Next**.

The next TaskWizard screen explains what information fields it will include in the database. There aren't any choices for you to make on this screen, so just read the information and click **Next** again.

The Address Book du jour

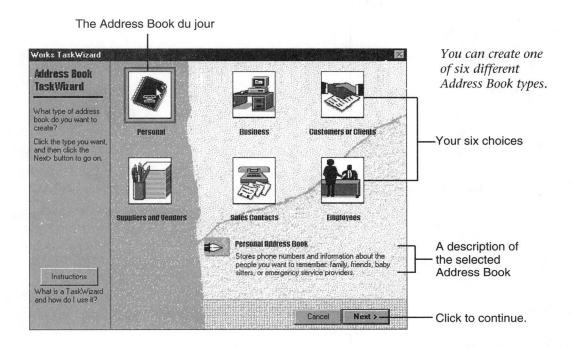

You can create one of six different Address Book types.

Your six choices

A description of the selected Address Book

Click to continue.

Adding Details

A sample page

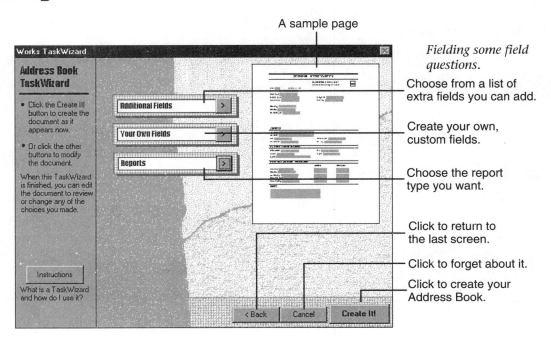

Fielding some field questions.

Choose from a list of extra fields you can add.

Create your own, custom fields.

Choose the report type you want.

Click to return to the last screen.

Click to forget about it.

Click to create your Address Book.

315

The next page is the last before you actually create your Address Book. Here, you can choose from a list of additional fields Works can add to your database, add your own fields, and select the type of report(s) Works will generate from your Address Book.

Additional Fields

Works assumes that you want the usual range of information (broken down into over a dozen fields) included in your Address Book: Name, address, home phone number, business name, Company, position. It even includes a "Category" field where you can classify folks as, well, whatever you want, but things like "relative," "co-worker," "in-law," and "business contact" leap to mind.

But, even though the TaskWizard assumes you want to include employment information (Company, position, and the like) it doesn't include a field for a work telephone number (go figure). To add one, click **Additional Fields** and Works will pop up the dialog box shown here.

Additional fields forever...

Adds work phone, fax, beeper, and e-mail fields

Adds fields for a spouse and children

Adds a freeform area you can use as you like

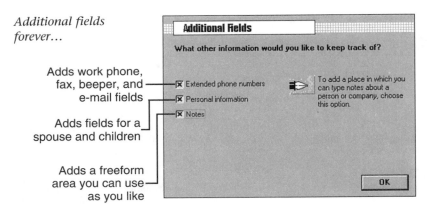

Click on the check box in front of the additional field category/categories you want to add; then click **OK**.

Do Your Own Fields

If you want to add a field or two that the Wizard hasn't thought of (although I can't think of any—the TaskWizard is pretty complete), click the arrow beside Your Own Fields. You see a dialog box in which you can enter up to four more fields. Just type the field name(s) in the text box(es) and click **OK** when you're done.

Reports Will Tell

Finally, if you want to be able to generate prepared reports from your Address Book, click the arrow beside Reports. Works lets you choose from two reports: an Alphabetized directory (everybody arranged alphabetically by last name), or a Categorized directory (everybody arranged by the categories you enter in the Category field).

You can choose one, the other, or both. You can also choose none of the above, and create your own reports later. Click on the report type you want (if any); then click **OK**.

Are You Sure About That?

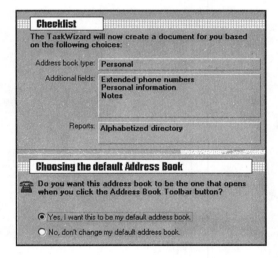

Last chance to change your mind...

Before Works actually creates your Address Book, it gives you a quick recap of what options you've selected (in the Checklist box, shown in preceding figure). You can check to make sure you've added everything you need. Look it over.

Below that (in the Choosing the default Address Book box), Works wants to know if the Address Book you're creating should be your default Address Book.

Your default Address Book is the one that opens automatically when you click on the **Address Book** button in the toolbar. If you want this one to be your default, click **Yes, I want this to be my default address book.** If not, click **No, don't change my default address book.**

If the Checklist meets with your approval, click **Create Document**. If you've forgotten to add something, or you added a field you don't really want, click **Return to Wizard** and you can go back and make whatever changes you like.

The Address Book Proper

Automatically shows today's date

Birthday and Anniversary reminders

The basic Address Book information, Part I.

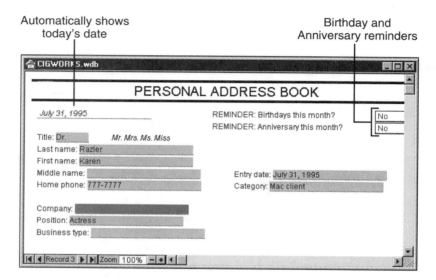

When you finally click **Create Document**, Works takes a few moments to assemble the database with the standard fields and then any of the extras you've added. The finished product looks like the preceding figure (except it won't have any data entered in it yet), and the next figure.

(By the way, if all this "field" and other database babble is baffling you, that means you probably skipped or skimmed Chapters 18–21, which cover introductory through advanced database doo-doo.)

The last field (not shown in either preceding figure) is the Notes field. It's just four shaded lines in which you can enter any information you care to about the person.

For example, in the Notes field on Karen's record (shown in the two preceding figures), I noted that she's fond of silver and turquoise jewelry and likes alternative-type music.

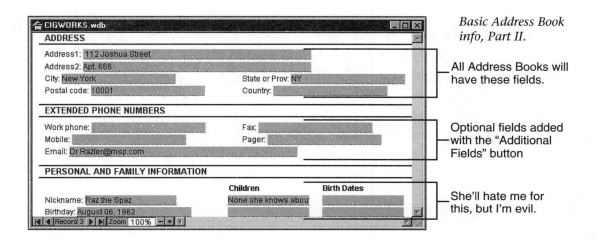

Basic Address Book info, Part II.

All Address Books will have these fields.

Optional fields added with the "Additional Fields" button

She'll hate me for this, but I'm evil.

Save It or Lose It

Works creates your Address Book for you, but it doesn't name it or save it. Before you do anything else, save it. Chapter 5 tells you how, if you've forgotten. Call it something that will let you figure out what names are in it (Family, Work, Support Group, Garden Club—whatever is appropriate).

You should also save your file regularly while entering data (I'd do it after entering each new record—to keep from having to re-enter more than one, should something untoward happen).

Entering Names and Such

When your Address Book file opens, and after you've saved it (nudge, nudge), you can begin to enter the information on your usual cast of characters.

Entering data in your Address Book works the same as entering data in any Works data-base file (Chapter 19 has all the details on entering and editing database data). Works starts you out with the Title field selected, so type the title (Mr., Mrs., Ms., whatever) and press **Enter** or **Tab**. A tab moves the cursor to the next field.

Customizing the Address Book

The Address Book TaskWizard only allots a certain amount of space for each field and a set number of fields that may or may not meet your needs.

For example, I could (and usually do) run out of space when entering "Pivovarnick" in most standard-sized name fields. If I need to, I can increase the size of the Last name field to accommodate all those extra syllables.

319

For another example, the Personal and Family Information section only includes fields for five children and their birthdays. One family of my acquaintance has (please, no gasping aloud) eleven children. I'd have to add a dozen more fields just to keep up.

And, finally, since I resist the urge to categorize my family and friends (it gives me a headache), the Category field is a waste of space for me. I may as well delete it.

The point is, that once Works hands you your Address Book file, it's yours to do with as you please. You can add and delete fields, redesign it, do whatever you want with it. Chapters 19 and 20 cover all the information you'll need to customize Works' Address Book to meet your particular (or, in my case, peculiar) needs.

The Report Report

My Address Book in report view. Needs work.

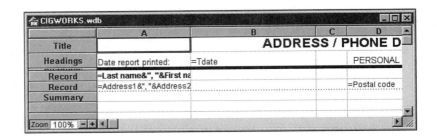

If you elected to have Works create an Alphabetized or Categorized directory report, you can check it out in *report view*—click on the **Report View** button in the toolbar. That will show you a report similar to the one shown in the preceding figure.

To actually see how your records will look in the report, you need to print it, or save the paper and use Print Preview. That will give you a chance to see your records and see whether or not you need to tinker with the report format (field width, record height, and so on) so you can read all the information in the report.

Additionally, you may want to create your own reports from your Address Book. You most certainly can. All of the report-related information is in Chapter 21.

Address Book Suggestions

These are some random ideas for practical ways to use your address book; you may like them, you may not. If nothing else, they may suggest other uses to you that haven't occurred to me.

The Obvious Idea: Birthday/Anniversary Warnings

At the end of each month, filter your address book for any birthdays and anniversaries that are coming up in the next month. That way, there won't be any last-minute gift and card crises.

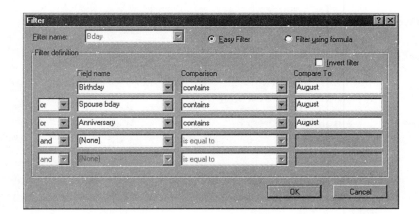

Stay out of the dog house with a Birthday/Anniversary filter.

You can do one filter (like the one shown here) for a record's **Birthday** or **Spouse Bday** or **Anniversary** in the coming month.

You'll need to create a second filter for the children's birthdays, if you opted to add the Personal and Family information fields. Each filter can only accommodate five fields, and there's a total of seven birthday fields in each record.

Phone Lists

If you belong to a couple of clubs and organizations, you could create an Address Book that includes all the members.

While creating a Clubs Address Book, specify a Categorized Directory when you select the report options. Then, while entering data, use the Category field to enter the club and organization names.

You can use the Categorized Directory report to print out phone lists for each club. Each club will be a category. Distribute copies of the category lists to each club's members, and everyone will be able to keep in touch. The membership will be so impressed, they'll elect you President.

Emergency Numbers

Keep an Address Book that contains names, addresses, and phone numbers for trusted neighbors, family members, your family doctor, police and fire, ambulance service, the hospital you prefer, and other potentially life-saving information.

You can print out a fresh copy to hand your baby-sitter when you're going out for an evening, and you won't ever have to write one out again.

Holiday Card Craziness

I don't know about you, but I have such a varied circle of friends, I go nuts around the holidays trying to remember who celebrates which holiday.

This year, I resolve to create a holiday Address Book that uses a few fields to specify Christmas, Chanukah, or Kwaanza; Easter or Passover; or, for my truly *outré* friends, the solstices.

I can generate a report for each, do a summary counting how many of each, and know how many particular holiday cards (yeah—try and find a "Happy Vernal Equinox!" card at the local Hallmark store) I need to buy.

Year-in-Review Letters

Some folks are fond of sending Year-in-Review letters to all their friends and family, sharing the highs and lows of their lives. (Personally, my response has always been: *If this was so important when it happened, why am I just hearing about it now? You couldn't call? Drop me a line?* I guess that's the Jewish Grandmother in me.)

You can use your Address Book, the word processor, and mail merge (covered in Chapter 24) to create personalized mailings so each letter doesn't begin "Dear Family and Friends" (which is about as warm as "To Whom It May Concern").

With Works' page layout powers (covered in Chapter 11) you can create a family news-letter that will really knock their socks off.

The Least You Need to Know

Your Address Book, though handy, is just another database file. You can do anything you like with it—anything at all. Customize it to suit your needs. If you need help, all of Part 4 is devoted to the ins and outs of database design.

Once you've customized it, *use* it. Update it regularly. Delete old, unwanted records. Enter those odd scraps of paper you've accumulated with names and phone numbers on them. Make the Address Book work for you; don't work to find addresses.

Chapter 26

Communications Basics

In This Chapter

➤ Computer communications demystified

➤ What you need before you start

➤ A simple, sample online session (say that three times fast)

Computers keep getting more science fiction-ish all the time. It's almost scary. Some can talk and take verbal commands, just like the "Star Trek" computers. Some take dictation (with transcription software). Some answer the phone and take messages (with a modem and special software).

Then there's all that buzz about the Internet, online services, and the Information Super Highway—which is supposed to be a cure for all of society's ills (I'll believe *that* when I see it).

Works may not talk back to you, take a memo, or bring you a cup of coffee (I *wish*), but it will provide you with basic communications software that will hook you into a lot of the digital information flying around the planet.

Before You Get Your Hopes Up...

Stop drooling. We need to take care of some business, first.

In order to use the Works communication tool, there are a few things you need first. Some of them you have already. Others, you may not.

Stuff You Need

In very basic terms, these are the extra accessories you need to have or get before you can become an information diva (like my dear friend and goddess-babe, Juliet Cooke).

Check This Out...

Internet A world-wide network of computers that grew from old military and educational networks. It's a challenge to use effectively. If you're interested in trying, get a good book on the subject (maybe *The Complete Idiot's Guide to the Internet?*) before you take the plunge.

➤ A computer (which I'll assume you have, or you wouldn't be reading this).

➤ Microsoft Works for Windows 95 (ditto).

➤ A modem.

➤ A telephone line.

➤ Information. You need to know whether your telephone line is Touch Tone (it beeps once for each dialed number), or pulse (it clicks nine times when you dial a "9," six for a "6," and so on). You also need to know if you have Call Waiting (you hear a beep in your ear if someone else calls when you're on the phone).

➤ More information. Once you're all set to use Works' communication module, you need another computer to communicate with. It could be one at your job, or a local electronic bulletin board.

Call Waiting?

If you have Call Waiting, you need to let Windows 95 know that, and how to turn it off while you're using your modem. If you don't, the clicking noise an incoming call makes, might disrupt your connection—in short, hang up on you.

This is putting the cart in front of the horse, since I haven't even told you how to start the Communications module. So, don't do this until you've read the rest of the chapter, but, to turn off Call Waiting from Works:

1. Select **Modem** from the **Settings** menu. That will open the Modems Properties Control Panel.

2. Click on the **Dialing Properties** button. The Dialing Properties Control Panel appears.

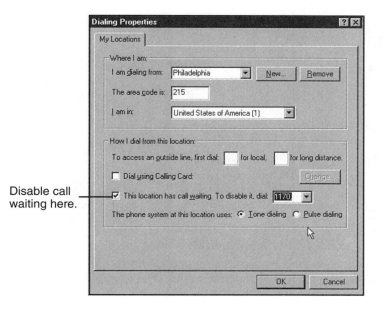

Windows 95's Dialing Properties Control Panel.

Disable call waiting here.

3. In the lower half of the control panel (the part labeled How I dial from this location), click on the **This location has call waiting** check box.

4. Select a disabling method from the pop-up list called **To disable it, dial**. (*70 or 1170, work for most locations).

5. If you haven't already, you might as well tell Windows if you have Tone or Pulse dialing. If you need to change or add any of the other settings, see your Windows 95 manual or online help for more details.

6. Click **OK**.

7. Click **OK** again (this time on the Modems Properties Control Panel) and you're back in Works.

Electronic bulletin board
Similar in nature to an *online service*, but usually much, much smaller. Most are run by individuals (called a *sysop*, for SYStem OPerator) as a hobby.

Where to Find the Items You Don't Have

If you don't have one or more of the items previously listed, you should take the time to track them down. You can order a modem through most computer mail-order companies or purchase one in most computer and office supply stores.

Buying a Modem? Some Info You Can Use

Modems are described in terms of their speed and capabilities. Their speed is expressed in terms of *baud rate* or *bits per second* (*bps*). You don't really need to know what those mean, except the higher the number given, the faster the modem. I wouldn't buy a modem that didn't operate at *least* at 14,400 bps, though a 28,800 bps modem wouldn't be out of the question. Faster modems can save you time and money, especially on commercial services where you pay for each minute of online time.

You probably have a telephone line already, since 95 percent of Americans do, according to AT&T.

If your computer isn't set up next to a convenient phone jack, you may need a *really* long phone cord, or you may want to invest in installing another jack near your computer (you can also plug a phone into most modems, so it will be a nice convenience being able to answer your phone at your desk).

A Phone of One's Own

For addictive personalities out there, and you *know* who you are, you're probably going to get hooked on modem communications. Eventually, you'll want to put in a telephone line *just for your computer* (called a dedicated phone line). I've seen it happen. I've done it. It also happens in families with teenage children where it's already a struggle to get the use of the phone.

Don't invest in one until you're sure you want and need it. They're expensive, even if they're horribly convenient.

Finding a computer to connect with is a harder nut to crack. If your computers at work aren't modem equipped, you can't use them. You can call a friend's modem-equipped computer, and you can type messages back and forth to each other, but after the initial thrill is gone, it's more fun just to talk to him on the phone, regular-like.

A local bulletin board is probably your best bet. You can ask around at your favorite computer store, check the classified sections of your newspaper, or ask around at the local high school, college, or computer club. You'll need the bulletin board's phone number and the correct modem settings (more on those in a bit).

Things You Won't Be Able to Do (Sorry)

Works' communication tool is a generic/general communications package. If you have your hopes all set to use it to access CompuServe, eWorld, The Microsoft Network, or America Online, I have some bad news: You can't use Works to access The Microsoft Network or America Online, and you probably won't *want* to use it with CompuServe.

The Microsoft Network and America Online (among others) require special software (such as a custom communications package called *proprietary software*) to use the services. CompuServe doesn't require special software, but it is available. The special CompuServe software (there are two packages called CompuServe Information Manager and CompuServe Navigator) makes the service much, much easier to use. All these online services, plus Prodigy and others, have software available in your favorite computer or software store.

Never One to Resist a Shameless Plug...

If you're interested, there's a *Complete Idiot's Guide to America Online* available now (written by yours truly), and there will be one for the Microsoft Network, in the not too distant future (also written by yours truly). Hey, a geek's got to eat.

Computer Communications Explained

Here's how all these accoutrements work together to let computers (and their users) communicate.

The central piece is the modem. A *modem* (which is a contraction of *MOdulating* and *DEModulating*) is a device which converts information from your computer into sound waves (that's the modulating bit) that can be sent over telephone lines to another modem. The receiving modem then turns the sounds back into information (that's the demodulating bit) that the computer at the other end can use.

The communication starts with you. You fire up Works and create a communications document with information about the computer you want to call. You tell Works to go ahead and call, and it activates your modem. The modem, acting like a phone, dials the computer's phone number.

When the other computer's modem answers the phone, they chat for a second (you hear it as a series of high-pitched squeals, much like a reunion of cheerleaders). The two modems compare their powers and capabilities, and negotiate a common ground where they can both give you the best connection possible. (That common ground is usually the maximum capacity of the weakest modem. You know what they say: a chain is only as strong as its weakest link.)

At this point, the other computer will ask you to identify yourself, and enter your password. When you do (or when you provide your name and create a password for the very first time), that's the end of the sign on process.

Check This Out...

Password
Like on the old game show of the same name, a password is a secret word that grants you (and only you) access to your account with a bulletin board or online service. If other people know your password, they can sign on and pretend they're you. Not a good thing.

Then the computer at the other end (assuming it's a bulletin board or online service), sends you a list (menu) of things you can do while online (connected to their service). You send commands back (usually typed), and the receiving computer obeys.

After you do all the things you like to do online, you sign off. Signing off is the process of your computer telling the other computer, "Okay, lady. Love ya. Bye-bye." (So I watch "Animaniacs." You wanna make something of it??)

That's an online session in a nutshell, and without many specific details. The things you need to do to prepare Works and your modem are pretty consistent, and I'll talk about them in the next chapter.

What actually happens when you're online—how you do the stuff you want to do, move around, and sign off—varies from bulletin board to bulletin board. There's usually information online to explain how each system works.

The Least You Need to Know

Oh, it's a big, wide, digital world we live in. The Internet is *the* geeky fashion accessory of the 90s and folks without e-mail addresses are just *so last Tuesday*. Don't worry, Works Communications module will keep you *chic* for years to come.

In order to use Works' communications tool, you need a computer, a modem, and a telephone line. In the next chapter, we'll get into the communications tools in detail.

➤ Information about your telephone line. Is it Touch Tone or pulse dial? Do you have Call Waiting?

➤ More information. You need the telephone number of a local (or national) bulletin board system, or another computer with communications software, to call.

Chapter 27

Communication Skills: The Next Generation

> **In This Chapter**
>
> ➤ Getting to Works' communication tools
>
> ➤ Toying with my emotions...I mean *settings*
>
> ➤ The communications toolbar, button by button
>
> ➤ Sending and receiving text and files

In the last chapter, you got a brief, basic overview of communicating with other computers via Works and your modem. Now we get to the nub, the crux, the down-and-dirty details. Drivers, start your modems!

Your First Time Online

To access Works' communication features, start with the Task Launcher. Click on the **Works Tools** tab, and then click on the **Communications** button.

Start here: the Works Tools page of the Task Launcher.

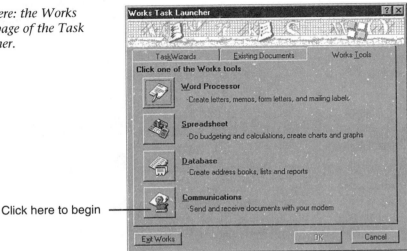

Click here to begin

Where Are You Calling?

Works wisely assumes that if you're opening up the communications package, you want to communicate with someone. It immediately presents you with the Easy Connect dialog box shown here.

Works' Easy Connect dialog box—making it easy to get out and sign on.

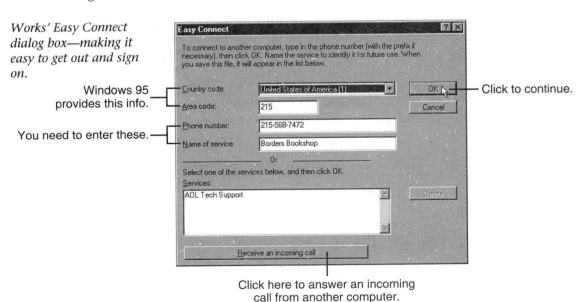

Windows 95 provides this info.

You need to enter these.

Click to continue.

Click here to answer an incoming call from another computer.

At the top of the dialog box, Works will have already filled in the information in the Country code and Area code boxes. It cribs it from the information you provided to Windows 95 when you installed your modem. You can change either one if it's not appropriate for your outgoing call.

Enter the number you need to dial to connect with this service or bulletin board in the Phone number text box. In the figure, I've entered the number for the bulletin board at my local Borders Bookshop. Which is also why I typed: **Borders Bookshop** in the Name of service text box. Funny how that works.

When you finish typing, click **OK**. Works saves the information you entered in a communications document. The next time you want to use this number, you can select it from the list of Existing Documents in the Task Launcher, or from the Services box at the bottom of the Easy Connect dialog box. (Notice that I've already saved a previous call to AOL Tech Support.)

Dialing...

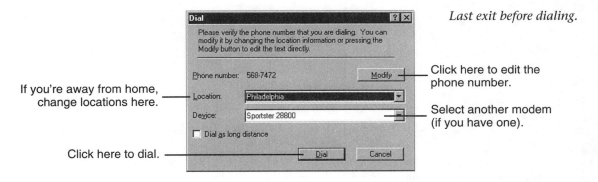

Last exit before dialing.

Click here to edit the phone number.

If you're away from home, change locations here.

Select another modem (if you have one).

Click here to dial.

When the Easy Connect dialog box closes, Works gives you a chance to verify the phone number (with the Dial dialog box).

With the Dial dialog box, you can edit the Phone number (click **Modify** to do that) in case you entered it incorrectly, or need to remove an area code. You can also change your Location (if you're on the road with a portable computer, for instance); just click on the **Location** drop-down menu.

You can also select another modem or communications port from the Device drop-down menu.

Why Select a Port, Not a Modem?

You can select any of your COM ports from the Device drop-down list instead of your modem. You would select a COM port if you were trying to connect with another computer in the same room with you. You don't need a modem for that, only a *null modem cable* connected to a COM port on the back of each computer. You also need communications software (such as Works) installed on both PCs.

If you click on the **Dial as long distance** check box, Works will dial using calling card or other long distance numbers (even plain old 1+ an area code) that you provided Windows 95's Dialing Properties Control Panel (seen earlier in this chapter).

Click **Dial** and Works will try to reach out and touch someone via modem. As it tries, it shows you the Dial Status window.

One ringy-dingy. Two ringy-dingies...

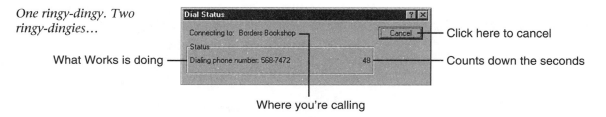

What Works is doing ── Dialing phone number: 568-7472

Click here to cancel

Counts down the seconds

Where you're calling

With the Borders bulletin board, I never did get through. Nobody answered the phone and Works gave up after 50 seconds (which is a long time, in terms of phones ringing). That's called a *timed-out*. Apparently, Borders lost interest in running their bulletin board, so they packed up their modem and went home. The employee in charge may have quit, and no one wanted to step in and play sysop.

That happens *a lot* to small, home-grown bulletin board systems, too. Hobbies turn into work, and stop being fun, so folks close up shop. Thus, the next section.

If At First You Don't Succeed...

... try, try again.

There are a few ways things can go wrong when trying to connect with an online service or bulletin board. Likewise, there are a couple of things you can do to try and correct the problem. This section is about what to do when things go wrong before you connect, or while you're connected.

Number Is Busy or No Answer

If the number you're trying to dial doesn't answer, the service may be offline for repair, upgrading, or the sysop may just need to do some homework on it (it happens). Try again later. If you can never get an answer, the bulletin board may be out of business. Try to find another.

A busy signal, however, is usually a good sign—*somebody's* using the service. You can set Works to try dialing again, automatically, in a few minutes. Here's how:

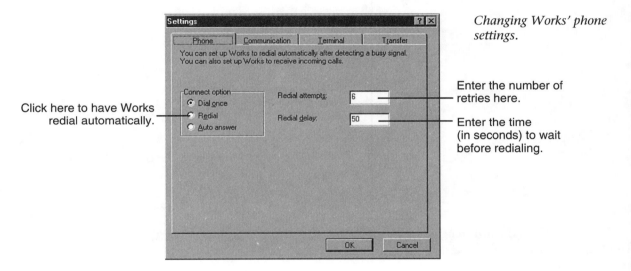

Changing Works' phone settings.

Click here to have Works redial automatically.

Enter the number of retries here.

Enter the time (in seconds) to wait before redialing.

1. Select **Phone** from the **Settings** menu. That calls up the preceding dialog box.

2. Click **Redial** in the Connect options box.

3. Type the number of times Works should try to redial in the Redial attempts box. It says **6** in the figure, but that seems excessive to me. Try **3**, maybe.

4. Enter the amount of time Works should wait between attempts (in seconds) in the Redial delay box. In the figure it says **50** seconds. That sounds too short to me; I'd make it 90–120 seconds. (But that's just me.)

5. Click **OK**.

The **Auto answer** option (in the Connect options box) is for Works to answer an incoming call from another computer. Personally, I don't set mine to Auto answer. I like to know in advance when someone wants to tap into my computer (not that it happens that often). Call me paranoid.

Works Can't Find My Modem

If Works tells you it can't find your modem, it's probably because you didn't tell it where it is (or changed it for some reason and forgot to change it back). Whatever happened, you tell Works where to find your modem with the Communication settings.

Communicating with the Communication settings.

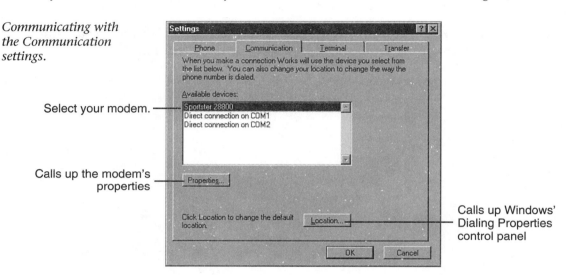

Select your modem.

Calls up the modem's properties

Calls up Windows' Dialing Properties control panel

Select **Communication** from the **Settings** menu. The Settings dialog box appears. Click on the name of your modem in the Available devices list box.

If you need to fiddle with the settings, the Properties button calls up the selected modem's properties without having to go through Windows 95's Modems Control Panel. In most cases, though, you probably won't need to fiddle.

Use the **Location** button and the Windows 95 Dialing Properties Control Panel appears, where you can change your location (if you've moved or are traveling with a portable computer). You saw it earlier in this chapter in the section on turning off Call Waiting.

I See Garbage Characters on My Screen

Calling into a new bulletin board is a crap shoot, really. You don't really know what kind of computer you're calling, nor how it's set up. If you dial into a computer and page after page of gibberish scrolls across your screen, you *probably* need to change Works' Terminal settings.

Whenever you create a new communications document, Works automatically sets the terminal settings to standard, "they work most of the time" settings—"most of the time" being the operative phrase.

The settings that are the culprits most often are the actual Terminal setting, and sometimes the ISO translation. To change these settings, select **Terminal** from the **Settings** menu. That calls up the dialog box.

You can customize the font and
size Works uses here, too.

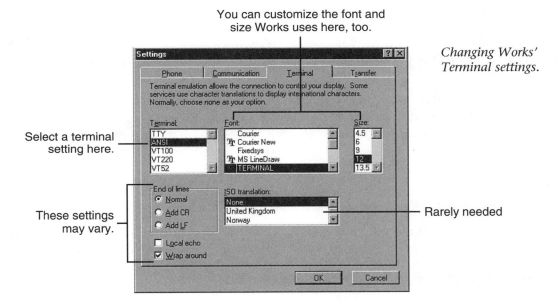

Changing Works' Terminal settings.

Select a terminal setting here.

These settings may vary.

Rarely needed

In the Terminal list box, you have five terminal emulations to choose from. You don't really need to know what they are, or even do. You *do* need to know that the most commonly used are ANSI and VT100. Try those first. If they don't work, try each of the others in turn. Keep track of your attempts; it's a process of elimination.

The ISO translation box lists a bunch of foreign countries. If you're calling a bulletin board outside your own country (whatever that may be) and get a lot of extra garbage characters on-screen, select the appropriate country's name from the list. Generally, you won't need it.

Check This Out...

Terminal
As in "computer terminal," not as in "terminate" or "terminally ill." Since there's a whole mess of different computers and bulletin boards out there, to simplify connecting to an unknown computer, communications software pretends to be one of a few standard computer types. This pretending is called *terminal emulation.* VT100 and ANSI are the two most commonly used terminal emulations.

335

You Can Make Your Eyes Happy, Too...

It doesn't affect any connection problem whatsoever, but you can use the Terminal settings to change the font, and the size of that font, that Works uses to display your session on-screen. Just select a new font from the Font list, and a size from the Size list, and your tired eyes will heave a sigh of relief.

The other Terminal settings (End of lines box, and the Local echo and Wrap around check boxes), generally, won't need to be altered unless you dial into a very old bulletin board system.

If the text you receive on your screen just piles up in an illegible mess and overwrites itself, you may need to select **Add LF** (for Line Feed, which adds a blank line after a carriage return). If the text you receive scrolls okay but doesn't start properly on the left side of your screen (there are words obviously missing), you may want to select **Add CR** (for Carriage Return, like hitting the return key on a typewriter).

Wrap around is the Works default setting. It wraps the text you receive so it doesn't run off the right side of your screen. You probably won't need to change it.

Click **Local echo** if the text you type doesn't appear on your own screen. If the text you type appears twice on your screen, turn Local echo off (by clicking on the check box).

Transfer Settings

Transfer settings allow you to send and receive files.

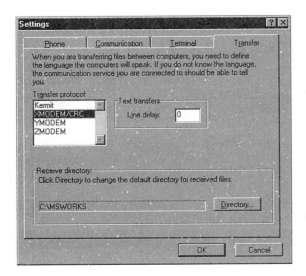

Just like it does with the Terminal settings, Works automatically selects a common Transfer setting (XMODEM/CRC, as shown in the preceding figure) for each new communications document.

The Transfer settings (shown in the Transfer protocol list box) are standard methods for sending a file, by modem, from one computer to another. That's what a protocol is, a standard method of doing things.

Both computers have to use the same protocol or hijinks will ensue. Beyond that, you don't really need to know any more about these protocols than the following:

➤ **XMODEM/CRC** is a venerable and reliable protocol that lets you send/receive one file at a time. It's a good choice.

➤ **YMODEM** lets you transfer several files at once but isn't as reliable as XMODEM.

➤ **ZMODEM** is fast, reliable, and allows you to transfer several files at once, but some bulletin boards don't use it.

➤ **KERMIT** (yes, as in "the Frog") is slow and steady, like the proverbial tortoise, but some bulletin boards don't use it.

Beyond that, you don't really need to know anything else. The technical details about what each is and does (and how they do it) would sedate even the worst insomniac.

Most bulletin board systems are capable of using several transfer protocols. You just need to remember which one Works is set for, so you can select the same one from the bulletin board's list of protocols.

Works' default choice, XMODEM/CRC, is pretty common and generally a hassle-free transfer method. Me, I'd leave it set as is, until you find out the bulletin board you're calling can't handle it. Then select another protocol from the list that the bulletin board *can* use.

The Text transfers box allows you to specify how much time Works will wait before it sends the next line of a file to the other computer. You'll only need to do this if the receiving computer can't accept the text as fast as your computer can send it. If you do need to use it, type the amount of pause time you want in the Line delay box. Entering a **1** causes a tenth of a second delay—a **2**, two-tenths of a second, and so on.

At the bottom of the dialog box there's the Receive directory box. This shows where any files you transfer will be stored on your hard drive. The default, as shown in the figure, is your MSWORKS directory. If you want your received files stored elsewhere, click Directory. That gives you a dialog box similar to your typical Save dialog box. Use it to navigate to the directory or subdirectory where you want to store your received files; then click **OK**.

Save Your Settings

As always, Mr. Phelps, whenever you change any of your settings, you should save them immediately. To save your settings, Select **Save** from the **File** menu, just as you would to save any other Works document.

If, by some chance, you forget to save your settings and then go to close a communications document (or exit Works completely), Works will ask you if you want to save your file then. Click **Yes** to save. Clicking **No** will exit Works without saving the changes you made, and clicking **Cancel** will return you to Works without closing the document.

The Communications Toolbar

Works' toolbar: the communications variation.

The toolbar, in communications, has the same buttons for the Task Launcher, saving files, copy, and paste, as it does in every other Works module. They're the first four buttons on the left.

The Address Book button, also standard, is the last button on the left.

In between these standard buttons are the communications-only buttons. The table below shows these buttons in order of appearance.

The Communications Toolbar Buttons

Icon	Function
Communication Settings	Clicking this is the same as selecting Communication from the Settings menu.
Terminal Settings	Clicking this is the same as selecting Terminal from the Settings menu.
Phone Settings	Clicking this is the same as selecting Phone from the Settings menu.

Icon	Function
Transfer Settings	Clicking this is the same as selecting Transfer from the Settings menu.
8,n,1	The shorthand way of expressing the standard modem setting used for most bulletin board services. The 8 is for the number of data bits, "n" means no parity, and the 1 is for "1 stop bit." Do you need to know what any of that means? No, you don't.
7,e,1	The counterpart to the 8,n,1 button. This is the other standard modem setting you might need—but in 10 years of modeming, I've never used it. So there. It stands for "7 data bits, even parity," and "1 stop bit." You really don't need to know what it means.
Easy Connect	Calls up the Easy Connect screen you saw back at the beginning of this chapter.
Dial/Hangup	A click on this will dial the telephone number for the currently open communications document, and connect you to the service. If you're already connected, this will hang up your phone and disconnect you.
Pause	Pauses the online proceedings while you get ready to, say, send a file, or capture incoming text. More on both of these shortly.
Capture Text	Saves any and all text that gets sent to your screen from the bulletin board you've connected with. It's a handy feature that can save you time online—more in a moment.
Send Text	Starts the process of sending a text file from your computer to the other computer
Send Binary File	Starts the process of sending an application or other file to the remote computer. It's also known as *uploading* a file.

continues

The Communications Toolbar Buttons   Continued

Icon	Function
⬚ Receive Binary File	Starts the process of getting an application or other file from the remote computer. It's also known as *downloading*.

The buttons in the toolbar make it much easier changing settings offline and accomplishing other tasks while online. Let's look at some of the online business (since I think I've beaten the settings to death).

Sending and Receiving Text

Everything you see when you're logged onto a bulletin board is text that's being sent to and from your computer—actual text information, yes, but also the menu choices, the questions you are asked, and even the answers you type are all text. This section is about the various ways to send and receive text with the Works communications tool.

Sending Text

There are three ways to get text from your computer to the computer you connect with via modem. One is simple typing. When you're linked to another computer, everything you type appears on a monitor at the receiving end. If you want to tell your life story to someone via modem, you can just type and type and type.

An easier way of sending your life story would be to write it with Works' word processor (that way you can check your spelling and consider cutting embarrassing information). When you later sign on to whatever bulletin board with which you're sharing the saga of your life, you can open the word processing document, and copy and paste it (a few lines at a time, probably) into the communications module. Here's how:

1. Write your life story with the word processor and save it to your hard drive (or a floppy disk). Leave the document window open.

2. Launch the communications module and connect to the bulletin board or online service.

3. Navigate to wherever you need to be (a live chat area, perhaps where users can talk (type) to each other).

4. Using the **Window** menu, switch to your life story.

5. Select the first bit of text; then select **Copy** from the **Edit** menu.

6. Switch back to the communications window (just select its name from the **Window** menu).

7. Make sure the cursor is where it needs to be (this varies between bulletin boards); then select **Paste Text** from the **Edit** menu. Your text will appear.

8. Press **Enter** to send the text.

9. Repeat the process until you've run out of your life story.

The copy and paste method is good for situations where you want (or can at least expect) questions from the person reading the text you're sending. If you're in a situation where someone says, "Send me your life story—I'll read it and get back to you," (and that happens all the time, doesn't it?), there's an even easier way.

You can send the text file directly from your hard drive to the other person's screen. You don't even need to read it again, yourself (why should you want to, it's your life—you know what happened).

To do that, select **Send Text** from the **Tools** menu. Works will give you a standard Open file dialog box. Use it to navigate to the text file you want to send. Click on the file name to select it, and then click **OK**. Works will send that life story faster than you can say "It all began in a 5,000-watt radio station in Fresno, California."

Receiving Text

Fair's fair. If you subject someone to your life story, you should be prepared to read hers as well. When she chooses to send it to you, this is what happens:

When Works receives text, it saves it in a smidgen of memory it has set aside, called a *text buffer*. Text fills the buffer until there's no more room. Then the new text replaces the old text, line by line. If it doesn't matter that you don't have a copy of all that text you're getting, you don't need to do any more than read it. If you want to save your friend's life story (for later blackmail usage, maybe), you need to *capture* that text to a file (which is then saved on your hard drive).

It's a good idea to capture your incoming text, especially when you're signing on to a new bulletin board. You can have a record of everything you've seen and done, and it can save you time later. Likewise, if you like to read information files online, you don't actually have to spend the time *reading* them. Works can capture them almost as fast as the other computer can send them. That will save you money on your phone bill, and that's a good thing. (What, suddenly I'm Martha Stewart??)

Here's how to capture text (you can do this before you sign on or after you're connected to the bulletin board):

Start to capture text, NOW!

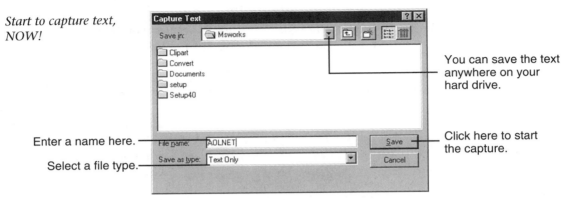

You can save the text anywhere on your hard drive.

Enter a name here.

Select a file type.

Click here to start the capture.

1. Click on the **Capture** button in the toolbar (the one with the camera on it). Works will present you with a standard Save-type dialog box.

2. Type a name for the capture file in the File name box. Works automatically calls it "capture," but you can call it anything you like.

3. Select a file type from the Save as type pop-up menu. *Text Only* is the default.

4. If you care to, you can navigate to the directory or sub-directory where you want the file saved. As long as you can remember where the file is, it doesn't much matter. You can always move it later. Just a point of personal preference.

5. Finally, click **Save**. Works will begin to write the file to your hard drive.

If you begin the capture while online, Works will automatically press the **Pause** button in the toolbar (the one with the hourglass on it). Before you can do anything else online, you need to click on **Pause** to get things going again. If you forget, Works will flash a cranky message that says something like, "How can I do that when the Pause button is pressed?" It's such a gentle, sensitive application.

To turn Capture off, click on the **Capture** button on the toolbar (the one with the camera on it). Later, you can view your captured file with Works' word processor. It will look a little something like the following figure.

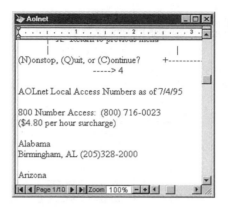

Viewing captured text...sort of a text zoo, really.

If You Start Up Capture Again...

If you start to capture text again (in the same session online, or a later one), you can add the new text to the end of an existing capture file. Just enter the name of the existing file in the Capture dialog box. When you click **Save**, Works will ask if you want to Replace the existing file, or Append the new text to the end of it. Click **Append**, and Works will add to the existing file, instead of erasing it.

Sending and Receiving Files

One of the most popular features of bulletin boards and online services are the file libraries. These are locations online where other members of the service have uploaded files of their own creation to share them with other members. You can find all manner of files online: photographic images, clip art, fonts, sample documents, and more.

As you start your online adventures, you're more likely to be downloading (receiving) files (until you get the hang of things), so let's look at that first.

Gimme Files!

Generally, most bulletin boards have file libraries where you can peruse brief descriptions of the available files. The file libraries, like regular libraries, are broken down into categories (Communications, Desktop Publishing, Graphics, Text files, and so on). The first step is finding a file that you want to have for your very own.

The actual process of indicating which file(s) you want varies from service to service. Check out any Help, or "Read Me" files online before you try this.

After you've indicated your file choice, you tell the bulletin board to send you the file. It will then ask you how you would like that sent (by what protocol; see the transfer settings section earlier for details)? Select the transfer protocol you set in Works' Transfer Settings dialog box, and the bulletin board will respond: Okay, beginning transfer (or words to that effect).

Downloading a file—the service is asking which transfer protocol I want to use.

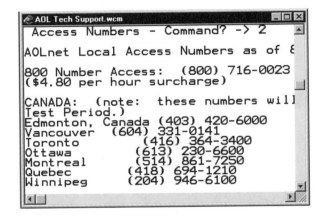

```
AOL Tech Support.wcm                          _ □ ×
 Access  Numbers  -  Command?  -> 2

AOLnet Local Access Numbers as of 8

800 Number Access:   (800) 716-0023
($4.80 per hour surcharge)

CANADA:  (note:   these numbers will
Test Period.)
Edmonton, Canada (403) 420-6000
Vancouver   (604) 331-0141
Toronto       (416) 364-3400
Ottawa        (613) 230-6600
Montreal      (514) 861-7250
Quebec        (418) 694-1210
Winnipeg      (204) 946-6100
```

You then have to tell Works that there's a file coming. To do that, select **Receive File** from the **Tools** menu.

Works will give you a standard Save-type dialog box (only it's called Receive file, now) where you can tell Works where you want the file stored, and what you want it called. When you have it set, click **Save**. Works will then start to receive the file, giving you a little status display (see the following figure).

Incoming!

Where it's going on your computer

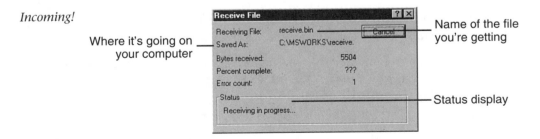

Name of the file you're getting

Status display

Receive File	? ×
Receiving File:	receive.bin
Saved As:	C:\MSWORKS\receive.
Bytes received:	5504
Percent complete:	???
Error count:	1
Status	
Receiving in progress...	

When the transfer is complete, you'll be returned to the bulletin board's menu and you can proceed on your merry way.

It's Better to Send Than to Receive

Well, maybe not. However, if you do want to share some of your original creations with other members of a bulletin board, here's how to do it. The process is remarkably similar to the downloading process, it just works in the other direction.

1. First, you need a file to send, and you need to know where it is on your hard drive.

2. While signed on to the bulletin board, navigate to the file *uploading* area. There may be more than one.

3. Tell the bulletin board you want to send a file. The process varies: it may ask you to enter a file name and description, or it may just ask you to select a transfer protocol and begin the transfer.

4. Tell Works you want to send a file: select **Send File** from the **Tools** menu.

5. Works will give you a standard file open-type dialog box (but called Send File, this time). Use it to navigate to the file you're sending, and click **Send**.

6. You'll get a Send File status display, very similar to the Receive File one we saw in the last section.

7. When the transfer finishes, the status display will vanish and you'll return to the uploading area on the bulletin board.

Be Legal In All Things

The federal government is going out of its way to try to moderate and control the kinds of things that are sent and received via electronic bulletin boards. Personally, I don't think they can do it—it's just too Herculean a task, and controlling it just stomps all over our right to freedom of speech.

Some things are illegal to transmit via modem, and most of them fall under the heading of copyrighted material, which can be: books, such as this one, photographs from a magazine, commercial products you'd normally buy in a store (software, clip art, fonts, games, and more).

If the material you want to send isn't completely your own from start to finish or you didn't receive permission from the person who owns the material, don't send it. It's just that simple.

The Least You Need to Know

That's an impossible goal. This is a big, fat, hairy, information-packed chapter. If I were you, this is what I'd do:

➤ Read the sections in the last chapter on finding and signing onto a bulletin board in your area, and use them to find one and sign on. Explore the service.

➤ If the service behaves badly for you, tinker with your communications settings as described in this chapter.

➤ Explore some more. Capture the text of your explorations so you'll have a record of where things are and how to get to them. Combine that information with the information in this chapter.

➤ When you're ready to upload or download a file, reread the appropriate section, and then take a shot at it.

➤ There's too much variation between services to say, "Here you go; here's the only information you need—go conquer the online world." There is a learning curve, but you'll be a modem maven in short order.

Chapter 28

Works' Customizing Options

In This Chapter

➤ Adding buttons to the toolbar

➤ Removing buttons from the toolbar

➤ Other customizing options

I saved this one for last because you really should get some quality work-time in with Works, so you can make informed choices about your customizing options. Not that the world will end if you don't, or you won't ever be able to change them again, if you want.

Basically, your customizing options fall into two broad categories. First is the toolbar; you can add and remove buttons so you can have your frequently used tools just a mouse-click away. The second set of options lets you customize how Works looks and behaves.

Customizing the Toolbar

After you get a little more experience with Works, you may find yourself reaching (clicking?) for some toolbar buttons more than some others. At this point, for example, I rarely use the Task Launcher after Works' initial startup. I have enough of my own files built up on my hard drive that I tinker with them, rather than resorting to a TaskWizard. For me, then, it would be more helpful to have a generic Open File button on the toolbar, instead of the Task Launcher button. It can be done.

We'll remove a button and then add a button to the word processor toolbar. First, open any old word processing document (or start a new one). Then, select **Customize Toolbar** from the **Tools** menu to open the Customize Works Toolbar dialog box.

Go Customizing Crazy!

You can customize the toolbars for each of Works' main components. Just open a document appropriate to the module you want to change (a spreadsheet, database, or communications) before you select **Customize Toolbar** from the **Tools** menu. Otherwise, the procedure is exactly the same as previously described.

Removing Buttons

First, send your toolbar to the dry cleaners—that's usually good for removing at least one button. (Kidding! I'm kidding. No letters from irate dry cleaners, please.) (Or if you must, write it with a TaskWizard so I know the book worked.)

Removing a button from the toolbar is a simple affair. With the Customize Works Toolbar dialog box open, click and drag the offending (or unused) button from the toolbar. Then release the mouse button. The button magically disappears from the toolbar and reappears in the customizing dialog box. Meanwhile, the buttons remaining on the toolbar all shift to fill in the void the removed button left. In my case, I dragged the Task Launcher button from the toolbar. Now I want to add the Open File button.

Adding a Button

A custom toolbar is just a click-drag away.

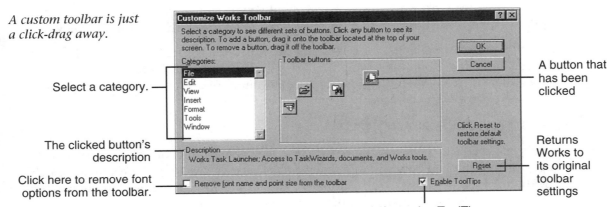

Select a category.

The clicked button's description

Click here to remove font options from the toolbar.

A button that has been clicked

Returns Works to its original toolbar settings

Click here to turn off those helpful/annoying ToolTips.

As you can see in the Customize Works Toolbar dialog box (shown here), there is a set of buttons available for each of Works' menus (except the Help menu). The ones shown in the figure are for commands in the word processor's File menu.

To add a button, do the following:

1. Select a command category from the Categories list box.

2. Click on a button in the Toolbar buttons box. That will show you a description of the button in the description box.

3. When you find the button you want, click-drag the button off of the dialog box and onto the toolbar.

4. When you have the button positioned where you want it on the toolbar, release the mouse button.

It's new! And improved!

My toolbar after switching buttons— oooh, pretty.

You can repeat the add/remove process as often as you like. You don't even have to add or remove anything.

With the Customize Works Toolbar dialog box open, you can add buttons, remove unused buttons, or any combination thereof. You can even rearrange the buttons that are already there: drag them to more convenient positions on the toolbar.

The ease of juggling things around on the Works toolbar lets you put everything right where you need it. And there are still more options you can customize to your liking.

Other Toolbar Options

If you look back at the picture of the Customize Works Toolbar dialog box, you'll notice three more little options hiding at the bottom of the dialog box.

The check box labeled Remove font names and point size from the toolbar will (oddly enough) remove the font name and size drop-downs from the toolbar, leaving you gobs more room for buttons. (I left them there, though. I fool around with fonts too much to do without them. But that's just me.)

The Enable ToolTips check box is automatically checked when you install Works. It enables Works to show you those helpful tips windows each time you select a new tool. After a certain point, however, they may become annoying. To make them go away, click in the check box and make the check mark disappear. Those ToolTips are history (at least until you enable them again).

The Reset button will undo all of the changes you've ever made to the toolbar, and reset it back to its virginal, just-installed-on-your-hard-drive configuration. My kitchen should have such a button.

Options, Options, And More Options

You can access all the remaining customizing options you have at your disposal (there I go, back in the kitchen again) by options that include: Editing, Data Entry, Address Book, General, View, and Proofing Tools. To bring the various options forward, just click on the appropriate tab.

Unlike the toolbar options in the last section, these options are (mostly) standard no matter which Works module you're currently using. Let's look at each.

Editing Options

Your Editing options customize how you select and replace text with the word processor.

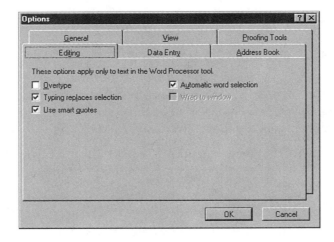

To call the Editing options (shown in the figure) to the front, click on the Editing tab. Here, you'll find five basic editing options:

Overtype puts Works permanently into overstrike mode (as discussed back in Chapter 6). I don't like it, won't use it—but you're a mature person, you can do whatever you like. You can drink out of the milk carton if you want to. Go ahead. Just don't offer me a glass of milk at your house.

Typing replaces selection configures Works so that when you select a word, a line, or paragraph, whatever you type next replaces it. If you click on this option (so it isn't checked) Works will insert whatever you type in front of the selection.

Use smart quotes automatically replaces straight, typewriter-type quotation marks (") with quotation marks that curl to the right in front of a quote, and to the left after. It's more professional looking.

Automatic word selection helps you select a word more quickly. You may notice, as you start to drag-select a word, that Works jumps to the conclusion you want the whole word selected. That's this option at work. If that annoys you (it does me, sometimes), click on the option to remove the check mark, and it will stop.

Wrap to window is the grayed-out option that you probably can't read in the figure. Since word wrap is an automatic feature of the word processor, you can't fool around with this option.

However, if you call up this option while using the communications tool, you *can* set it to wrap text to the window. Be warned: there's a 50–50 chance it will make your on-line session difficult to read (especially bulletin board menus).

Data Entry

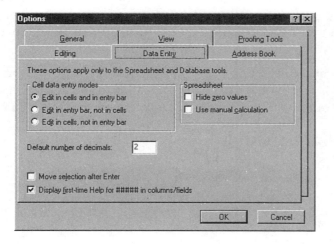

These options only affect spreadsheets and databases.

The Data Entry options, shown in the preceding figure, fiddle with how you enter information in spreadsheets and databases.

The Cell data entry modes options set where you can edit your entries in a spreadsheet. You have three options here: editing in both individual cells and the entry bar (also known as the formula bar); in cells alone; or in the entry bar alone. Click the option you want to use.

The Spreadsheet options, on the right, will hide zero values in spreadsheets (which can save you time and ink when printing). You can also set spreadsheets to do *manual calculations*.

Generally, when you enter data in a spreadsheet cell, Works checks to see if it's something that should be added (subtracted, multiplied, or whatever) in a formula somewhere in the spreadsheet. On slower computers, that can eat up time and slow down your work.

If you click the **Use manual calculation** check box, Works ignores any and all new entries until you select **Recalculate Now** from the **Tools** menu. Only then does it do the math.

This is an option you may want to check out, especially if you own an older PC or if you create large, mathematically complex spreadsheets.

At the center of the Data Entry options page, you can set the default number of decimal places for all of your spreadsheets. If you work with numbers with more (or less) than two decimal places on a regular basis, you may want to change the default setting of **2**.

The remaining two options are Move selection after Enter and Display first-time Help for ##### in columns/fields.

The first, when selected, automatically selects the *next* cell or field in a spreadsheet or database after you press the Enter key. As it stands now, you have to use the Tab or an arrow key to select the next cell or field (or use the Enter key on your numeric keypad, if you have one). Try it both ways and see which you prefer.

Display first-time Help is the option that warns you politely when you enter a formula that doesn't quite work. Once you get the hang of creating formulas (formulae?), you may want to turn this option off. Just click in the box to remove the check mark.

The Default Address Book

Which Address Book should Works open?

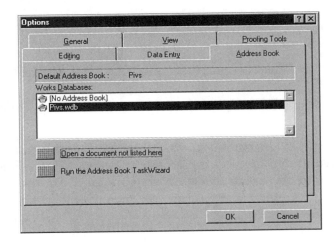

The Address Book options page really only gives you one option: selecting which Address Book file Works opens when you click the Address Book button. Just click on the file name of the Address Book you want Works to use.

If the Address Book you want to use isn't shown in the list, click **Open a document not listed here** and show Works where the file you want is located. Or, if you don't already have an Address Book, click **Run the Address Book TaskWizard** and create one.

Generally Speaking...

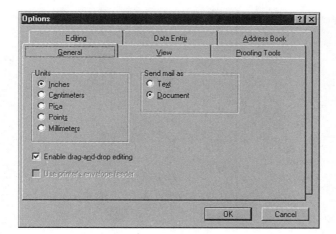

A mixed bag of general options.

The General options affect all of Works' tools: the word processor, database—everything.

You can set what unit of measurement Works uses throughout (and displays in the ruler). Just click on the option you want in the **Units** box. You can choose from: Inches, Centimeters, Pica (a printer's measurement), Points (as in the point size of fonts), and Millipedes... meters, Millimeters. (A minor bug phobia rears its ugly head once more. *Ew, ew, ew.*)

If you installed the Microsoft Exchange software (included with Windows 95, but optional), you'll have the Send mail as options shown in the preceding figure. You can send mail as Text (which insert text from a Works document into a mail message) or as a Document (which attaches a Works document to your e-mail like a pilot fish to a shark).

At the bottom of the General page, there are two more options: Enable drag-and-drop editing and Use printer's envelope feeder. (My printer doesn't have a built-in envelope feeder, so it's grayed out in the figure. Yours may or may not be, depending on your printer.)

Drag-and-drop editing (covered in Chapter 8) is the way-cool feature that allows you to select text and, rather than cutting and pasting it to a new location, just drag it to its new home. I can't work without it.

If your printer has a built-in (or even an add-on option) envelope feeder, you should click the **Use printer's envelope feeder** check box. It will make printing envelopes so much easier.

A View to a Window

How do you want Works to look?

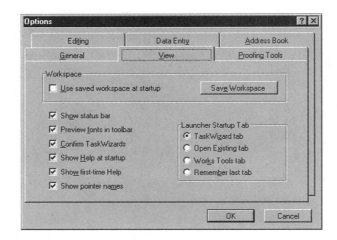

The View options (in the preceding figure) are where you customize how Works looks and behaves while you're using it.

The Workspace options set what files (if any) Works will open every time you launch Works. It's very convenient if you're working on a long project that involves the same set of files day-in and day-out. To use it, do this:

1. Close the Options display (click **OK** if you've made changes you want to keep; otherwise click **Cancel** or the close box).

2. Open all the files you want opened every time you start Works.

3. Select **Options** from the **Tools** menu again.

4. Click on the **View** tab.

5. Click the **Save Workspace** button.

6. Click **Use saved workspace at startup**.

7. Click **OK**.

Now, whenever you start Works, that set of files will automatically open. To change the set of files at a later date, repeat steps 2 through 5, and step 7.

Below the Workspace box, there's a list of six check boxes that turn various options on and off (they're all turned on (like, wow, man) in the figure). They are:

Show status bar   The status bar is the bar that runs across the bottom of the Works screen, above Windows 95's Start and application/window buttons. It displays information about the file you're working with (like what page you're on), and whether your NUM and Caps lock keys are pressed.

Preview fonts in toolbar   Shows you a sample of what your installed fonts look like when you select them from the toolbar's pop-up font listing. I like the font preview, but it can slow down the font selection process.

Confirm TaskWizards   Prompts Works to ask you if you're really, really sure you want to use the TaskWizard you selected before starting it up.

Show Help at startup   Tells Works to make sure the Help panel is up and running when you launch works. Very useful at first but a waste of monitor real estate, later.

Show first-time Help   Brings up those offers of help every time you try a new thing with Works.

Show pointer names   The option that pops up the names under the pointer.

You can probably do very nicely without a few of these options, once you're more familiar with Works features.

The last set of View options are for the Task Launcher. In the Launcher Startup Tab box, you can tell Works which tab you want foremost when the Task Launcher appears at startup. Select from the three tabs (TaskWizard, Existing documents, or Works Tools), or tell Works to use whichever tab was the last one you selected. Select whichever tab you use the most. I prefer the Remember last tab option myself.

Finally: Proofing Tools

That's "finally" as in the last one, not as in "it's about time we got to this one." The last set of options are for which dictionary and thesaurus files Works will consult automatically. This is pretty much of a Hobson's choice, which is to say, no choice at all. Works comes packaged in language-specific editions.

In the Spelling box, you can choose between an American English dictionary or a British English dictionary. That's it. The only difference between the dictionaries is that the British English dictionary won't call you on the carpet for spelling color "colour," or theater "theatre."

The Proofing Tools—not much of a choice, really.

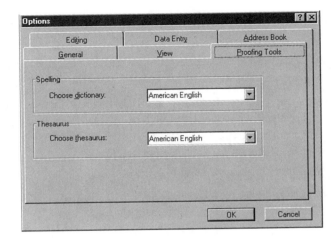

If you're an American, the British spellings will give your readers the impression that you're a pretentious goof (okay, okay, it gives *me* that impression—this is a pet peeve of mine), so don't use them (if you're writing to me) unless you're in the United Kingdom.

The Thesaurus drop-down list only has an American English option, so it's really no option at all.

If you're multilingual, or write in lawyer-, doctor-, or techno-speak, you can find other language dictionaries and thesauri for sale in many mail-order catalogs and software stores. That way you won't have to teach Works' American English dictionary how to spell *framboise* (which it wants to correct to "farmhouse") or *polyethylene glycol* (which is my favorite ingredient in Dr. Pepper).

The Least You Need to Know

You can easily customize Works to meet your needs. I wouldn't, however, mess with the customization options until you know that the default settings aren't cutting it for you.

You need to discover how *you* work, and what you do while working before you can effectively tailor Works to your performance peculiarities.

Speak Like a Geek: The Complete Archive

absolute text wrap   See *text wrap*.

active cell   The cell in a spreadsheet surrounded by a thick box for easy identification. This is the cell in which you can enter data, or edit existing data.

active window   The document window that is foremost on your screen, the one you're working with. You can also tell it's the active window because its title bar is a vibrant color (*what* color depends on the color scheme you've selected in Windows' Display Control Panel).

address plate   An area set aside in a document to hold a mailing label, stamp, and your return mailing address in the typical envelope-type arrangement.

alphanumeric   Generally, anything that is a combination of letters and numbers. With Works' spreadsheet, some alphanumeric data needs special handling, so Works knows what you expect to be done with the information.

application   A fancy way of saying "software" or "program." It has come into vogue, I think, because you use software to "apply" the power of your computer. Or I could be making it up.

argument   In the "logic" sense, not the "you are so wrong" sense, an argument is a logical construction often incorporating the words "if" and "then." It tells your database or spreadsheet to look for entries that meet certain criteria: IF this is true, THEN do that. IF this is not true, THEN don't do that.

baud rate   A measure of a modem's speed. The higher the baud rate, the faster the modem.

bits per second   Another measurement of modem speed, often abbreviated to BPS. The higher the modem's BPS rating, the faster the modem operates.

bookmark   An invisible marker that helps you quickly return to important parts of your document. You place a bookmark by selecting **Bookmark** from the **Edit** menu.

BPS   See *bits per second.*

buffer   A bit of memory that Works sets aside to store incoming text when you're connected to a bulletin board. When the buffer is full, new text deletes the text at the top of the buffer, unless you capture it to a file.

bullet   A typographical eye-catcher like this: ➤. Use bullets to set off important, short lists of information. See also *dingbat.*

cell   The basic unit of a spreadsheet designed to hold one piece of information. Each rectangle in the light gray grid-work is a cell. You can identify cells by the letter of the column they are in, followed by the number of the row. A1, for example.

cell alignment   How the contents of a cell are placed in relation to the cell wall (what is this, biology?). Cells, like text, can be aligned left, center, right, but also by decimal place. You use the Font and Alignment dialog box (under the Format menu) to change cell alignment.

cell reference   The column letter and row number (A1, B12, and so on) used to identify cells.

chart   A graphical representation of the data from a Works spreadsheet. Charts make it easier for people to interpret your data, but they can also be misleading if there's no real relationship between the charted data...datums...doo-doo.

Clear command (shortcut: Del)   Deletes the selection (text or other something else) without sending it to Windows' Clipboard. Kiss it good-bye.

Clipboard   A bit of your computer's memory that Windows (and Windows applications) use to temporarily store information that you cut or copy from documents. The Clipboard only holds one item at a time. You can paste that item (sometimes called a "clip") into the same Works document, a different Works document, or a document created with another Windows application. Very convenient.

column   A vertical line of cells in a spreadsheet, such as the columns that hold up the roof over your front porch. You can identify columns by letters.

Copy command (shortcut: Ctrl+C)   Found in the Works Edit menu; copies selected text (leaving the original text in your document) and places the copy in Windows' Clipboard for later use.

Cut command (shortcut: Ctrl+X)   Found in the Works Edit menu; removes the selected text from your document and places it in Windows' Clipboard for later use.

database   A collection of information that you can easily search and sort for whatever information you need.

dedicated telephone line   A telephone line whose only purpose in life is to connect your computer modem and/or fax machine to the outside world. It's a real badge of geek-dom. Needless to say, I have one.

default   Usually refers to software settings: the way your software was set up when you bought it, or standard options (such as margins) that Works assumes you want to use unless you tell it otherwise.

design view   See *form design view*.

desktop publishing   Literally, publishing from the top of your desk. Personal computers, software, and other hardware have made it possible for common folks like you and me to design, edit, print, and duplicate professional-looking documents without resorting to typesetters, printers, and all the old-fashioned headaches and hassles of printing. Desktop publishing software is also sometimes referred to as *page layout software*.

dialog box   Sometimes, when you tell your computer to do something, it needs more information to follow your orders. When that happens, a dialog box appears on your screen, asking for the additional information.

dingbat   a specialty font composed entirely of symbols instead of the usual assortment of letters, numbers, and punctuation marks.

document   Any file you create with Works or any software: a spreadsheet, a letter, a novel, an address database. They're all documents. It's used to distinguish data files from software and system files, since "file" is too generic to be meaningful.

downloading   The process of retrieving an application or other file from a remote computer.

drawing program   A drawing program, such as Microsoft Draw, is an application designed to let you create simple graphics from discrete pieces (a circle, a box, a chunk of text, and so on.) that you can easily move and arrange into a pleasing arrangement.

electronic bulletin board   Similar in nature to an *online service*, but usually much, much smaller. Most are run by individuals (called *sysops*, for SYStem OPerators) as a hobby.

embedded, embedding   An object inserted into a Works document (from a file created with another application) is *embedded* if it is not linked to the original application. The object is like a fly trapped in amber: it's unchangeable unless you delete the object and start over. See also *linked* and *OLE*.

end of line mark   A special character that looks like an arrow bent at a 90-degree angle; it forces Works to start a new line of text without starting a new paragraph.

field   The portion of a database designed to hold one bit of information in every record.

field entry   The data you type into a field.

file format   Different applications store their files differently when they write them to a disk. How the file is stored is called its file format. You don't need to know the details, really.

filter   One or more logical statements (IF this, then do THAT) used by Works' database to sift through records to find the ones that meet the filter's criteria.

folder   Part of Windows' metaphor for filing things on your computer. Like paper file folders, a folder on your computer represents a place you can save a file to. In ultra-geeky terms, it represents a subdirectory on your hard drive.

font   Generic word for a digital typeface. A font is a complete set of letters, numbers, punctuation, and commonly used symbols (all the stuff you find on your keyboard). The differences between fonts, visually, are how the letters are drawn: thick or thin, slanted or not, and so on. Fonts are identified by names that usually tell you nothing about what the font looks like.

footer   A line of text at the bottom (foot) of each page of a Works document. You enter a footer by using the Footer command in the View menu.

form   A single database record, as seen in form view.

form design view   A way of displaying a database file. It allows you to arrange fields on the page, add graphic elements (boxes, shading, and such), and generally beautify your finished database.

form letter   What Works calls the process of creating a database with name and address information, writing a letter *without* name and address information, and then mashing the two files together to produce a copy of the letter for each name and address record in your database.

form view   The way of displaying a database file that shows (pretty much) what a record will look like when printed; allows you to enter and edit information in individual fields.

format, formatting   The process of taking your plain, vanilla document, and spicing it up with fancy margins, fonts, and other typographic effects, most of which are created with the Works toolbar or the Format menu.

formula   A shorthand way to express a mathematical operation. Like a grammatical sentence, a formula usually includes a command (a subject), and then something on which to perform the command (an object). All formulas begin with an equal sign (=).

function   A generic mathematical formula that's already built into the Works spreadsheet. You access functions through the Easy Calc button on the toolbar (it's the one with the calculator on it).

handles   Little boxes on each side, and in each corner, of a graphic. Click-dragging on a handle lets you resize the graphic to the size you need (but may also distort the graphic, so be careful).

hanging indent   An indentation that's tired of living. No, no—it's a start-of-paragraph indentation that sticks out toward the left margin, as opposed to the regular indent, which moves in toward the right margin.

header   A line of text at the top (head) of each page of a Works document. Enter a header by using the **Header** command in the **View** menu.

icon   A graphical representation of a computer command (launch this application) or feature (open this folder). Usually, you issue a command by double-clicking on the appropriate icon with your mouse.

inactive window   A document window that you have moved to the background. Normally, an inactive window's title bar will turn gray (or a grayish color, depending on the color scheme you've selected in Windows' Display Control Panel). You can't work with an inactive window. To activate an inactive window, just click on any part of it, or select its name from the Window menu.

inline text wrap   See *text wrap*.

insertion point   The blinking vertical line that shows you where what you type will appear in your document.

Internet   A world-wide network of computers that grew from old military and educational networks. It's a challenge to use effectively.

keyboard shortcut   a combination of keystrokes (such as Ctrl+S) that you can use instead of a menu item (in this case, selecting **Save** from the **File** menu). Most use the Control or Alt keys on a standard keyboard, plus a letter, number, or function key (such as the F1 key).

landscape   Page orientation where an 8 1/2-by-11-inch page is wider than it is tall. See also *portrait*.

Launch, launching   A fancy way of saying "starting up." You can launch Works either by selecting it from the Programs menu from the Start menu, or you can double-click the Works shortcut icon on your desktop (if you choose the shortcut option during installation).

leading   An old word borrowed from typesetters that refers to the amount of space between lines of type.

legibility   A measure of how easy it is to identify letters, number, and characters of a font. Sans serif fonts are very legible.

linked   A linked file is one that is still connected with its original application after being inserted into a Works file. Changes made to the original file appear in the object, and changes made to the object appear in the original file.

linking   See *OLE*.

list view   The way of displaying a database file that shows you all of your records in a spreadsheet-like table. You can enter and edit information in individual fields, as well as edit and format the fields themselves.

mail merge   See *form letter.*

margin(s)   Margins are the white spaces that surround text on the printed page. Traditionally, margins are set at 1 inch at the top, bottom, and sides of the page. Works' default margins are set at 1" at the top and bottom, and at 1.25" to the left and right.

modem   A contraction of *MOdulating* and *DEModulating.* A modem is a device that converts information from your computer into sound waves (that's the modulating bit) that can be sent over telephone lines to another modem. The receiving modem then turns the sounds back into information (that's the demodulating bit) that the computer at the other end can use.

monospaced font   A font in which characters (letters and blank spaces) take up the same amount of space on the page.

MS-DOS   An acronym for Microsoft Disk Operating System (pronounced "em-ess-doss" to rhyme with "toss").

network   Two or more computers linked to each other to make it easier for them to share data. These computers may be in the same room or spread out over a wider area. Printers and other devices may also be part of a network.

nonbreaking hyphen   Special character that keeps hyphenated words together on the same line, even if it means leaving empty space at the end of the previous line.

nonbreaking space   Special character that keeps the two words at either side of the space together on the same line, even if it means empty space at the end of the previous line.

object   A document, or part of a document, created with another application, which has been prepared for inclusion in a Works document. See also *OLE.*

offline   Term to describe the condition of being disconnected from a bulletin board or online service. If you aren't connected, you'd say "I'm offline right now."

OLE   (pronounced "OH-lay," like what gets shouted at bullfights) An abbreviation that stands for Object Linking and Embedding. OLE gives you the ability to place things (called objects) created with another OLE-compatible application in a Works document, and vice versa.

online   Term for computer communications as they happen. When you are connected to another computer, bulletin board, or online service, you are *online.*

online service   A commercial company (it costs you money) that provides a variety of news, entertainment, and computer-related services via modem. It can usually accommodate a large number of users at the same time.

optional hyphen   A special character used to place a hyphen in a word; Works will hyphenate that word only when the word is at the end of a line. See also: *nonbreaking hyphen.*

OS   Operating System. The basic set of instructions that tell a computer how to deal with software, hardware, and commands. All computers require an operating system. PCs can use MS-DOS or Windows 95, among others.

overstrike mode (OVR)   Overstrike mode means that newly typed text doesn't push existing text along, instead it types over existing text. You turn overstrike mode on and off by pressing the **Insert** key on your keyboard.

OVR   Abbreviation for *overstrike mode.*

page break   The point where one page ends and the next begins. You can force a page break by using the **Page Break** command in the **Insert** menu. An inserted page break says to Works, "I don't care if this page isn't full; start a new one." And Works does.

page layout   See *desktop publishing.*

page orientation   The direction in which words and images appear on the printed page. There are two page orientations: *portrait* and *landscape.*

password   Like on the old game show of the same name, a password is a secret word that grants you (and only you) access to your account with a bulletin board or online service. If other people know your password, they can sign on and pretend they're you. Not a good thing.

paste special command   Found in the Edit menu; lets you paste special characteristics (font and paragraph formatting) onto other text in your Works documents. It also lets you retain special formatting when you're pasting items copied or cut from other applications. For instance, you may want the pasted text to retain your font choice or other formatting applied in the other application.

place holder   The bracketed field entries in a form letter (<<First name>> and the like) are called *place holders* because they hold the place for the actual data that will be added from your database.

plunk   A technical term meaning "to place discretely." Not to be confused with "punk" or "pluck" which both mean something else entirely.

point   Font sizes are measured in *points*, from an old typesetting term. One point (abbreviated pt.) equals about 1/72 of an inch. A 72 point character would be about an inch tall. 10 and 12 points are common for most word processing uses.

portrait   This page orientation is the way most folks think of a sheet of paper. That is, with an 8 1/2-by-11-inch page. A page in portrait orientation is taller than it is wide.

proportional font   A font in which letters only take up the amount of space they need. Most computer fonts are proportional. See also *monospaced fonts.*

proprietary software   Special software required to use an online service (such as America Online or Prodigy) that can only be used with that particular service. It's called "proprietary" because it is, in essence, their property (since it's useless for anything else).

pt.   Abbreviation for *point*.

RAM (random-access memory)   Like humans' short-term memory, RAM is a temporary storage area for application and document information. The contents of RAM disappear when you turn your computer off. To prevent the loss of your documents, you must save them either to your hard drive or a floppy disk.

range   Two or more cell references used to indicate the first and last cell of a series of cells, to be used by a spreadsheet formula.

record   One complete set of fields in a database is a record.

readability   How difficult or easy it is to read a particular font for a long period of time. Serif fonts are very readable.

result   The answer to a spreadsheet formula. While the formula appears in the formula bar, the result appears in the appropriate cell.

row   A horizontal (side to side) line of cells in a spreadsheet, like rows in a theater. Numbers identify rows.

RTF (Rich Text Format)   A special file saving method that not only saves your actual text but also all of the formatting information (font, margins, indents, and so on) regardless of which application you use to view or edit the file.

sans serif   Literally translated, it means *without serifs*; a font that does not include the tails and curlicues (the serifs) that improve the readability of text. The chapter names and headings in this book are in a sans serif font.

save, saving   The process of telling Works (or any application) to store a copy of your document on your hard drive or floppy disk. If you don't save a file, it exists only as electronic burps and beeps in your computer's *RAM* (random-access memory), and the file will be lost forever if you turn off your computer or the power goes out. Ctrl+S is the keyboard shortcut for the Save command.

scale, scaling   A really techno-geeky way of saying "resize" a picture. Use it. It will make you sound *soooo* smart at cocktail parties, or wherever geeks collide.

script   A font that duplicates the look of hand-written documents or calligraphy. Very fancy and formal, usually you'll only find it on wedding invitations and business cards.

series   A row or column of data in a spreadsheet, represented by one line, bar, or other indicator in a chart.

series indicator   A line, bar, or other graphic element (such as a pie wedge in a pie chart) used to represent numerical data from a spreadsheet.

serif   Fonts whose letters have little tails and curlicues (the serifs) that make them easy to read and identify quickly. The text of this book is set in a serif font.

Shortcut   A desktop icon that allows you to launch Works (or any application) simply by double-clicking on it. (Don't confuse it with a *keyboard shortcut*.) Shortcuts save you steps with applications and folders you use all the time. You can create your own shortcuts with the File menu in the Windows Explorer window.

sign off   The process of ending your session with a bulletin board or online service.

sign on   The process of connecting to a bulletin board, including entering your name and password.

sort   The sort command automatically rearranges information in a spreadsheet or database according to your ordering criteria. You can sort information alphabetically (A to Z), chrono-logically (January 1 to December 31), or numerically (1 to 100).

spot color   A technical term for using teeny-tiny bits of color (even gray) on an otherwise black-and-white page. Usually, it's applied to the first letter of a main paragraph or to other attention-getting typography, such as bullets.

spreadsheet   A tool that helps you organize and present a lot of numerical information in a way that's easy for the reader to understand. Additionally, you can perform mathematical operations on the numbers in the spreadsheet.

Start button   Windows 95's funky new application launching tool. It's the button, typically on the bottom left corner of your screen, which reveals a menu of all the applications on your hard drive.

Start menu   The menu that pops up from Windows 95's Start button. It contains a list of all the applications on your hard drive for easy launching.

subscript   Text formatted (with Works' Font and Style dialog box) to fall below the rest of a line of text, for example: H_2SO_4.

superscript   Text formatted (with Works' Font and Style dialog box) to rise above the rest of a line of text for example: $10^2 \times 6^4$.

sysop   Pronounced "sis-op." See *system operator*.

system operator (usually abbreviated to sysop)   The person in charge of an electronic bulletin board.

taskbar   The bar that runs across the bottom of the Windows 95 screen. It contains buttons for all of your currently open windows and/or applications so you can easily switch between them. To go to an item in the taskbar, just click on it.

Terminal   As in "computer terminal" not as in "terminate" or "terminally ill." Since there's a whole mess of different computers and bulletin boards out there, to simplify connecting to an unknown computer, communications software pretends to be one of few standard computer types. This pretending is called "terminal emulation." VT100 and ANSI are the two most commonly used terminal emulations.

terminal emulation   See *terminal*.

text buffer   See *buffer*.

text wrap   How text flows around a picture (or other object) inserted into a Works document. Inline text wrap places text above and below the object. Absolute text wrap also places text on either side of the object (if space allows).

tick   NOT the comic book and cartoon character who shouts "Spoon!" as he leaps into action. A tick is one of the little hash marks that appear in the X- and Y-axes of a graph that show what increments the chart is measuring. They're like inch-marks on a ruler.

timed-out   Works' communications package has only a set amount of time (50 seconds) to connect with the computer you're calling. If the other computer doesn't answer in that time, the call is timed-out, and Works hangs up the phone.

translator   Works uses a file translator (like a language translator) to change a Works format file into the file format used by another application.

uploading   The process of sending an application, or other file, to a remote computer via modem. See also *downloading*.

Word processor   A software tool that simplifies the editing process, freeing up brainpower for the difficult part of writing: thinking of something to say in an informative, entertaining way.

word wrap   The technical name for how Works automatically continues a long line of text on the next line of a word processing document without you having to hit the Enter key. It's automatic in the word processor; you have to tell Works to do it in the spreadsheet. Don't confuse *word wrap* with *text wrap*—they're two different things.

Index

Symbols

" (double quotation mark),
157, 226
( ) (parentheses), 166
* (asterisk), 149
+ (plus sign), 149
- (minus sign), 149
/ (slash mark), 149
= (equals sign), 149, 157
? (question mark), 44
3-D charts
    area charts, 197
    bar charts, 197
    line charts, 198
    pie charts, 198

A

About Microsoft Works 4.0
  command (Help menu), 34,
  43
absolute text wrap, 140
  see also text wrap
accessories
    communications
      accessories, 324
    graphics accessories
      ClipArt, 278-279
      Draw!, 272-275
      WordArt, 279-281
account IDs, inserting in form
  letters, 305
Accounts TaskWizard, 217
active cells, 146, 150
  defined, 357
active windows, 63
  defined, 357

adding cells
  three-cell calculations, 166
  two-cell calculations, 165
Address Book
  building, 318
  customizing, 316
    field insertion, 316,
      319-320
    reports, building, 317
    selected options,
      viewing, 317-318
    viewing reports, 320
  names, inserting, 319
  opening, 314
  options page,
    custom-izing Works, 353
  saving, 319
  selecting, 314
  uses, 320
    birthdays/anniver-
      saries, 321
    emergency numbers,
      322
    holiday cards, 322
    phone lists, 321
    Year-in-Review letters,
      322
Address Book TaskWizard, 217
address plates, 133
  defined, 357
addressing form letters,
  300-302
aligning
  cells (defined), 358
  fields, 243-244
  paragraphs, 106-107
  spreadsheet alignment,
    187-189
  tabs, 109

Alignment command (Format
  menu), 188, 231, 243
alphanumeric data, 157
  defined, 357
applications
  data sharing, 284-285
  defined, 357
  integrated applications,
    46-47
  launching with Start
    button, 13-14
applying
  AutoFormats, 184
  fonts to spreadsheets,
    184-185
  styles, 121
area charts, 197
arguments (defined), 357
Arrange Icons command
  (View menu), 22
Ascending sort order, 179, 249
assigning
  names
    charts, 201
    fields, 229
    files, 54-55
    titles (database reports), 260
asterisk (*), 149
author initials (form letters),
  305
AutoFormat command
  (Format menu), 182
AutoFormats, 182-184
  applying, 184
  undoing, 183-184
AutoSum feature, 148,
  163-164
Average summary, 265
averaging cells

Easy Calc feature, 167
multiple math operations, 166
ranges, 166
three-cell calculations, 166
two-cell calculations, 165
AVG( ) function, 167

B

Backspace key, 172
bar charts, 197
baud rates
    defined, 357
    modems, 326
Bids TaskWizard, 151
bits per second (bps), 326
    defined, 357
bookmarks (defined), 357
Bookshelf program, 38
Border command (Format menu), 246
borders, inserting
    around text, 133-134
    charts, 201-212
    databases, 246-247
    pages, 135-136
    spreadsheets, 189-190
Borders and Shading command (Format menu), 133
Borders and Shading dialog box, 134
boxes, inserting in database fields, 244-245
bps (bits per second), 326
    defined, 357
Bring to Front command (Edit menu), 275
buffers
    defined, 358
    text buffers, 341
building
    Address Book, 318
    bulleted lists, 107-108
    charts, 199-200
        Advanced Options tab, 201-202
        Basic Options tab, 200-201
        data, selecting, 200
    columns, 130-131
    databases, 218-220

dummy documents, 131-132
Easy Formats, 117
files, 55-56, 128
filters, 256-257
    database reports, 263-264
form letters, 296-297, 299
    addressing options, 300-301, 305
    fields, inserting in addresses, 301-302
    font selection, 304
    greetings, 303
    letter contents, 304
    manual creation, 308-309
    stationery, designing, 299-300
    logos (Draw! program), 276-278
    mailing labels (form letters), 309-311
    OLE objects, 291
    reports (Address Book), 317
    spreadsheets, 151, 155
    see also writing formulas
bulleted lists
    building, 107-108
    defined, 358
bulletin boards
    defined, 359
    dialing, 330-332
        busy signals/no answer, 333
        modems, searching, 334
        Terminal options, setting, 334-336
        Transfer options, setting, 337
    files
        receiving, 344-345
        sending, 345-346
    searching, 326
    text
        capturing, 341-343
        sending, 340-341
Bullets command (Format menu), 108
Business Inventory TaskWizard, 217
buying, see purchasing

C

calculations
    cell ranges, averaging, 166-167
    manual calculations, 352
    multiple math operations, 166
    spreadsheet planning, 155
    three-cell calculations, 166
    two-cell calculations, 165
Call Waiting, disabling, 324-325
captions, 122
Capture dialog box, 343
capturing text (bulletin boards/online services), 341-343
carbon copies (CC), 305
Carriage Return (CR), 336
CD-ROMs
    Bookshelf program, 38
    icons, 18
    installing Works from, 32-37
cells, 146
    aligning, 187-189
        defined, 358
    averaging
        Easy Calc feature, 167
        multiple math operations, 166
        ranges, 166-167
        three-cell calculations, 166
        two-cell calculations, 165
    converting to currency format, 159
    defined, 358
    entries
        cutting/copying/pasting, 172
        deleting, 172
        restoring, 173
    references (defined), 358
    selecting, 150-151
    sorting, 178-179
center paragraph alignment, 107
Change Easy Formats dialog box, 116
Change Folder dialog box, 35

Character Map, 108
characters, *see* special
  characters
Chart command
  Insert menu, 287
  View menu, 204
Chart Type dialog box, 205
charts, 196
  building, 199-200
    Advanced Options tab,
      201-202
    Basic Options tab,
      200-201
    data, selecting, 200
  defined, 358
  displaying, 204
  formatting, 203-206
    fonts, switching, 210
    KISS principle, 211
    labels, editing, 204
  printing, 212
  selecting, 204-206
  series indicators,
    210-211
    defined, 365
  types, 197-198
  X/Y axes, 198-199,
    207-209
checking spelling, 90-92
Checklists
  Address Book, 317-318
  form letters, 306
  TaskWizards, 52
Clear command (defined), 358
clearing, *see* deleting
clicking mouse, 14
ClipArt
  customizing, 278-279
  inserting, 137-138
    in databases, 248-249
  sizing, 138-139
  text wrap, 140
ClipArt command (Insert
  menu), 137, 248, 279
Clipboard, 84-85
  defined, 358
Close command (File menu),
  20
closing
  minimized windows, 64
  Windows 95, 23-24
  Works, 71-72

color
  font colors, selecting, 120
  red spreadsheet numbers,
    186
  selecting (chart series
    indicators), 210-211
  shading patterns,
    134-135
  spot color, 136-137
    defined, 365
  switching (Line/Fill color
    palettes), 274-275
Color dialog box, 274
Column Width command
  (Format menu), 176
columns, 146
  building, 130-131
  defined, 358
  deleting, 174
  dragging-and-dropping,
    174-175
  headers, printing, 193
  inserting, 173-174
  labels, freezing, 192
  selecting, 150-151
  spreadsheet columns,
    labeling, 156-157
  widths, setting, 176-178
Columns command (Format
  menu), 130
COM ports, selecting, 332
combination charts, 198
comma format (spreadsheets),
  186
commands
  Clear command
    (defined), 358
  Draw menu commands,
    276
  Edit menu, 21
    Bring to Front, 275
    Copy, 85, 164
    Cut, 84
    Find, 88
    Paste, 85, 165, 172
    Paste Special, 86, 289
    Replace, 88
    Select All, 67, 84
    Send to Back, 275
    Undo, 87, 173
    Undo Editing, 68
  File menu, 19-20
    Exit and Return, 277
    Exit Works, 72

  Import Picture, 275
  Open, 61
  Page Setup, 99, 128
  Print, 71, 193
  Print Preview, 70, 191
  Save, 53, 69
  Save As, 94, 284
  Update, 275, 292
Format menu
  Alignment, 188,
    231, 243
  AutoFormat, 182
  Border, 246
  Borders and
    Shading, 133
  Bullets, 108
  Column Width, 176
  Columns, 130
  Easy Formats, 114
  Field, 229
  Field Size, 232
  Field Width, 230
  Font and Style, 120, 137,
    184, 242
  Freeze Titles, 192
  Horizontal (X)
    Axis, 207
  Number, 185
  Paragraph, 103
  Picture, 139
  Record Height, 231
  Row Height, 177
  Send To Back, 249
  Set print area, 191
  Shading, 190
  Shading and
    Color, 210
  Snap to Grid, 239
  Tabs, 109
  Text Wrap, 140, 278
  Vertical (Y) Axis, 208
Help menu, 22, 42-43
  About Microsoft Works
    4.0, 34
Insert menu
  Chart, 287
  ClipArt, 137, 248, 279
  Date and Time, 123
  Delete Column, 174
  Delete Row, 174
  Document Name, 123
  Drawing, 272
  Footnote, 124
  Insert Column, 174

Insert Row, 174
Label, 240
Object, 291
Page Break, 125-126
Page Number, 123
Rectangle, 244
Special Character, 126
WordArt, 279-282
Record menu
Delete Field, 233
Delete Record, 234
Insert Field, 232
Insert Record, 234
Sort Records, 249
selecting, 19-23
Settings menu
Communication, 334
Modem, 324
Phone, 333
Terminal, 335
Start menu
Programs, 38
Run, 32
Tools menu
Create New
Chart, 200
Envelopes, 310
Form Letters, 308
Labels, 310
Options, 354
Recalculate Now, 173,
352
Receive File, 344
ReportCreator, 259
Send File, 345
Send Text, 341
Sort, 178
Spelling, 90, 227
Thesaurus, 93
View menu, 21-22
Chart, 204
Display View as Printed,
212
Footer, 123
Header, 123
Window menu (Minimize),
63
Communication command
(Settings menu), 334
communications, 46
accessories, 324
bulletin boards
dialing, 330-332
files, sending/receiving,
343-345

searching, 326
text, sending/receiving,
340-343
Call Waiting, disabling,
324-325
modems, purchasing,
325-326
online services
access limita-
tions, 327
dialing, 330-332
files, sending/
receiving, 343-345
text, sending/receiving,
340
phone lines, purchasing,
326
sample online session,
327-328
settings, saving, 338
software, 29-30
toolbar buttons, 338-340
troubleshooting, 332
busy phone signals/no
answer, 333
modems, search-
ing, 334
Terminal options,
setting, 334-336
Transfer options, setting,
337
Complete installation, 35
connections (bulletin boards/
online services), 330-332
busy phone signals/no
answer, 333
modems, searching, 334
Terminal options, setting,
334-336
Transfer options,
setting, 337
Contents command (Help
menu), 42
Control menu, 16
Control Panel icons, 18
converting cells to currency
format, 159
Copy command (Edit menu),
85, 164
defined, 358
Copy Disk command (File
menu), 20
copying
cell entries, 172
formulas, 164-165

text, 85
bulletin boards/online
services,
340-341
copyrighted material, sending/
receiving,
345-346
correcting spelling errors,
90-92
Count summary, 265
CR (Carriage Return), 336
Create Database dialog
box, 218
Create New Chart command
(Tools menu), 200
Create Shortcut command
(File menu), 20
creating, *see* building
currency format
converting cells to, 159
spreadsheets, 186
cursors, *see* I-beam cursors
Custom Dictionary (spell
checks), 91-92
Custom installation, 35
Customers or Clients
TaskWizard, 217
customizing
Address Book
field insertion, 316,
319-320
reports, building, 317
selected options,
viewing, 317-318
viewing reports, 320
charts, 204-206
Advanced Options tab,
201-202
Basic Options tab,
200-201
ClipArt, 278-279
database reports, 267
fonts in databases,
241-242
form letters, 299, 305
addressing options,
300-301
building addresses,
301-302
fonts, 304
greetings, 303
letter contents, 304
stationery, designing,
299-300

Start menu, 14
TaskWizard options,
  51-52
toolbar, 347-350
  deleting buttons, 348
  inserting buttons, 349
Works
  Address Book
    options, 353
  Data Entry options,
    351-352
  Editing options,
    350-351
  General options,
    353-354
  proofreading options,
    355-356
  View options,
    354-355
  see also formatting
Cut command (Edit
  menu), 84
  defined, 358
cutting
  cell entries, 172
  text, 84

D

data
  alphanumeric data
    (defined), 357
  chart data, selecting, 200
  database data
    editing, 227
    inserting, 225-227
    viewing, 227-228
  grouping (database reports),
    263
  inserting
    Address Book, 319
    form letters, 308
    spreadsheets, 157
Data Entry options, customizing Works,
  351-352
data series (defined), 364
data sharing, 283
  between PCs, 284
  OLE objects, inserting,
    289-292

to other applications
  opening foreign file
    formats, 286-287
  saving file formats,
    284-285
  within Works, 287-288
databases, 28
  building, 218-220
  components, 216
  data
    editing, 227
    inserting, 225-227
    viewing, 227-228
  defined, 358
  fields
    defined, 359-360
    deleting, 233
    inserting, 232-233
    moving, 234
    naming, 229
    width, setting,
      230, 232
  filters
    building, 256-257
    Easy Filters, 254-255
    Filter using formula
      option, 257-259
  form letter addresses,
    300-302
  formatting
    aligning fields,
      243-244
    borders/shading,
      inserting, 246-247
    boxes, inserting,
      244-245
    ClipArt, inserting,
      248-249
    fields, moving,
      238-239
    fonts, switching,
      241-242
    gridlines, enabling/
      disabling, 239
    sorting fields/records,
      249-250
  labels, inserting,
    240-241
  planning, 216-218
  printing
    form view, 235
    list view, 234-235

records
  defined, 364
  deleting, 234
  displaying, 221
  height, setting,
    230-232
  inserting, 234
  moving, 234
  searching, 254-259
reports, 254, 259
  customizing, 267
  data, grouping, 263
  fields, inserting,
    260-261
  filters, building,
    263-264
  fonts, selecting, 260
  page orientation,
    selecting, 260
  previewing, 266
  records, sorting, 262
  summary information,
    collecting, 265-266
  titles, assigning, 260
  saving, 223
  TaskWizards, 217-218
  tools, 222-223
Date and Time command
  (Insert menu), 123
date format
  databases, 219
  spreadsheets, 187
dedicated phone lines, 326
  defined, 358
deductions (spreadsheet
  planning), 155
default settings (defined), 359
defining fields, 218-220
Delete Column command
  (Insert menu), 174
Delete command (File menu),
  20
Delete Field command (Record
  menu), 233
Delete Record command
  (Record menu), 234
Delete Row command (Insert
  menu), 174
deleting
  cell entries, 172
  fields, 233
  records, 234
  rows/columns, 174

Start menu items, 14
tabs, 109, 111
text, 67, 86
toolbar buttons, 348
words (Custom Dictionary),
    92
Descending sort order, 179,
    249
design view, 228
    defined, 360
    formatting databases,
        238-239
    printing databases, 235
desktop, 10
desktop publishing,
    127-141
    defined, 359
Details command (View
    menu), 22
Dial dialog box, 331
dialing bulletin boards/online
    services, 330-332
    busy signals/no
        answer, 333
    modems, searching, 334
    Terminal options, setting,
        334-336
    Transfer options, setting,
        337
dialog boxes, 23
    Borders and Shading, 134
    Capture, 343
    Change Easy Formats, 116
    Change Folder, 35
    Chart Type, 205
    Color, 274
    Create Database, 218
    defined, 359
    Dial, 331
    Easy Calc, 167
    Easy Connect, 330
    Enter Your Text Here, 281
    Existing Documents, 60
    Field Width, 230
    Filter, 255
    Filter Name, 254
    Find, 88
    Form Letters, 309
    Format, 231, 243
    Format Bullet, 108
    Format Cells, 185
    Format Field, 229
    Format Font and Style, 120,
        137, 210

Format Horizontal
    Axis, 207
Format Paragraph, 103
Format Picture, 140
Format Record
    Height, 231
Format Row Height, 177
Format Shading and Color,
    210
Format Tabs, 109
Format Vertical
    Axis, 208
Insert Field, 232
Insert Function, 170
Insert Object, 291
Labels, 310
New Chart, 200
New Easy Format, 117
Open, 61
Other Options, 193
Page Setup, 99, 130,
    191, 235
Replace, 89
Report Name, 259
ReportCreator, 259
Run, 32
Save As, 53, 284
Settings, 334
Sort, 178
Sort Records, 249
Spelling, 92-93
Thesaurus, 93
Transfer Settings, 344
Dictionary, *see* Custom
    Dictionary
dingbat fonts, 119
    defined, 359
disabling
    Call Waiting, 324-325
    gridlines, 239
    ToolTips, 349-350
Display View as Printed
    command (View
    menu), 212
displaying
    charts, 204
    records, 221
    see also viewing
distortion, sizing
    ClipArt, 139
dividing cells
    three-cell calculations, 166
    two-cell calculations, 165

Document Name command
    (Insert menu), 123
document windows, 63
documents, *see* files, dummy
    documents
DOS, 10
    defined, 362
double line spacing,
    77-78, 102
double quotation mark ("),
    157, 226
double-clicking mouse, 15
downloading (defined), 359
drag-and-drop method, 15
    fields/records, 234
    rows/columns, 174-175
    text, 87
dragging mouse, 14
Draw menu com-
    mands, 276
Draw!, 272
    ClipArt, customizing,
        278-279
    Line/Fill color palettes,
        switching colors,
        274-275
    logos, building, 276-278
    menu commands,
        275-276
Drawing command (Insert
    menu), 272
drawing programs (defined),
    359
dummy documents, building,
    131-132
dynamic copies, 288

E

Easy Calc dialog box, 167
Easy Calc feature, 148, 167
Easy Connect dialog
    box, 330
Easy Filters, 254-255
Easy Formats, 114-117
    building, 117
    editing, 116
Easy Formats command
    (Format menu), 114
Edit menu commands, 21
    Bring to Front, 275
    Copy, 85, 164
        defined, 358

Cut, 84
  defined, 358
Find, 88
Paste, 85, 165, 172
Paste Special, 86, 289
  defined, 363
Replace, 88
Select All, 67, 84
Send to Back, 275
Undo, 87, 173
Undo Editing, 68
editing
  ClipArt, 278-279
  Custom Dictionary (spell
    checks), 92
  databases
    data, 227
    reports, 267
  Easy Formats, 116
  files
    deleting text, 67
    inserting text, 66
    replacing text, 68
    selecting text, 66-67
    typing vs. word
      processing, 76
  form letters, 307
  spreadsheets, 172
    cutting/copying/pasting
      cell
      entries, 172
    deleting cell
      entries, 172
    labels, 204
    restoring cell
      entries, 173
Editing options, customizing
  Works, 350-351
electronic bulletin boards
  (defined), 359
embedding
  defined, 359
  OLE objects, 290
Employee Profile TaskWizard,
  217
Employee time sheet
  TaskWizard, 151
enabling gridlines, 239
enclosures (form
  letters), 305
end of line marks
  (defined), 359
Enter Your Text Here dialog
  box, 281

entry bar (database
  tools), 222
envelopes, printing, 310
Envelopes command (Tools
  menu), 310
Envelopes TaskWizard, 310
equal sign (=), 149, 157
errors, correcting (spelling
  errors), 90-92
Existing Documents dialog
  box, 60
Exit and Return command
  (File menu), 277
Exit Works command (File
  menu), 72
expenses (spreadsheet
  planning), 154-155
Explore command (File menu),
  20
exponential format
  (spreadsheets), 186

F

Field command
  (Format menu), 229
Field Size command
  (Format menu), 232
Field Width command
  (Format menu), 230
Field Width dialog
  box, 230
fields, 216
  aligning, 243-244
  boxes, inserting,
    244-245
  defined, 359
  defining, 218-220
  deleting, 233
  inserting, 232-233
    Address Book, 316,
      319-320
    database reports,
      260-261
    form letter addresses,
      301-302
  moving, 234, 238-239
  naming, 229
  sorting, 249-250
  width, setting, 230, 232
File menu commands,
  19-20
  Exit and Return, 277

Exit Works, 72
Import Picture, 275
Open, 61
Page Setup, 99, 128
Print, 71, 193
Print Preview, 70, 191
Save, 53, 69
Save As, 94, 284
Update, 292
  Draw! program, 275
files
  building, 55-56
    TaskWizards, 128
  capturing text to,
    341-343
  database files, searching,
    301
  defined, 359
  editing
    deleting text, 67
    inserting text, 66
    replacing text, 68
    selecting text, 66-67
    typing vs. word
      processing, 76
  formats
    defined, 359
    foreign file formats,
      opening, 286-287
    saving, 284-285
  formatting, 113-114
    Easy Formats,
      114-117
    fonts, 118-121
    guidelines, 124-125
    headers/footers/
      footnotes, 122-124
    headings/subheadings/
      captions,
      121-122
  indents, setting, 104-106
  line spacing, setting,
    103-104
  linked files (defined), 361
  margins, setting, 99-100
  multiple files, opening,
    62-64
  naming, 54-55
  OLE objects, building,
    291-292
  printing, 71
  receiving (bulletin boards/
    online services), 344-345

saved files, opening, 60-61
saving, 52-55, 68-69, 94-95
searching, 87-88
sending (bulletin boards/ online services), 345-346
spell checks, 90
Transfer options, setting, 337
translators (defined), 366
WELCOME.EXE, 11
Fill color palette, switching colors, 274-275
Filter dialog box, 255
Filter Name dialog box, 254
Filter using formula option, 257-259
filters
building, 256-257
database reports, 263-264
defined, 360
Easy Filters, 254-255
Filter using formula option, 257-259
Find command
Edit menu, 88
File menu, 20
Find dialog box, 88
fixed format (spreadsheets), 186
floppy disks
files, saving, 52-55
icons, 18
installing Works from, 32-37
folders (defined), 360
Font and Style command (Format menu), 120, 137, 184, 242
fonts, 118-119
applying to spreadsheets, 184-185
defined, 360
dingbat fonts (defined), 359
formatting, 120-121
legibility (defined), 361
monospaced fonts, 78
defined, 362
pasting formats, 85-86
points (defined), 363

proportional fonts (defined), 363
readability (defined), 364
sans serif fonts, 119
defined, 364
script fonts (defined), 364
selecting, 69
database reports, 260
form letters, 304
serif fonts (defined), 365
sizing, 69-70
specialty fonts, 119
switching
charts, 210
databases, 241-242
text fonts, 118
Footer command (View menu), 123
footers, 122-123
defined, 360
Footnote command (Insert menu), 124
footnotes, inserting, 124
form design view, *see* design view
Form Letter TaskWizard, 296
form letters, 295
building, 296-297
manual creation, 308-309
customizing, 305
addressing options, 300-301
building addresses, 301-302
fonts, 304
greetings, 303
letter contents, 304
stationery, designing, 299-300
data insertion, 308
defined, 360
editing, 307
envelopes, printing, 310
mailing labels, building, 309
place holders (defined), 363
types, selecting, 298
uses, 296
see also mail merges

Form Letters command (Tools menu), 308
Form Letters dialog box, 309
form view, 221, 228
databases
printing, 235
sorting, 249-250
defined, 360
Format Bullet dialog box, 108
Format Cells dialog box, 185
Format command (File menu), 20
Format dialog box, 231, 243
Format Field dialog box, 229
Format Font and Style dialog box, 120, 137, 210
Format Horizontal Axis dialog box, 207
Format menu commands
Alignment, 188, 231, 243
AutoFormat, 182
Border, 246
Borders and Shading, 133
Bullets, 108
Column Width, 176
Columns, 130
Easy Formats, 114
Field, 229
Field Size, 232
Field Width, 230
Font and Style, 120, 137, 184, 242
Freeze Titles, 192
Horizontal (X) Axis, 207
Number, 185
Paragraph, 103
Picture, 139
Record Height, 231
Row Height, 177
Send To Back, 249
Set print area, 191
Shading, 190
Shading and Color, 210
Snap to Grid, 239
Tabs, 109
Text Wrap, 140, 278
Vertical (Y) Axis, 208

Format Paragraph dialog box, 103
Format Picture dialog box, 140
Format Record Height dialog box, 231
Format Row Height dialog box, 177
Format Shading and Color dialog box, 210
Format Tabs dialog box, 109
Format Vertical Axis dialog box, 208
formats
  currency format, converting cells to, 159
  file formats
    defined, 359
    foreign file formats, opening, 286-287
    saving, 284-285
  see also Easy Formats
formatting
  charts, 203-206
    fonts, switching, 210
    KISS principle, 211
    labels, editing, 204
    series indicator color, selecting, 210-211
    X/Y-axes, 207-209
  databases
    aligning fields, 243-244
    borders/shading, inserting, 246-247
    boxes, inserting, 244-245
    ClipArt, inserting, 248-249
    fields, moving, 238-239
    fonts, switching, 241-242
    gridlines, enabling/disabling, 239
    sorting fields/records, 249-250
  defined, 360
  files, 113-114
    Easy Formats, 114-117

fonts, 118-121
guidelines, 124-125
headers/footers/ footnotes, 122-124
headings/subheadings/ captions, 121-122
pages
  borders, 133-136
  ClipArt, 137-140
  columns, 130-131
  guidelines, 141-142
  margins, 129-130
  orientation, 128-129
  page breaks, 125
  shading text, 134-135
  special characters, 126
  spot color, 136-137
paragraphs
  alignment, 106-107
  bulleted lists, 107-108
  Easy Formats, 114-117
  indents, 104-106
  line spacing, 101-104
  margins, 98-101
  right mouse button, 111
  tabs, 108-111
spreadsheets, 181-185
  alignment, 187-189
  AutoFormats, 182-184
  borders/shading, 189-190
  fonts, applying, 184-185
  numbers, 185-187
  see also customizing
forms
  defined, 360
  see also *fields*
formulas, 148
  defined, 360
  editing, 173
  inserting, 162
    AutoSum feature, 163-164
    copy-paste method, 164-165
    in databases, 227
    manual insertion, 163
  results (defined), 364

writing
  cell ranges, averaging, 166-167
  filtering databases, 257-259
  multiple math operations, 166
  three-cell calculations, 166
  two-cell calculations, 165
  see also functions
fraction format
  databases, 219
  spreadsheets, 187
Freeze Titles command (Format menu), 192
freezing spreadsheet labels, 192
functions, 167, 170
  defined, 360
  see also formulas

G

general format
  databases, 219
  spreadsheets, 186
General options, customizing Works, 353-354
Grade Book TaskWizard, 151
graphical user interface (GUI), 13
graphics, 29
  accessories
    ClipArt, 278-279
    Draw!, 272-275
    WordArt, 279-281
  scaling (defined), 364
greetings (form letters), 303
gridlines
  enabling/disabling, 239
  inserting in charts, 201
  spreadsheet printing, 192-194
Group command (Draw menu), 276
grouping data in database reports, 263
GUI (graphical user interface), 13

H

handles
  defined, 360
  sizing handles, 138
hanging indents, 105
  defined, 360
hard disks
  files, saving, 52-55
  icons, 18
Header command (View
  menu), 123
headers, 115, 122
  defined, 361
  inserting, 123
  row/column headers,
    printing, 193
headings, 121
headline fonts, 119
Help menu commands, 22,
  42-43
  About Microsoft Works 4.0,
    34
Help system, *see* online help
Help window, 41-42
Hide Help command (Help
  menu), 42
highlighting, *see* selecting
Home Inventory TaskWizard,
  217
Horizontal (X) Axis command
  (Format
  menu), 207
horizontal axes, *see* X axes
How to use Help command
  (Help menu), 42

I

I-beam cursors, 64-65
icons, 11-12, 16-17
  defined, 361
Imager program, 290
Import Picture command (File
  menu), 275
inactive windows, 63
  defined, 361
indents, 78-79
  hanging indents, 105
    defined, 360
  setting, 104-106

Index command (Help menu),
  42
initialing form letters, 305
inline text wrap, 140
  see also text wrap
Insert Column command
  (Insert menu), 174
Insert Field command (Record
  menu), 232
Insert Field dialog box, 232
Insert Function dialog
  box, 170
Insert menu commands
  Chart, 287
  ClipArt, 137, 248, 279
  Date and Time, 123
  Delete Column, 174
  Delete Row, 174
  Document Name, 123
  Drawing, 272
  Footnote, 124
  Insert Column, 174
  Insert Row, 174
  Label, 240
  Object, 291
  Page Break, 125-126
  Page Number, 123
  Rectangle, 244
  Special Character, 126
  WordArt, 279-282
Insert Object dialog
  box, 291
Insert Record command
  (Record menu), 234
Insert Row command (Insert
  menu), 174
inserting
  borders
    around text, 133-134
    charts, 201-212
    databases, 246-247
    pages, 135-136
    spreadsheets, 189-190
  boxes in database fields,
    244-245
  ClipArt, 137-138
    in databases, 248-249
  data
    databases, 225-227
    form letters, 308
    spreadsheets, 157
  fields, 218, 232-233
    Address Book, 316,
      319-320

database reports,
  260-261
form letter addresses,
  301-302
footers, 123
footnotes, 124
formulas, 162
  AutoSum feature,
    163-164
  copy-paste method,
    164-165
  manual insertion, 163
gridlines in charts, 201
headers, 123
labels
  database labels,
    240-241
  spreadsheet columns,
    156-157
names (Address
  Book), 319
numbers, 66
OLE objects
  Copy/Paste Special
    method, 289-290
  Insert Object dialog box,
    291-292
page breaks, 125
records, 234
rows/columns, 173-174
shading
  databases, 246-247
  spreadsheets, 189-190
special characters (page
  formatting), 126
spreadsheet receipts
  multiple-category
    receipts, 159-160
  single-category receipts,
    158
Start menu items, 14
summary information
  (database reports),
    265-266
text, 66
  I-beam cursors, 64-65
  overstrike mode,
    65-66
toolbar buttons, 349
WordArt, 279
words (Custom Dictionary),
  92-93
insertion point
  (defined), 361

installing Works, 32-37
integration, 46-47
Internet (defined), 361
Introduction to Works command (Help menu), 42
Invert Filter option, 255
Invert Selection command (Edit menu), 21

J-K

justifying, *see* aligning

KERMIT protocol, 337
keyboard shortcuts (defined), 365
KISS (Keep It Simple, Stupid), 124
    charts, building, 211
    page layout, 141

L

Label command (Insert menu), 240
labeling spreadsheet columns, 156-157
labels
    database labels, inserting, 240-241
    freezing (spreadsheet printing), 192
    mailing labels (form letters), 309-311
    spreadsheet labels, editing, 204
Labels command (Tools menu), 310
Labels dialog box, 310
Labels TaskWizard, 309
landscape print orientation, 128, 191
    defined, 361
Large Icons command (View menu), 22
Launch Works Forum command (Help menu), 43
launching
    applications with Start button, 13-14

defined, 361
    Windows 95, 10
    Works, 37-38
leader tabs, 110
leading (defined), 361
leading zeros format (spreadsheets), 187
left paragraph alignment, 106
legal-sized paper (spreadsheet printing), 192
legibility (defined), 361
line charts, 197
Line color palette, switching colors, 274-275
Line Feed (LF), 336
line spacing, 101-104
Line Style command (Draw menu), 276
Line tool, 273
Line up Icons command (View menu), 22
linked files (defined), 361
List command (View menu), 22
list view, 221, 227
    databases
        printing, 234-235
        sorting, 249-250
    defined, 361
lists, *see* bulleted lists
logos, building (Draw!), 276-278

M

mail merges, 295
    defined, 360
mailing labels, building (form letters), 309
manual calculations, 352
margins, 98
    defined, 362
    setting, 129-130
        files, 99-100
        paragraphs, 100-101
markers, selecting (chart series indicators), 210-211
math operations, performing (formulas), 165
    cell ranges, averaging, 166-167

multiple math operations, 166
    three-cell calculations, 166
    two-cell calculations, 165
math symbols, 149-150
maximizing windows, 17
Maximum summary, 265
memory
    buffers (defined), 358
    defined, 364
menus, 16-17, 19, 56-57
    command selection (Draw!), 275-276
    Edit menu, 21, 56
    File menu, 19-20, 56
    Format menu, 56
    Help menu, 22, 57
    Insert menu, 56
    Tools menu, 57
    View menu, 21-22, 56
    Window menu, 57
Microsoft Draw!, *see* Draw!
Microsoft Imager, 290
Minimize command (Window menu), 63
minimizing windows, 17, 63-64
Minimum summary, 265
minus sign (-), 149
Modem command (Settings menu), 324
modems, 327
    baud rates (defined), 357
    dedicated telephone lines (defined), 358
    defined, 362
    purchasing, 325-326
    searching, 334
monospaced fonts, 78
    defined, 362
Mortgage/Loan analysis TaskWizard, 151
mouse
    clicking, 14
    double-clicking, 15
    drag-and-drop method, 15
    dragging, 14
    right mouse button, formatting paragraphs, 111
    triple-clicking, 15

moving
    fields/records, 234,
        238-239
    tabs, 111
MS-DOS, 10
    defined, 362
multiplying cells
    three-cell calculations, 166
    two-cell calculations, 165
My Computer, 16

N

names, inserting (Address
    Book), 319
naming
    charts, 201
    fields, 229
    files, 54-55
networks (defined), 362
New Chart dialog box, 200
New Easy Format dialog box,
    117
nonbreaking hyphens
    (defined), 362
nonbreaking spaces (defined),
    362
novelty fonts, *see* specialty
    fonts
null modem cables, 332
Num Lock key, 66
Number command (Format
    menu), 185
number crunching, 27-28
number format (data-
    bases), 219
numbers
    inserting in databases, 226
    right alignment, 189
    spreadsheet numbers,
        formatting, 185-187
    starting page numbers,
        selecting, 193

O

Object command (Insert
    menu), 291
Object Linking and Embed-
    ding, *see* OLE objects
offline (defined), 362

OLE objects, 47-48
    defined, 362
    embedding (defined), 359
    inserting
        Copy/Paste Special
            method, 289-290
        Insert Object dialog box,
            291-292
    linked objects (defined),
        361
    management, 293
online (defined), 362
online help
    ? button, 44
    first-time help, 43
    Help window, 41-42
    menu commands, 42-43
Online Registration, 37
online services, 26
    access limitations, 327
    defined, 362
    dialing, 330-332
        busy signals/no answer,
            333
        modems, searching, 334
        Terminal options,
            setting, 334-336
        Transfer options, setting,
            337
    files
        receiving, 344-345
        sending, 345-346
    text
        capturing, 341-343
        sending, 340-341
online sessions, 327-328
Open command (File menu),
    20, 61
Open dialog box, 61
opening
    Address Book, 314
    files
        multiple files, 62-64
        saved files, 60-61
    foreign file formats,
        286-287
    see also launching, starting
Operating System
    (defined), 363
operations, *see* math
    operations
optional hyphens
    (defined), 362

Options command
    Tools menu, 354
    View menu, 22
ordering modems, 325-326
orientation (print jobs)
    defined, 363
    landscape (defined), 361
    portrait (defined), 363
    selecting
        database reports, 260
        spreadsheet printing,
            191
    setting, 128-129
OS (defined), 363
Other Options dialog box, 193
Oval tool, 273
overstrike mode, 350
    defined, 363
    text, inserting, 65-66

P

Page Break command (Insert
    menu), 125-126
page breaks
    defined, 363
    inserting, 125
Page Number command (Insert
    menu), 123
page numbers, selecting, 193
Page Setup command (File
    menu), 99, 128
Page Setup dialog box, 99, 130,
    191, 235
pages
    formatting
        page breaks, 125
        special characters, 126
    layout options
        borders, 133-136
        ClipArt, 137-140
        columns, 130-131
        margins, 129-130
        orientation, 128-129
        shading text, 134-135
        spot color, 136-137
    sizing, 129
palettes, switching colors,
    274-275
Paragraph command (Format
    menu), 103

paragraphs
   aligning, 106-107
   bulleted lists, building,
      107-108
   formatting
      alignment, 106-107
      bulleted lists, 107-108
      Easy Formats,
         114-117
      indents, 104-106
      line spacing, 101-104
      margins, 98-101
      right mouse button, 111
      tabs, 108-111
   indents
      hanging indents, 106
      setting, 104-106
   line spacing, setting, 104
   margins, setting,
      100-101
   pasting formats, 85-86
   splitting, 104
   tabs, 108-109
      moving, 111
      setting, 109-110
parentheses ( ), 166
passwords (defined), 363
Paste command (Edit menu),
   85, 165, 172
Paste Special command (Edit
   menu), 86, 289
   defined, 363
pasting
   cell entries, 172
   formulas, 164-165
   paragraph/font formats,
      85-86
   text, 85
      bulletin boards/online
         services,
         340-341
Pattern command (Draw
   menu), 276
patterns
   selecting (chart series
      indicators), 210-211
   shading patterns, selecting,
      134-135
percent format (spreadsheets),
   186
Personal Address Book, 314
Phone command (Settings
   menu), 333

phone lines, purchasing, 326
Phone List TaskWizard, 217
phone numbers (bulletin
   board/online services)
   busy signals/no answer, 333
   dialing, 330-332
Picture command (Format
   menu), 139
pictures, *see* graphics
pie charts, 198
place holders (defined), 363
planning
   databases, 216-218
   spreadsheets, 151-152,
      154-155
plunk (defined), 363
plus sign (+), 149
pointer tool, 272
points (defined), 363
portrait print orientation, 128
   defined, 363
previewing
   database reports, 266
   print jobs, 70-71
Print command (File menu),
   71, 193
print jobs, previewing,
   70-71
Print Preview command (File
   menu), 70, 191
Printers folder icon, 18
printing
   charts, 212
   databases, 234-235
   envelopes, 310
   files, 71
   spreadsheets, 190
      labels, freezing, 192
      legal-sized paper, 192
      orientation, selecting,
         191
      Other Options dialog
         box, 192-193
      print areas, selecting,
         191
programs, *see* applications,
   drawing programs
Programs command (Start
   menu), 38
proofreading tools
   options, customizing,
      355-356

spell checker, 90-92
   thesaurus, 93-94
Properties command (File
   menu), 20
proportional fonts
   (defined), 363
proprietary software (defined),
   364
protocols, *see* transfer
   protocols
pt., *see* points
purchasing
   modems, 325-326
   phone lines, 326

Q-R

question mark (?), 44
Quotations TaskWizard, 151

radar charts, 198
RAM
   buffers (defined), 358
   defined, 364
ranges
   defined, 364
   selecting, 150
readability (defined), 364
Recalculate Now command
   (Tools menu), 173, 352
receipts (spreadsheets),
   154-155
   multiple-category receipts,
      159-160
   single-category
      receipts, 158
Receive File command (Tools
   menu), 344
receiving files/text (bulletin
   boards/online services),
   341-345
   legal issues, 345-346
Record Height command
   (Format menu), 231
Record menu commands
   Delete Field, 233
   Delete Record, 234
   Insert Field, 232
   Insert Record, 234
   Sort Records, 249
records, 216
   defined, 364
   deleting, 234

displaying, 221
height, setting, 230-232
inserting, 234
moving, 234
searching, 254-259
sorting, 249-250
    database reports, 262
summarizing, 265-266
Rectangle command (Insert
    menu), 244
rectangles, *see* boxes
references (defined), 358
Refresh command (View
    menu), 22
registering Works, 37
Rename command (File
    menu), 20
renaming, *see* naming
Replace command (Edit
    menu), 88
Replace dialog box, 89
replacing text, 68, 88-89
Report Name dialog box, 259
ReportCreator, 259
    customizing reports, 267
    data, grouping, 263
    fields, inserting, 260-261
    filters, building, 263-264
    fonts, selecting, 260
    orientation, selecting, 260
    previewing reports, 266
    records, sorting, 262
    summary information,
        collecting, 265-266
    titles, assigning, 260
ReportCreator command
    (Tools menu), 259
ReportCreator dialog box, 259
reports, 254, 259
    Address Book reports
        building, 317
        viewing, 320
restoring
    cell entries, 173
    records, 234
    text, 68, 86
    windows
        maximized
            windows, 17
        minimized windows,
            17, 63
results (defined), 364
Rich Text Format (defined),
    364

right paragraph alignment, 107
Rotate/Flip command (Draw
    menu), 276
Rounded rectangle tool, 273
Row Height command (Format
    menu), 177
rows, 146
    defined, 364
    deleting, 174
    dragging-and-dropping,
        174-175
    headers, printing, 193
    height, setting, 177-178
    inserting, 173-174
    labels, freezing, 192
    selecting, 150-151
RTF (defined), 364
ruler
    margins, setting, 100
    tabs, setting, 110
Run command (Start menu),
    32
Run dialog box, 32

S

Sales Contacts TaskWizard,
    217
sans serif fonts, 119, 184
    defined, 364
Save As command (File menu),
    94, 284
Save As dialog box, 53, 284
Save command (File menu),
    53, 69
saving
    Address Book, 319
    communications settings,
        338
    databases, 223
    defined, 364
    file formats (data sharing),
        284-285
    files, 52-55, 68-69, 94-95
    spreadsheets, 152
scaling, 138
    defined, 364
Schedule TaskWizard, 151
script fonts, 118-119
    defined, 364
scroll bars, 18

searching
    bulletin boards, 326
    files, 87-88
        database files (form
            letters), 301
    modems, 334
    records, 254-259
    synonyms, 93-94
    text, 87-88
Select All command (Edit
    menu), 21, 67, 84
selecting
    Address Books, 314
    charts, 197-198,
        200-201, 204-206
    colors
        font color, 120
        Line/Fill color palettes,
            274-275
    COM ports, 332
    database formats, 219
    fonts, 69, 120
        database reports, 260
    form letter options, 305
        addresses, 300-302
        fonts, 304
        greetings, 303
        letter contents, 304
        stationery, 299-300
    form letter types, 298
    functions, 170
    mailing label options,
        309-311
    menu commands, 19-23
    orientation
        database reports, 260
        spreadsheet printing,
            191
    paper size, 129
    print areas (spreadsheet
        printing), 191
    shading patterns,
        134-135
    spreadsheet components,
        150
    starting page numbers, 193
    styles, 121
    summaries (database
        reports), 265-266
    text, 66-67, 83-84
    windows, 62
Send File command (Tools
    menu), 345

Send Text command (Tools menu), 341
Send To Back command
  Edit menu, 275
  Format menu, 249
sending files/text (bulletin boards/online services), 340-346
serialized format (databases), 219
series indicators (charts), 210-211
  defined, 365
series, *see* data series
serif fonts, 118, 184
  defined, 365
Set print area command (Format menu), 191
setting
  alignment options (database fields), 243-244
  chart options
    Advanced Options tab, 201-202
    Basic Options tab, 200-201
  column width, 176-178
  field width, 230, 232
  form letter options, 305
    addressing options, 300-301
    building addresses, 301-302
    fonts, 121-124, 304
    greetings, 303
    letter contents, 304
    stationery, designing, 299-300
  indents, 104-106
  line spacing, 103-104
  mailing label options, 309-311
  margins, 129-130
    files, 99-100
    paragraphs, 100-101
  orientation (print jobs), 128-129
  record height, 230-232
  row height, 177-178
  tabs, 109-110
  TaskWizard options, 51-52

Terminal options (communications), 334-336
Transfer options (communications), 337
  X-axes options, 207-208
  Y-axes options, 208-209
Settings dialog box, 334
Settings menu commands
  Communication, 334
  Modem, 324
  Phone, 333
  Terminal, 335
Setup program, 32
shading
  inserting
    databases, 246-247
    spreadsheets, 189-190
  text, 134-135
Shading and Color command (Format menu), 210
Shading command (Format menu), 190
sharing data, 283
  between PCs, 284
  OLE objects, inserting, 289-292
  to other applications
    opening foreign file formats, 286-287
    saving file formats, 284-285
  within Works, 287-288
shortcuts
  defined, 365
  Works installation, 36
Show Guides command (Draw menu), 276
Show Help command (Help menu), 42
shutdown, 23-24, 71-72
signing off, 328
  defined, 365
signing on (defined), 365
single line spacing, 102
sizing
  ClipArt, 138-139
  columns, 176-178
  fields, 229-232
  fonts, 69-70, 120
  pages, 129
  records, 229-232
  rows, 177-178

sizing handles, 138
  defined, 360
slash mark (/), 149
Small Icons command (View menu), 22
smart quotes, 351
Snap to Grid command
  Draw menu, 276
  Format menu, 239
software
  communications software, 29-30
  proprietary software (defined), 364
Sort command (Tools menu), 178
Sort dialog box, 178
Sort Records command (Record menu), 249
Sort Records dialog box, 249
sorting
  cells, 178-179
  databases, 249-250
  defined, 365
  records, 262
spacing, *see* line spacing
special characters
  end of line marks (defined), 359
  nonbreaking hyphens (defined), 362
  nonbreaking spaces (defined), 362
  optional hyphens (defined), 362
  page formatting, 126
Special Character command (Insert menu), 126
specialty fonts, 119
spell checker tool, 90-93, 227
Spelling command (Tools menu), 90, 227
Spelling dialog box, 92-93
splitting paragraphs, 104
spot color, 136-137
  defined, 365
spreadsheets, 27-28, 145
  building, 151, 155
  columns
    deleting, 174
    dragging-and-dropping, 174-175

inserting, 173-174
labeling, 156-157
widths, setting, 176-178
components, selecting, 150
data, inserting, 157
defined, 365
editing cell entries
cutting/copying/pasting, 172
deleting, 172
restoring, 173
formatting, 181-185
aligning cells, 187-189
AutoFormats, 182-184
borders/shading, 189-190
fonts, applying, 184-185
numbers, 185-187
formulas, 162
labels, editing, 204
math symbols, 149-150
planning, 151-152, 154-155
printing, 190
labels, freezing, 192
legal-sized paper, 192
orientation, selecting, 191
Other Options dialog box, 192-193
print areas, selecting, 191
ranges (defined), 364
receipts
multiple-category receipts, 159-160
single-category receipts, 158
rows
defined, 364
deleting, 174
dragging-and-dropping, 174-175
height, setting, 177-178
inserting, 173-174
saving, 152
sorting cells, 178-179
terminology, 146
tools, 147-148

stacked line charts, 197
Standard Deviation summary, 266
Start button, 13-14
defined, 365
Start menu
commands
Programs, 38
Run, 32
customizing, 14
defined, 365
launching Works from, 38
starting TaskWizards, 48-49
see also launching, opening
stationery design (form letters), 299-300
Status Bar, 18, 23
Status Bar command (View menu), 22
Student & Membership Information TaskWizard, 217
styles, applying, 121
subheadings, 121-122
subscripts, 121
defined, 365
subtracting cells
three-cell calculations, 166
two-cell calculations, 165
Sum summary, 265
summary information, collecting (database reports), 265-266
superscripts, 121
defined, 365
Suppliers & Vendors TaskWizard, 217
switching
between windows, 62
chart types, 204-206
colors (Line/Fill color palettes), 274-275
fonts, 69
charts, 210
databases, 241-242
SYD( ) function, 167
symbols
math symbols, 149-150
see also special characters
synonyms, searching (thesaurus tool), 93-94
system operator (defined), 365

T

tabs, 108-109
moving, 111
setting, 109-110
Tabs command (Format menu), 109
Task Launcher, 40
files, opening, 60-61
spreadsheets, building, 155
taskbar, 11
defined, 366
TaskWizards, 30
Address Book, 314
databases, 217-218
Envelopes, 310
files, building, 128
Form Letter, 296
Labels, 309
options, customizing, 51-52
spreadsheets, building, 151
using, 48-49
Terminal command (Settings menu), 335
terminal emulation (defined), 366
terminals, setting options, 334-336
text
borders, inserting, 133-134
capturing (bulletin boards/online services), 341-343
copying, 85
cutting, 84
deleting, 67, 86
dragging-and-dropping, 87
inserting
I-beam cursors, 64-65
in databases, 226
overstrike mode, 65-66
pasting, 85
receiving (legal issues), 345-346
replacing, 68, 88-89
searching, 87-88
selecting, 66-67, 83-84
sending
bulletin boards/online services, 340-341

legal issues, 345-346
shading, 134-135
spell checks, 90
spreadsheet text, inserting, 157
word wrap (defined), 366
WordArt text, inserting, 279
wrapping (ClipArt), 140
text buffers, 341
text fonts, 118
text format
    databases, 219
    spreadsheets, 187
text wrap (defined), 366
Text Wrap command (Format menu), 140, 278
Thesaurus command (Tools menu), 93
Thesaurus dialog box, 93
thesaurus tool, 93-94
ticks (defined), 366
time format
    databases, 219
    spreadsheets, 187
timed-out, 332
    defined, 366
Tip of the Day, 11
title bar, 16
titles
    assigning (database reports), 260
    freezing (spreadsheet printing), 192
toggle buttons, 17
Toolbar command (View menu), 22
toolbars
    buttons, 57-58
    Communications toolbar, 338-340
    customizing, 347-350
        deleting buttons, 348
        inserting buttons, 349
tools
    database tools, 222-223
    proofreading tools
        options, customizing, 355-356
        spell checker, 90-92
        thesaurus, 93-94
    spreadsheet tools, 147-148

WordArt tools, 280-281
Tools menu commands
    Create New Chart, 200
    Envelopes, 310
    Form Letters, 308
    Labels, 310
    Options, 354
    Recalculate Now, 173, 352
    Receive File, 344
    ReportCreator, 259
    Send File, 345
    Send Text, 341
    Sort, 178
    Spelling, 90, 227
    Thesaurus, 93
Tooltips, disabling, 349-350
touring Works, 39-40
Transfer options (communications), 337
transfer protocols, 337
Transfer Settings dialog box, 344
translators
    data sharing, 285
    defined, 366
triple line spacing, 102
triple-clicking mouse, 15
troubleshooting communications, 332
    busy phone signals/no answer, 333
    modems, searching, 334
    terminal options, setting, 334-336
    Transfer options, setting, 337
True/False format (spreadsheets), 187
typefaces, *see* fonts
typing vs. word processing, 76
typist initials (form letters), 305

U-V

Undo command (Edit menu), 87, 173
Undo Editing command (Edit menu), 68
Ungroup command (Draw menu), 276

Update command (File menu), 292
    Draw! program, 275
uploading (defined), 366

Variance summary, 266
Vertical (Y) Axis command (Format menu), 208
vertical axes, *see* Y-axes
View menu commands, 21-22
    Chart, 204
    Display View as Printed, 212
    Footer, 123
    Header, 123
View options, customizing Works, 354-355
viewing
    Address Book options, 317-318
    database data, 227-228
    form letter options, 306
    reports (Address Book reports), 320

W

WELCOME.EXE file, 11
Window menu commands (Minimize), 63
windows
    active windows (defined), 357
    components, 16-18
    Help window, 41-42
    inactive windows (defined), 361
    minimizing, 63-64
    switching between, 62
Windows 95, 9-10
    closing, 23-24
    launching, 10
word processing, 26, 75
    double-spaces, 77-78
    indents, 78-79
    vs. typing, 76
    word wrap feature, 79-80
word processors, 46
    as writing tool, 77
    defined, 366
    text, sending, 340-341

word wrap feature, 79-80, 351
  defined, 366
WordArt
  inserting, 279
  tools, 280-281
WordArt command (Insert
  menu), 279-282
words
  synonyms, searching
    (thesaurus), 93-94
  see also text
Works
  communications software,
    29-30
  customizing
    Address Book options,
      353
    Data Entry options,
      351-352
    Editing options,
      350-351
    General options,
      353-354
    proofreading options,
      355-356
    View options,
      354-355
  databases, 28
  demonstration tour,
    39-40
  exiting, 71-72
  graphics, 29
  installing, 32-37
  launching, 37-38
  online services, 26
  registering, 37
  spreadsheets, 27-28
  toolbar buttons, 57-58
  word processing, 26
wrapping text (ClipArt), 140
writing formulas
  cell ranges, averaging,
    166-167
  databases, filtering,
    257-259
  multiple math operations,
    166
  three-cell calculations, 166
  two-cell calculations, 165

X-Y-Z

X-axes (charts), 198-199
  formatting, 207-208
X-Y scatter charts, 197
XMODEM/CRC protocol, 337

Y-axes (charts), 198-199
  formatting, 208-209
YMODEM protocol, 337

ZMODEM protocol, 337
Zoom tool, 272